Explore

NELLES

GW00871354

COSTA RICA

Authors:
Dr. Klaus Boll, Ortrun Egelkraut, Detlev Kirst

*An Up-to-date travel guide with 167 color photos
and 10 maps*

**First Edition
1999**

Dear Reader: Being up-to-date is the main goal of the Nelles series. Our correspondents help keep us abreast of the latest developments in the travel scene, while our cartographers see to it that maps are also kept completely current. However, as the travel world is constantly changing, we cannot guarantee that all the information contained in our books is always valid. Should you come across a discrepancy, please contact us at: Nelles Verlag, Schleissheimer Str. 371 b, 80935 Munich, Germany, tel. (089) 3571940, fax. (089) 35719430, e-mail: Nelles.Verlag@T-Online.de

Note: Distances and measurements, including temperatures, used in this guide are metric. For conversion information, please see the *Guidelines* section of this book.

LEGEND

▦	Public or Significant Building	Uvita	Place Mentioned in Text	▨▨▨	National Border	
▪	Hotel	♣	National Park	┄┄┄	Provincial Border	
▩	Shopping Center	✈	International Airport	══════	Tollway	
○	Market	✈	National Airport	═════	Expressway	
✝	Church	10	Route number	─────	Principal Highway	
∴	Ancient Site	\25/	Distance in Kilometers	─────	Main Road	
✳	Place of Interest	Volcán Turrialba 3328	Mountain (Altitude in Meters)	─────	Provincial Road	
🖾	Plage			┄┄┄┄	Other Road	
				━▪━▪━	Railway	

COSTA RICA
© Nelles Verlag GmbH, 80935 Munich
    All rights reserved

First Edition 1999
ISBN 3-88618-127-8
Printed in Slovenia

Publisher:	Günter Nelles	**Translation:**	M. & H. Schroe
Editor-in-Chief:	Berthold Schwarz	**Photo Editor:**	K. Bärmann-Thümr
Project Editor:	Dr. Klaus Boll	**Cartography:**	Nelles Verlag Gm
English		**Color Separation:**	Priegnitz, Mun
Edition Editor:	Chase Stewart	**Printing:**	Gorenjski

TABLE OF CONTENTS

LAND AND PEOPLE

TRAVELING IN COSTA RICA

GUIDELINES

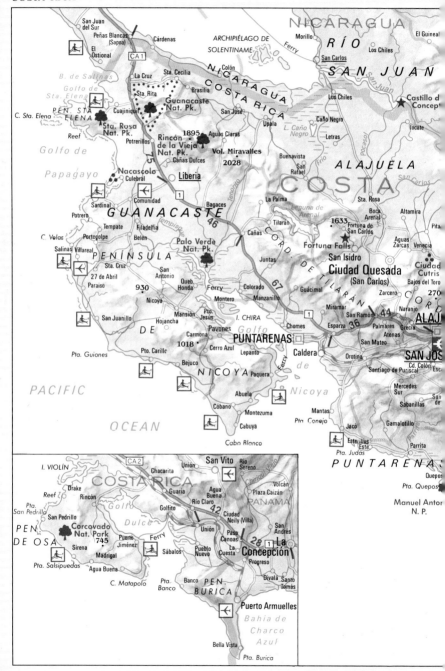

719
608

Bahía de Punta Gorda

Barra del Río Maíz

Pta. Castilla

San Juan del Norte

I. MACHUCA

Barra del Colorado

Pavas · Tigra · Colorado

L. Astillero

Puerto Viejo de Sarapiquí

Tortuguero

Canta Gallo

La Virgen · San Miguel · Las Horquetas · Cariari · Tortuguero Nat. Pk. · Siete

HEREDIA · Rita · Guapiles · Guácimo · Río Jiménez · Irlanda · Parismina

Volcán Barva 2906 · Braulio Carrillo Nat. Pk. · Pocora · Perla

Heredia · CENTRAL · Batán · Matina

Guadalupe · Guayabo Nat. Monument · Florida · Siquirres · Swamp Mouth

Curridabat 3432 · Basilica

CARTAGO · Turrialba · Platarillo · Playa Hermosa · Puerto Limón · Westfalia

Paraíso · Platarillo · Bomba

Orosi · Tapanti · CARTAGO · Reserva Indígena Chirripó · Miramar · Cahuita N. P.

Colonial Town · Vesta · Hortensia · Pta. Cahuita · Cahuita

San Andrés · San Marcos · Santa María · 109 · 3394 · Bribrí · Puerto Viejo de Talamanca · Pta. Mona

SAN JOSÉ · Teliré · San José Cabécar · Suretka · Margarita · Gandoca

Piedra · Cerro Chirripó 3819 · Amubre · Sixaola · Guabito

Rivas · Chirripó Nat. Pk. · Cerro Durika 3280

San Isidro de El General · Gral. Viejo · Palmares · La · Co. Kámuk 3549 · Changuinola

Platanillo · San Pedro · Convento · Amistad · Almirante · Bocas del Toro

Dominical · Unión · Inter-national · CRISTOBAL

San Rafael · Buenos Aires · Cerro Fábrega 3335 · BOCAS

Uvita · Marino Ballena N.P. · Brujo · Mosca · Park · DEL TORO

Bahía de Coronado · I. BOCA BRAVA · Palmar Norte · Palmar Sur · Boruca · Potrero Grande · Punta Róbalo

Ciudad Cortés · Coto Brus · PANAMÁ

I. VIOLÍN · Stone Spheres · Unión · San Vito · Cerro Punta

I. DEL CAÑO · Drake · Rincón · Chacarita · Guaria · Agua Buena · Río Sereno · Plaza Caizán

Reef · Golfito · Río Claro

Pta. San Pedrillo

CARIBBEAN SEA

COSTA RICA · PANAMA · LIMÓN · CARTAGO · SAN JOSÉ · CORDILLERA DE TALAMANCA

COSTA RICA

0 · 20 · 40 km

LAND AND
PEOPLE

IMPORTANT FACTS

Costa Rica is in many ways a country of superlatives. Almost 25 percent of the land consists of nature areas protected by law; 11 percent has been set aside as national parks containing a phenomenal variety of tropical plants and animals. Mountains and volcanoes rising up to an altitude of 3,000 meters are perfect for hiking, and their streams provide kayakers an opportunity for year-round adventure.

Lake Arenal, which is of volcanic origin, is very popular with windsurfers. Surfers enjoy ideal conditions riding the long, high waves that pound the Pacific coast. Fishing enthusiasts from all over the world come to try their luck at game fishing. The east coast is the perfect place to enjoy the casual, easy-going lifestyle for which the Caribbean is famous.

Hundreds of beautiful beaches invite vacationers to bathe under the tropical sun. Fortunately, there are no high-rise hotels or oversize hotel complexes in Costa Rica because local building regulations forbid tourist compounds that rise above the palm trees. More than 90 percent of Costa Rica's tourist accommodations are in private hotels or inns in idyllic fishing villages and picturesque small towns. Costa Rica is a small country offering ideal conditions for great vacations. And that isn't all: for decades Costa Rica has had one of the most stabile governments in Latin America. It has achieved political stability without the help of a military (its army

Previous pages: The virgin rain forest attracts tourists. The Volcán Arenal region is an El Dorado for mountain-bikers. Left: A procession in honor of the Blessed Virgin.

was disbanded in 1948). The low rate of illiteracy in Costa Rica compares favorably with that of the United States (five percent). The inhabitants like to point out that Costa Rica has more teachers than soldiers. Each year these friendly and hospitable people welcome more than 600,000 foreign visitors to their country.

GEOGRAPHY

Costa Rica, meaning "rich coast" in Spanish, has a land area of 51,100 square kilometers and is slightly smaller than Switzerland, a country with which it is often compared. Its 3.5 million inhabitants (an average population density of 67 people per square kilometer) are ethnically homogenous but live in a country that varies greatly from one area to another. In the north the Rio San Juan forms most of the 300-kilometer-long border to Nicaragua. The border to the south and southeast separates Costa Rica from Panama. The vast La Amistad National Park is shared by the two countries and spreads out on both sides of the border. The 200-kilometer-long Caribbean coast is to the east and the 1,000-kilometer-long Pacific coast is to the west.

Topography

Costa Rica can be divided into three major topographic areas: The Cordilleras (mountain chains), which are of volcanic origin, the alluvial Caribbean Lowland Plains and the hilly Pacific Region.

The Cordilleras

The Cordilleras run from the northwest to the southeast of the country and consist of four mountain chains. The Cordillera de Guanacaste stretches from the Nicaraguan border to Lake Arenal. The Tenorio (1,916 m), Rincón de la Vieja (1,096 m), Orosi (1,487 m) and Arenal (1,633 m) volcanoes make up the verte-

brae of its spinal column. The Cordillera de Tilarán includes the cloud forest preserve of Monteverde, and reaches heights of up to 1,500 meters. The 70-kilometer-long Cordillera Central rises to its highest altitude at the inactive Poás volcano (2,704 m), and contains other dormant volcanoes. Costa Rica's four major cities: San José, Alajuela, Cartago and Heredia are situated between 1,000 and 1,500 meters altitude in the part of the Cordillera Central known as the Meseta Central (Central Plateau).

Finally, there is the Cordillera de Talamanca, a massive mountain chain made of fold mountains (not of volcanic origin) which contains the highest peak in Costa Rica, the Cerro Chirripó (3,820 m). From its summit the view spreads in all directions, taking in many mountains rising more than 3,000 meters skyward. The densely populated Cordillera Central separates the Cordillera de Talamanca from the Cordillera de Tilarán.

The Caribbean Lowland Plains

Banana plantations form the center of the Atlantic region or *región Atlántico*. Numerous lagoons and swamps, along with the Tortuguero National Park, make up the northern and western parts of this region. In the southeast, near the border to Panama, lies an enormous park, La Amistad, made up of vast areas of virgin jungle. Further west the forest becomes flatter and thicker.

The Pacific Region

The third area is the Pacific Region to the west. Great plains dominate the northern part where the historically important Santa Rosa National Park is located. This is also where the fertile valley of the Río Tempisque, which is so vital to the country, is located. In the south is the dry Península de Nicoya, with its wide

Above: Costa Rica features miles of beaches (Osa Peninsula/Pacific). Right: Tropical showers on the Caribbean coast.

valleys and hills reaching up to 1,000 meters skyward. The coastal lowlands become narrower in the central Pacific Region and end at the southern tip of the Península de Osa. Huge commercial banana plantations have replaced the virgin rain forest that once covered the southern Pacific Region of Costa Rica, surrounding the harbor town of Golfito.

Climate

Costa Rica has two rather than four seasons: the rainy season and the dry season. The dry season, known to the native inhabitants as *verano* (summer), lasts from December to April, during which it rains only once or twice a month. The rainy season, *invierno* (winter), lasts from May through November. The heaviest rainfall occurs during September and October, and supplies a large share of the country's annual rate of precipitation.

The Atlantic coast averages 20 rainy days per month, while the variable weather of the Pacific coast means fewer days of continuous rain, but more frequent tropical showers (*aguaceros*). Costa Rica ranks among the world's 10 rainiest regions.

Temperatures on the coast range from 20°C during the night to 30-35°C during the day. *Primavera eterna* (eternal spring) dominates the weather in San José, and in the Alajuela region where it is seldom cooler than 15°C at night or hotter than 26°C during the day.

The exception is the summits of the volcanoes, where cooler temperatures, due to the high altitudes, are the rule, especially at night or on cloudy afternoons when it can be surprisingly chilly.

The amount of annual precipitation varies from region to region. San José averages 2,000 mm annually (about three times the average of central Europe), while the Caribbean port city of Puerto Limón has twice as much rain, averaging 4,000 mm a year. Certain national parks and tropical rain forest preserves have twice as much precipitation, producing high humidity throughout the year.

15

HISTORY

Pre-Columbian Civilizations

The first humans inhabited Central America about 14,000 years ago. They were hunters and gatherers. Once these early nomads settled down in the land which is today known as Costa Rica to plant crops, they grew corn, yucca, chili peppers, beans, avocados, herbs and fruit in communal fields.

The migration of Indian tribes in Central America continued from north to south and vice versa. The Chibcha forced their way out of the Chilean Andes into Costa Rica. The Circumcarib came from the area which today forms Venezuela, and tribes from Mexico settled in the Guanacaste and Nicoya regions.

The South American ethnic influence reached its apex approximately three to five thousand years ago. Social structures were formed: a *cacique* served as the head of a tribe; chieftains were in charge of individual villages; political offices and property were inherited from the mother. Slowly religion, with its gods, shamans, medicine men and priests, came into being. Trade routes were laid out and markets established in which beautifully-ornamented pottery and polished stone figures were sold. Artisans manufactured valuable jewelry made of jade, obsidian and gold.

Perhaps it was during this period that the *Esferas de Piedra* came into being. The mysterious stone balls made of granite or basalt, ranging in size from six centimeters to 2.4 meters in diameter, are to be found throughout Costa Rica, and may have been used for astronomical research. Early Americans, such as the Maya, were very advanced in this field. Anthropologists estimate that before the arrival of the Spanish conquistadors, be-

tween 20 and 30 thousand people probably lived in the territory that is now known as Costa Rica.

Conquest and the Colonial Era

Christopher Columbus (1451-1506) reached the Atlantic coast of Central America in September 1502, during his fourth and final voyage to the New World. He went ashore on Isla Uvita, the small rocky island located in front of the modern harbor town of Puerto Limón. He spent two weeks exploring the mainland and trying to make contact with the native inhabitants.

In his report to King Charles V of Spain, he called the land *Costa Rica y Castillo de Oro* – "Rich Coast and Golden Castle." The name was more an expression of wishful thinking than an actual description of what Columbus found. Costa Rica would remain a poor country for another 300 years. Columbus had hoped to find a new route to India (there are also other theories about his voyage); perhaps he was really seeking El Dorado, the legendary city of gold.

The discovery of the New World brought Columbus very little good fortune, but others followed him and persisted in their search for wealth. Some 20 years later, Pedro Arias de Avilla, Governor of Panama, organized an unsuccessful and now nearly forgotten expedition to Costa Rica.

Six years after Avilla, Hernan Ponce de León, Juan de Castañeda and Gaspar de Espinoza, a group of Castilian explorers sailing along the Pacific coast between Panama and the Gulf of Nicoya, were more enthusiastic in the reports they sent home. The Spanish conquistadors spent several weeks with the Chorotega Indians, and baptized 30,000 of them before moving on to the territory now known as Nicaragua. Their attempts to make more conversions inspired the Nicaraguan Indians to flee southward.

The First Settlers

In 1540, having already transferred the administration of Central America to the authority of Guatemala (*Audiencia de Guatemala*), the King of Spain separated Costa Rica from Panama and ordered the colonization of the country, which would last for several decades and prove largely unsuccessful. The conquest of the new territory was delayed because Spanish knights, wearing armor and European clothing, were unaccustomed to the tropical climate. They also suffered from a variety of illnesses, were confronted by impenetrable jungle and encountered a hostile native population.

It was not until 1561, when Juan de Cavallón settled the Meseta Central, bringing soldiers, wheat, cattle and horses with him, that fortune began to favor the Spanish settlers. In 1564, he founded the capital city of Cartago on the site of a former Indian village.

La Encomienda

Dominican and Franciscan missionaries followed the soldiers and settlers. They built churches, and soon small villages and farm settlements grew up around them. As in its other Latin American colonies, Spain introduced the system of *Encomienda*, allowing officials, usually noblemen, to obtain cheap farm land and to use Indian slaves to plant and harvest their crops. In return, the missionaries gave the slaves a Christian education, which was for many a questionable gesture of generosity. Less privileged settlers were left to fend for themselves as well as they could.

Many Indians died fighting the Spaniards who swept through their villages in pursuit of slaves. Others fled into the hinterland and hid in the nearly impenetrable jungle. Some of the captured natives were sold and shipped off to Guatemala

Above: On Oct. 12, 1492, Columbus landed on the Bahama Island of Guahani. Right: Sir Francis Drake was a pirate for the British.

or South America. A large percentage died at the hands of the cruel conquistadors or succumbed to the diseases that the white conquerors had brought with them. According to estimates, only half the population survived the first century of Spanish rule.

The colony of Costa Rica developed slowly. Attacks by English pirates, such as Drake, Mansfield and Morgan, delayed its development.

The Misquito Indians from Nicaragua in the north continued their attacks, and the number of slaves able to withstand the hard labor steadily diminished. The hoped-for treasure of gold and silver remained illusive, and Costa Rica lost its charm for the Spanish settlers. Within 300 years of colonial settlement only 50,000 people, most of them mestizos (a mixture of Spanish and Indian blood), and a few thousand pure-breed Indians and whites lived in Costa Rica. Except for the central highlands, the land was largely unsettled.

Costa Rica's fortunes finally improved with the signing of the Constitution of Cadíz in 1812. It ended *Encomienda*, guaranteed the right to education and freedom of the press, liberalized trade, and suspended taxation on trade for 10 years. As a result, trade flourished, schools and newspapers were founded, and the native population was rewarded for showing initiative.

Independence

Unlike Mexico, Costa Rica did not have to fight for its independence. It became independent automatically at the *Declaración de la Independencia* of Guatemala, which took place on September 15, 1821. The politicians in Cartago, however, only learned about their independence a month later. They then set up a provisional government (*junta*) composed of representatives chosen from the largest settlements in the country. Costa

Rica had two choices: It could either join the Central American Federation along with the states of Guatemala, Honduras, El Salvador and Nicaragua, or it could become a part of the Kingdom of Mexico. The republican representatives of the cities of Alajuela and San José voted to join the federation. The monarchists from Heredia and Cartago chose Itúrbide, the future Emperor of Mexico.

It was impossible to find a peaceful solution, and the difference of opinion soon escalated into civil war. Fortunately, the war did not last long. On April 5, 1823, the republicans won the battle of Volcán Irazu. The victorious party chose San José as their new capital. The change, however, had to wait until the warring factions fought one more short civil war in 1835, the *Guerra de la Liga*. In September of the same year, troops from San José fought against forces from three hostile neighboring cities. Although Costa Rica became a member of the Central American Federation, it made little effort to integrate itself. Costa Rican

19

President Braulio Carrillo Colina followed his own independent political course and finally withdrew from the union in 1838. When he seized dictatorial powers in 1841 and dismissed the government, the republicans joined forces with the former Federation president, Francisco Morazán from Honduras. Morazán vanquished Carillo, seized power, and once again integrated Costa Rica into the Central American Federation. Six months later he, too, was overthrown in yet another revolution, and was eventually executed.

The Victory of Coffee

A few years later the situation had once again stabilized, and in 1848 the *República de Costa Rica* was officially proclaimed. Coffee baron Juan Rafael Mora Porras became the head of state and

Above: Coffee plantation, an illustration from 1907. Right: Juan Santamaría, the national hero of Costa Rica.

would remain in the office for the next 11 years. Under his regime coffee was planted as never before. The aromatic beans became the mainstay of Costa Rica's economy and would remain so for decades to come. Huge plantations, where valuable highland coffee was grown, were established in the Meseta Central. Initial investment was financed by British banks and by the discovery of gold at Alajuela.

A small number of rich, industrious – but also greedy – planters contrived to buy out or cheat smaller farmers of their land. This gave way to huge feudal land holdings called *latifundia*. As a result, the large landholders and coffee merchants gained political power at the expense of the poor farmers. Under its *aristocracia cafetalera* (coffee aristocracy), small farmers (*peones*) were further degraded and reduced to becoming seasonal agricultural workers. They slipped ever deeper into poverty. Even President Mora Porras, who wanted to found a national bank offering low interest loans to farmers with small land holdings, was unable to withstand the pressure exerted by the politics of coffee and was finally forced from power in 1860.

The coffee aristocracy brought Costa Rica enormous economic growth. Streets, schools and hospitals were built. Busy ports were established along the coast, and San José grew from a sleepy agricultural city into a gleaming middle-sized capital. Everywhere noble mansions seemed to sprout out of the ground.

The peace and prosperity lasted until the turn of the century, with only one short interruption when a former slave trader named William Walker arrived from the United States.

The William Walker Episode

In 1855, liberal Nicaraguan politicians asked William Walker and his 300 *filibusteros* (soldiers of fortune) to help them fight in the civil war between conservative and liberal forces in Nicaragua. He came, helped them, and used the opportunity to seize power and name himself president of the country. One of his first acts as the newly self-appointed president was to once more legalize slavery in Nicaragua.

In March 1856, William Walker set his sights on Costa Rica and marched his troops into Guanacaste, prompting Costa Rican President Porras to quickly organize the *Campaña Nacional* and to assemble an improvised volunteer army to defend the country. In the decisive battle that took place near the Hacienda Santa Rosa, in what is today the Santa Rosa National Park, Porras' troops forced Walker to retreat.

They trapped the fleeing mercenaries near Rivas. Juan Santamaría, a young drummer from Alajuela, set fire to Walker's camp and forced him to retreat. Santamaría lost his life in the battle, but he won immortality as a national hero of Costa Rica.

Bananas and Railroads

In the second half of the 19th century, bananas became the additional foundation supporting the Costa Rican economy. The success of bananas as a cash crop is inseparable from the establishment of a railroad network. President Tomás Guardia (1870-82), with the help of loans from a British bank, began construction of a railroad line from San José to Puerto Limón on the Atlantic coast. The railroad was to shorten the time required for shipping coffee to Europe by three months. Previously, sacks of coffee beans had to make the long journey via Puntarenas to Chile and then around Cape Horn to Europe.

The construction of the 160-kilometer-long track was difficult. More than 4,000 railroad workers died of malaria or yellow fever in the jungles and swamps, forcing a one-year halt in construction until an American named Minor Kooper Keith took over the project. His uncle, Henry Meiggs, had already made a name

for himself as the builder of the famous Andes Railroad in Peru. Keith negotiated with the government to let him use thousands of hectares of land which had been cleared for the railroad to plant bananas. He finished laying the track with the help of 1,000 Afro-Caribbean workers from Jamaica. They proved more resistant to tropical disease than white railway workers, and they remained once the construction was completed to work on Keith's banana plantations. In 1899, the United States of American United Fruit Company (UFC) was founded. For decades it would control the economy and politics of Costa Rica.

Democracy and Modern Costa Rica

The period between 1880 and 1940 was marked by continual disputes be-

Above: Almost all of the descendants of the Afro-Caribbean workers from Jamaica today live on the Caribbean coast. Right: Schools instead of military barracks is the rule.

tween large landholders, rich merchants, landed aristocrats and the church, on the one hand, and the liberal government on the other.

In the 1880s, President Bernardo Soto introduced legislation dedicated to the eventual separation of church and state. The clergy's monopoly on education was abolished, the Catholic University of Santo Tomás was closed, civil marriage was recognized, and the administration of cemeteries was taken away from church and turned over to the state.

The state had already introduced universal compulsory education and set up special training programs for technicians and other experts. Costa Rica began systematically to modernize: electrical plants were constructed, the postal system was widely extended, and a telephone network was built. The Atlantic railway was completed, and universal male suffrage was introduced. In San José, a national library was constructed, and the imposing building that is now the National Museum was erected.

Political Parties and Unions

This period was not without its problems. In order to strengthen the position of small farmers against the coffee aristocracy, huge areas of land were cleared and set aside for agricultural use. The population increased rapidly, and ever more migrants from Europe came to Costa Rica.

After many years marked by military takeovers and terrorism, political parties and unions finally came into existence in the 1930s. They were successful in denouncing the inhuman working conditions suffered by employees of the United Fruit Company.

The government of Angel Calderón Guardia (1940-44) could not escape modernization and was forced to introduce the eight-hour work day, the *salario mínimo* (minimum wage), the right to union representation and a primitive form of social security system. The revolutionary reforms soon became collectively known as *Calderonismo*.

When the conservative opposition succeeded in calling a general strike in 1947, the government liberal majority, which until that time had been a significant factor among the population, began to lose power. The elections of 1948 ended with both sides accusing each other of electoral fraud. The dispute quickly escalated into civil war (*Guerra de la Liberación*). On April 18, 1948, opposition forces led by former coffee aristocrat José Figueres Ferrer forced the government to accept defeat and sent President Calderón into exile in Nicaragua.

Surprisingly – and for his supporters among the coffee aristocracy incredibly – Figueres passed legislation recognizing the equality of blacks (they had supported him in the civil war), introduced universal suffrage and nationalized the banks. In order to finally break the power of the coffee barons, Figueres – in a now famous speech in front of the National Museum, then the headquarters of the military – disbanded the army and replaced it with a civilian police corps.

23

Industrialization and Neutrality

Figueres' successor Ulate used the money previously allocated to the military for his new education program, to improve health and to modernize the country's agriculture. In order to further finance his reforms, he introduced a value-added tax and levied duty on imports. He tried to divert land to forestry and cattle breeding in order to free Costa Rica from its dependence on coffee and bananas, which are sharply influenced by the rise and fall of world prices. A broader, educated middle class came into being, guaranteeing a firmer basis for democracy.

President José Figueres Ferrer (1953-57 and 1970-74) led the country into a significant period of economic recovery. His efforts to restore prosperity won him

Above: Cattle from one of Costa Rica's large Haciendas. Right: Almost 50 percent of all Ticos are younger than 20, putting great pressure on the government to create jobs.

the support and affection of his people. He would become known as "Don Pepe," and remain one of the country's most popular leaders.

In 1983, President Luis Alberto Monge declared Costa Rica neutral in the Nicaraguan conflict in order to avoid pressure from the United States and President Ronald Reagan, who wanted to use Costa Rican territory as a staging area to support the Contras in Nicaragua.

Monges' successor Oscar Arias Sánchez (1986-90) continued the former president's pacifistic policies. He succeeded in gathering the former members of the Central American Federation to meet and negotiate a peace plan for Central America. His efforts won him the Nobel Peace Prize in 1987.

The Social Democrats – *Partido de Liberación Nacional* (PLN) – won the next elections in 1994, putting President José María Figueres Olsen into office. The opposition candidate Miguel Angel Rodriguez (POSC) won the following election in 1998.

CULTURE

Ticas and Ticos – The People

The inhabitants of Costa Rica like to call themselves *Ticos* or (for women) *Ticas*, an abbreviation of *Hermaniticos* and *Hermaniticas* – little brothers and little sisters; an affectionate nickname popular throughout Central America.

According to the last census, taken in 1993, 3,135,000 people lived in Costa Rica. By 1997, the population of the country had grown to 3.5 million. Between 1960 and 1985 the population nearly doubled. In terms of land area, an average 67 people now occupy each square kilometer.

Within the country the population density varies from one region to another. In the heavily-populated Meseta Central an average 300 people live in each square kilometer; in the sparsely populated coastal regions the average is only 20 people per square kilometer. By comparison, Mexico has an average population density of 47 people per square kilometer; in Germany the figure is 229 per square kilometer, while in the Netherlands it is 369 per square kilometer. The population is growing at a rate of two percent per year based on an annual average of 25 births for every four deaths.

These statistics place Costa Rica in a relatively low place on the birth-rate scale of the Third World. The state health system, which has been in force since the 1950s, has significantly reduced infant mortality to 1.4 percent and children's mortality to 1.6 percent. In terms of life expectancy, Costa Rica also ranks well. The average life expectancy is 74 years for men and 79 for women.

More than half of all Costa Ricans live in cities, a trend which is typical in Latin America. The average age of its population, however, remains a serious problem: 60 percent of all Ticos are younger than 25 and almost 50 percent are younger than 20. This means that thousands of new jobs have to be created each year – no small task in times of recession.

25

Demographics

The native Indian inhabitants of Costa Rica now number approximately 15,000 and make up 0.5 percent of the population, as opposed to 100 percent in 1502. Descendants of the numerous Indian tribes now call themselves *Indígena* (indigenous), but are mostly of mixed race following 500 years of contact with the white inhabitants. The word *"Indio"* is considered by many to be an insult.

Whites and Creoles descended from the original white settlers make up 87 percent of the population. In 1800 they made up only 10 percent, but the flood of immigrants in the 1920s added substantially to their numbers. This group also includes mestizos, descendants of mixed white and Indian parentage, who now make up seven percent of the population. The highland inhabitants are an espe-

cially homogenous group because the Indians gradually withdrew into the impassable mountain regions, and blacks were not allowed to settle in the Meseta Central until 1949. The inhabitants of the highlands enjoy greater prosperity than the lowland inhabitants.

Blacks and Mulattos

Descendants of the 10 million African slaves brought to Costa Rica in the 18th and 19th centuries now make up approximately three percent of the population. In colonial times the blacks worked on the cocoa *fincas* (plantations) along the Caribbean coast and traded with the *zambos misquitos* (black-skinned mestizos) and English pirates.

The number of blacks increased with the expansion of the banana plantations. Costa Rica abolished slavery in 1824. In 1872, more than 1,000 Afro-Caribbeans from Jamaica were brought to the country to build the railroad. A short time later, Minor Kooper Keith imported an-

Above: A young Boruca Indian. Right: The majority of Costa Rica's blacks live in the Atlantic coast region.

other 10,000 to complete the difficult Atlantic stretch of the railroad.

The United Fruit Company again brought hundreds of blacks to Costa Rica in 1915 to expand and work on its banana plantations. Later, when illness and poor crops forced the UFC to move its center of operations from the Atlantic lowlands to the Pacific coast at Golfito, most of the blacks remained behind. Legally, they were forbidden to move. Until 1949, they were banned from settling in the highland regions. It was only after the civil war of 1948, which was won by José Figueres, that blacks were recognized and granted Costa Rican citizenship.

To this day 100,000 black and mulatto descendants still live in the Atlantic region. Despite the growing influence of the white population, the majority of Spanish-speaking inhabitants and the growing numbers of tourists, many of these black inhabitants still speak *patois*, a fascinating mixture of Spanish and English. Rice and beans, *ñame* (a spice made of roots that flavors many of their native dishes) and *pan bom* characterize their cuisine.

This minority, whose indigenous culture is unfortunately gradually disappearing, favors calypso and reggae music. They wear their hair in dreadlocks, and adhere to Rastifarian sects imported from Jamaica or the Obeah religion of the Caribbean. They often consume alcohol excessively and smoke *ganja*, or marijuana. In addition to the *Indígenas*, whites, mestizos, blacks and mulattos, Costa Rica is also home to thousands of Asians. Most of the Chinese and Indians now living in the country arrived during the 19th century as migrant workers, and many today run ethnic restaurants.

Another 250,000 foreigners have chosen Costa Rica as their long-term residence. These include pensioners from the United States and Canada who come to the country to enjoy the mild climate along the coast or in the highlands, the

high standard of living and the many affordable leisure activities available to them. Smaller groups of Italian farmers (for example, in San Vito), German coffee planters and other European and North American hotel owners round out the population.

Religion

The Roman Catholic faith has dominated Costa Rica ever since the arrival of Spanish missionaries during the colonial era. The majority of the population (89 percent) remain Catholic, eight percent are Protestant and three percent adhere to other religions and sects. Ticos are, however, not as dependent on traditional religion as their Mexican neighbors. Their long democratic tradition and their disinclination to tolerate dictators and demagogues may account for the difference.

With the exception of a brief interlude in the 19th century, the Church has steadily lost influence in Costa Rica since the 18th century.

27

Today, being Catholic means attending church services only on special holidays and family celebrations. These include Easter (*Semana Santa;* the entire week preceding Easter Sunday is a national holiday) and Christmas. Costa Ricans also attend church for christenings, funerals of family members or close friends, and for weddings.

Thousands take part each year in the all-day procession in honor of Costa Rica's national saint, *Nuestra Señora de los Angeles,* on August 2 in Cartago.

The religious sentiments of the population are evident in many unexpected places: every bus, every taxi, every truck and almost every public office has its holy pictures or flower-bedecked shrine featuring statues of religious figures, which are meant to bring luck to the drivers and workers. These symbols have become talismans of luck and rarely have a deeper religious significance.

Protestant religious observance is barely noticeable in daily life. About one-half of Costa Rica's 40,000 Protestants are black and live on the Atlantic coast. Their beliefs often combine elements of Afro-Caribbean religion.

Language

The official language of Costa Rica is *Castellano* (Spanish). The vast majority (97 percent) of the population speaks the Costa Rican variety of Spanish, which has lost some of the grammatical forms of the language of the Spanish nobility and substituted expressions from indigenous and Afro-Caribbean dialects.

Blacks living along the Atlantic coast speak patois, a mixture of English and Spanish which bears great similarity to the pidgin English spoken in Jamaica. Few of the indigenous people of Costa Rica have retained their languages. Of

Right: The family takes first place in Costa Rican life.

the native population, only the Bribrí, the Boruca and the Cabécar, who live in the Cordillera de Talamanca, speak their original languages.

**Characteristics and
Leisure Activities**

Although it is dangerous to make generalizations about the common mentality or characteristics of a people, a journey through Costa Rica demonstrates certain traits. Most Ticos are extremely polite and like to maintain a polite distance. *A sus ordenes!* and *Para servirle!* (at your service) are two of the most often heard phrases and imply more than just a polite formality. *Hospitalidad,* or hospitality, takes top priority. Guests enjoy many more privileges and far more freedom than their hosts. The natural consequence of such an attitude is a very careful selection of guests.

The background of such hospitality is the unwritten law of the Ticos: *Quedar bien* – behave yourself well. An important maxim in Costa Rica is to make a good impression and it is almost universally followed.

Costa Ricans spend a great deal of time at home. Home is central to their lives, and their homes are very well taken care of. The saying "my home is my castle," or *"mi casa es mi castillo,"* could have been invented in Costa Rica.

Costa Ricans are much more family oriented than their North American or European neighbors. Social occasions, such as the popular Sunday picnic lunch, usually involve large family gatherings. The only events that take place outside the family circle are the Sunday promenade through the town center and the weekend dances where young people gather. Single children usually live with their parents until their marriage, and they contribute a significant part of their earnings to their parents for room and board. Pre-marital sex is frowned upon

and usually takes place in the darker corners of city parks, in cars borrowed from richer friends and in the dark anonymity of the cinema.

Part of the Costa Rican sense of hospitality and politeness expresses itself in the cheerful readiness of the native residents to be helpful to foreign guests. These attempts at courtesy can sometimes be irritating, especially when asking directions. A Tico would rather make something up than admit to a foreigner that he also doesn't know his way around. It is important in all situations to save face. Loss of face can lead to emotional outbreaks among Costa Ricans.

Costa Ricans are also extremely self-critical, both individually and collectively. However, criticism from outsiders, especially from foreigners, is often not well accepted. It is better to avoid critical remarks and, when that is absolutely impossible, to formulate words of criticism in a polite and diplomatic way. The customary practice of keeping a polite distance is also very im-

portant in maintaining control over emotions. This is often not possible without a little help. According to a statistical report published in 1995, Costa Ricans resort to tranquilizers more often than any of their Latin American neighbors. Unfortunately, drivers in Costa Rica's major cities do not appear to use tranquilizers. Aggressive, offensive driving is the rule of the streets. Risky passing maneuvers and nerve-jangling use of the horn characterize native driving habits.

Poco a poco and *despacio, despacio* – "little by little" and "not so fast" or "never too much at once" – are the sayings that often determine the pace of life in Costa Rica. Beneath such gentle warnings is a democratic and conservative attitude that favors the status quo over any kind of rash change. In leisure activities, unlike the attitude in public offices and businesses, time is generously dispensed.

When things occasionally go wrong the almost universal response is a shrug of the shoulders and the expression "*Quien sabe,*" which translates to "who

knows," a form of expression which is prevalent throughout the Latin American world. It is based on the supreme confidence that somewhere, someone will worry about the problem – hopefully not for another day or two.

A favorite response to almost any problem is "*mañana*" (tomorrow). The national philosophy dictates that you should never rush ahead. Tomorrow is another day and problems seldom go away. Great value is placed on public and private festivities and visitors are often pleasantly surprised to be invited by a total stranger to a fiesta.

First time social or business meetings, whether accidental or planned, always end with an exchange of *tarjetas* (business or visiting cards). Unlike Europeans and Americans, who regard such exchanges as routine, Costa Ricans see them as a sign of respect and trust.

Above: This bar owner's hobby is collecting business cards. Right: A true macho always gets the best seat in the house.

Men and Women

The relationship between the sexes in Costa Rica has evolved over 500 years in which Spanish and native Indian cultures became intertwined and inseparable. These cultures have given birth to expressions such as *machismo* and *marianismo*, which have entered even the international vocabulary of sexual relationships. Although the sharply defined roles of the sexes are changing among the younger generation, especially among the educated middle class, most Ticos still maintain macho values. "*Este hombre es muy macho,*" (this man is very macho) is universally held to be a compliment. The opposite, borrowed from the moral integrity of the Virgin Mary, is the woman who offers herself for her husband, children and home. The more beautiful, delicate and vulnerable she appears, the closer she comes to the Costa Rican ideal for women.

The clear division of roles between the sexes is easily observed at family picnics

in the city's parks. The women do what Costa Ricans call *chinear* – they fuss over their husbands continuously and anticipate their every wish. The husbands, meanwhile, enjoy themselves and condescend to making the occasional compliment or bestowing short bursts of attention upon their children.

Despite this public appearance of domestic harmony and romantic bliss, violence is on the rise in Costa Rican families. According to a study published in 1994, one out of three people admits having experienced violent outbreaks at the hands of their father. Jealousy and lack of respect can turn a volatile macho, especially under the influence of alcohol, into an unpredictable and dangerous man within seconds.

Before marriage, flirting is trumps. *Dando cuerva* (make eyes at someone) is a popular pastime. Young men call out provocative expressions like *mi amor, machita* or *guapa* (pretty), and both sexes in Costa Rica indulge in the sport of flirting. In fact, Ticos and Ticas are world champions at flirting; they have turned it into a high art and practice it regardless of age.

Young Ticas with long black hair, wearing skin-tight jeans, often with knee-high leather boots, seem to ignore the remarks of their admirers. In reality, they never miss a word and know how to value such gallantry. For foreign women, especially if they are blonde and long-legged, the chorus of whistles can eventually become tiresome and annoying.

Flirting is often successful and can easily go beyond innocent remarks. Many married Costa Rican men have affairs with unmarried, divorced or widowed women. Wives, on the other hand, are expected to be eternally faithful to their partners and to tolerate the affairs of their husbands, as long as they bring home the paycheck and observe their duties at home. Extramarital sexual adventures account for the fact that 25 percent of all children born in Costa Rica are illegitimate, and five percent have no idea who their biological father is.

Literature and Music

Costa Rica has few internationally famous poets or authors. Even today, few writers in Costa Rica can live from literature alone. Nonetheless, there is a respectable body of Costa Rican literature that is worth exploring in preparation for your trip, or which makes good reading during a vacation in the country.

Carlos Luis Falla's *Mamita Yunai* is the story of workers of the United Fruit Company and their daily lives and struggles. Joaquím Gutierrez wrote *Puerto Limón*, published in 1950. It is a socially realistic novel, based on the lives of blacks who live on the Atlantic coast. *El Eco de los Pasos* by Julieta Pinto is a vivid account of the civil war of 1948. The essays and short stories of Roberto Brenes Mesen and Joaquín García Monge, Costa Rica's first poets, reveal

Above: Ticos love the exciting sounds of marimba music, which is played on a kind of xylophone with 77 keys.

important insights into the values and sensibilities of Costa Ricans.

Music and dance are ubiquitous in Costa Rica. Whether in a bar, restaurant, hotel lobby, by the swimming pool, on the street or in the central park that marks every town and city – everywhere there is music. At the slightest opportunity, in bars and discos, at family gatherings and folk festivals, couples dance the exciting dances of Latin America: *merengue, salsa, soca, cumbia* or *marcado*.

In town squares throughout the country, and in crowded restaurants during the evening hours, *mariachi* bands made up of a guitar, contrabass, four-stringed *cuatro, bandolón* (a form of harmonica), Italian violin and trumpet entertain with their lively melodies. They set the mood for dancing and fill the warm tropical air with delightful sounds.

The musicians usually wear richly embroidered jackets and skin-tight knee breeches, which are often decorated with silver buttons. What could be more romantic and exciting?

Costa Rica's most popular instrument is the *marimba*, a type of xylophone of African or Indian origin. The marimba, usually made of ebony, has 77 keys of various lengths and produces tones in six octaves. It can be played by two or four musicians, each using two to four wooden mallets.

Modern music is influenced by the inescapable sounds of Anglo-American pop. Folk music, which is usually accompanied by the guitar, and choral music remain popular and borrow their beat and rhythm from Mexican folk tunes.

Economy

Although only three families have supplied Costa Rica with heads of state since the country's independence in 1821, most Ticos would not hesitate to describe their country as a classless democracy. Although the ancient feudal divisions of society into *hidalgos* (aristocrats) and *peones* (farmers) have long since disappeared, in modern Costa Rica the profits from the coffee and banana plantations and cattle ranches still flow into the pockets of very few families. The per capita gross national product comes to US $2,610, putting Costa Rica into 76th place among the world's economies. The annual per capita income in 1994 was approximately US $3,000, well above the Latin American average. The division of economic sectors is typical for developing countries: in 1995, industry accounted for 17 percent of Costa Rica's gross domestic production, services 58 percent, and agriculture 23 percent. The most important industries are pharmaceuticals, textiles and food processing. Since 1990, modern tuna fish canneries and highly mechanized furniture factories have been gaining importance and may soon compete with agriculture as a major source of national income.

The dream of gold that has haunted Costa Rica's history was never realized, and, except for bauxite, Costa Rica has no significant mineral resources.

The unemployment rate in 1996 was 6.2 percent, which is far below the rate of many industrialized nations. The figure, however, is deceptive. The low rate of mechanization in industry and agriculture, and the fact that underemployment and hidden unemployment are not reported by the government, account for the relatively low figure. The foreign debt of US $3.8 billion is also responsible for the significant slowdown in the nation's economy.

Costa Rica's imports exceed exports, resulting in a balance of payments deficit. Its major imports include manufactured goods, machinery and fossil fuels, which amount to US $3.3 billion per year. The United States provides 26 percent of the country's imports. The high duty on imported automobiles, high-fidelity equipment and other luxury products results in double to quadruple prices that consumers have to pay. Costa Rica's exports amount to US $2.6 billion. Manufactured goods make up 46 percent of this sum; 18 percent comes from textile products; bananas account for 16 percent, and coffee beans bring in 11 percent.

In terms of living conditions, Costa Rica compares very well to other countries around the world, especially in terms of private housing. Ticos inhabit some 600,000 houses (5.5 people per house). Two-thirds of all houses are privately owned homes; 25 percent are rental properties and appartments. Costa Rica has the highest standard of living in Latin America. According to recent statistics: televisions are found in 70 percent of all households; 30 percent have telephones; 20 percent have bathrooms with running hot water. But slums continue to exist despite the affluence. The 10,000 *tugurios*, or illegally built shacks, that fill the slums surrounding San José have neither plumbing nor running water, and are home to more than 60,000 people.

Agriculture

In Costa Rica, every fourth citizen is employed in agriculture. By comparison, in Germany it is every 80th, in the U. S., every 200th person. Farm land accounts for 12 percent of total area, and 45 percent of it is used as pasture. Forests are on the decrease and now cover only 27 percent of the land (formerly it was 90 percent). Although many family farms still exist, it is the large agro-industrial concerns that account for the major exports so vital to the country's economy.

At present, 70 percent of the land in use for agriculture is used as pasture for the 2.5 million head of cattle (zebu, Charolais and Hereford). The province of Guanacaste, with lush meadows that remain green throughout the year, lays claim to 75 percent of the country's cattle

Above: Sugar cane, grown along the coast, is an important export. Right: Rental car drivers should be prepared for a variety of exciting driving conditions.

ranches. Other areas where cattle ranches are also found are in the Valle de El General and, most recently, in the newly cleared fields along the Atlantic coast. Meat, however, still accounts for only one percent of Costa Rica's exports. Most of the meat is sold to international hamburger chains.

Thanks to government subsidies, banana exports have increased by 50 percent since 1985 and now account for 16 percent of the nation's exports. The golden fruit, which was first planted by Minor Keith in 1890, is now a significant crop that covers 45,000 hectares of land.

The first coffee plants were probably brought to Costa Rica from Jamaica in the 17th century. The beans, which are grown mainly in the highlands, now comprise 11 percent of Costa Rica's exports. Coffee is grown on the larger *fincas*, or plantations, which employ hundreds of poorly paid seasonal workers. Sugar cane is grown along the coast and accounts for another US $50 million a year in exports.

Tourism

In contrast to industry and agriculture, which are big businesses in Costa Rica, tourism is, to a great extent, still in the hands of small private concerns. In 1997, a total of 580,000 visitors came to Costa Rica (52 percent were from North America). They spent a total of US $714 million, providing jobs for 130,000 Costa Ricans. The increase in tourism as an important source of income has prompted the government to add a new minister; since 1990, the country has had a Minister of Tourism in its cabinet.

While the number of available hotel rooms has increased to 25,000, the number of tourists has decreased over the past several years.

In a recent poll, 60 percent of all visitors cited "nature" as their primary reason for coming to Costa Rica. Beaches and sunshine attracted 50 percent. Only 18 percent are package tourists; 45 percent rent a car during their stay, and most of the visitors are under 40 years of age.

Most of the tourist accommodations continue to be small family-run hotels and inns, but major hotel chains, such as Marriott and Camino Real, have built hotels around San José. A gigantic, long-planned project, Golfo de Papagayo, on the Nicoya peninsula, has been scaled down following massive protests from inhabitants and regional hotel owners.

Almost 40 percent of all visitors say that ecologically sound tourism is important to them. Costa Rican travel agents responded by turning ecologically-oriented tourism into big business. They realized there was money to be made from organized trips to national parks, guided jungle tours, horseback-riding tours, kayak adventures and scuba diving courses. In areas such as the overcrowded Playa Grande, where sea turtles come to lay their eggs, the damage has already been done. New projects are being developed, but it isn't always easy to strike a balance between the interests of tourists and those of hotel owners, developers and farmers.

ALMACEN
EL EMPORIO

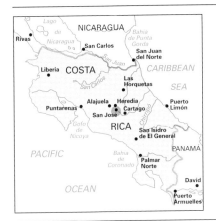

SAN JOSÉ

HISTORY
THE HISTORIC CENTER
SIGHTSEEING
OUTSIDE THE CENTER
NIGHTLIFE

Most visitors to Costa Rica first land in the capital city San José, and then take off for excursions to nearby beaches, mountains and national parks. The city, with its 300,000 inhabitants in the heart of the Meseta Central, offers travelers their first opportunity to sample the typical atmosphere of Central America and to gain an insight into the everyday life and culture of the Ticos.

Although San José, unlike most other major Latin American cities, does not possess a real *paseo* (the long avenue Paseo Colón is more a busy shopping street than an elegant boulevard for strolling), there are many exciting opportunities for travelers to take an active part in the daily life of the city or to settle down in one of the many city parks as silent observers of customs in the Costa Rican capital. From the benches of the Parque Central or the steps of the Plaza de la Cultura you can observe casually clad gentlemen who, upon spotting a tourist, plunge their hands into the bulging pockets of their pleated trousers with lightening speed and offer to *change-*

Preceding pages: A view over the roofs of San José. Fresh tropical fruit is available in the capital throughout the year. Left: Pretty Ticas turn the heads of home town men as well as visitors.

cambio-wechsel United States dollars into the local currency.

American and Canadian pensioners sit in the few sidewalk cafés that are open during the day. Surprisingly, Ticos tend to be homebodies, which is not what you would assume from the climatic conditions. The people in the cafés look slightly bored as they nibble their *bocas* (appetizers) and eat their hamburgers, stopping every now and then to take a sip of coffee. In the evenings there are concerts at the Soda Palace (Avenida Segunda), which offers welcome relief from the hectic nightlife in the loud bars, discotheques and casinos of the capital. *Mariachi* bands play day and night, livening up the scene and adding color and sound to the city. The musicians, usually good looking men dressed in Mexican-style clothing, play for a while, then move on to the next bar or café in the hope of earning a few colones.

HISTORY

With its relatively short history and the many earthquakes it has survived, San José (the city only got its present name in 1813) does not have many historical buildings nor famous sights to see. Nevertheless, there are many things to discover during the day and by night. The

41

development of the city is defined by its short but eventful history that begins in 1737. At that time Cartago, just 20 kilometers east of modern San José, was the capital of Costa Rica. In 1737, Cartago's church elders decided to build a parish church dedicated to St. Joseph. It would serve the 200 farms surrounding the small village of *Villa Nueva del Boca de la Monte* (New Town at the Mouth of the Mountain), and 2,000 other settlers scattered throughout the western part of the valley, saving them the long walk to attend Sunday church services in Cartago.

Years later, when the settlement failed to grow as expected because of the shortage of drinking water, the clergy and the mayor forced some farm families to settle

in San José. The city's water supply remained a problem until 1751, when the inhabitants finally managed to complete an eight-kilometer-long canal which brought water from the Río Torres to the city. By 1785, San José had more than 5,000 inhabitants and was larger than Cartago, the capital. But even in 1821, when Costa Rica gained its independence, San José remained little more than a collection of sprawling farms and workshops like so many other villages in the country.

But the idyllic rural character of the settlement was about to end. In 1821, the neighboring cities of Cartago and Heredia, led by monarchists, chose to join the Central American Federation

Avenida 13 LAISA
Avenida 11
Calle 5
Calle 7
Spirogyra
Jardín de
Mariposas
Parque Zoologico
Simón Bolívar
La Casa Verde
de Amón
OTOYA
L'Ambiance Avenida 11
Calle 13
Calle 15
Calle 17
AMON
Don
Carlos
Avenida 7
Calle 3
Aurola
Holiday Inn
Avenida 5
Museo
de Jade
Casa
Amarilla
Centro Nacional
de la Cultura
Edificio
Metálico
Parque
España
Museo
Nacional
de Ferrocarril
Avenida 3
Parque
Morazán
Centro Nacional de
Cultura,
Biblioteca
Nacional
Key Largo
Fábrica Nacional de
Licores
Parque
Nacional
Serpentario
Del Rey
Avenida 1
Balcón
de Europa
BELLAVISTA
Asamblea
Legislativa
San Pedro,
Museo de Insectos
Plaza
de la
Cultura
Museo del Oro
Precolombiano,
Museo Numismatico
Avenida Central
Teatro
Nacional
Instituto
Costaricense
de Turismo
Plaza
de la
Democracia
Museo
Nacional
Casa
429
Charleston
Avenida 4
Avenida 2
Teatro la
Mascara
Calle 15
Calle 17
Calle 19
Avenida 6
Iglesia
Soledad
Avenida 6
Avenida 8
Museo
Criminologico
SOLEDAD
Avenida 10
Calle 5
Calle 7
Calle 9
Calle 11
Calle 13
Calle 15
Avenida 10
Avenida 12
Teatro
Chaplin
Avenida 14

under the leadership of Mexico. San José and Alajuela preferred full independence for Costa Rica. The differences of opinion between the republicans of San José and the monarchists from Cartago soon escalated into a military confrontation that climaxed in the battle of April 5, 1823, in the hills of Ochomogo. Soldiers from San José and Alajuela fought troops representing Cartago and Heredia. San José's victory at Ochomogo established Costa Rica as an independent state.

The battle was barely forgotten before a new quarrel broke out among the cities of the high plateau. In addition to Cartago, Alajuela and Heredia now wanted the honor of becoming the new capital of the independent state. They joined forces against the upstart city of San José and kindled the conflict that would flare into the civil war of September 1837. To everyone's amazement San José's forces proved victorious, and the city became the new capital.

In the second half of the 19th century, income from coffee plantations (which had massive political support) brought new prosperity to the capital. San José blossomed and grew more beautiful every day. So much money from coffee exports flowed into the town that San José became only the third city in the world to light its streets with electricity. Its neighboring cities, already jealous of San José's status as a capital, were absolutely green with envy.

With money from the sale of coffee beans, the city's aristocrats financed the construction of libraries, museums and theaters. Concerts, opera performances featuring internationally-famous stars, lavish balls and sumptuous banquets won the new capital attention throughout Central America.

Famous architects from Paris and Milan traveled to San José, and demonstrated their skills in the public buildings and private mansions that they designed. In 1940, more than one hundred years following its elevation to capital, San José still only had 70,000 inhabitants. It was not until after World War II, when large numbers of poor European immigrants arrived in Costa Rica, that the city expanded appreciably.

The sudden increase in population led San José's politicians and city planners to make decisions that many of its citizens regret today. Countless beautiful historic buildings fell victim – especially in the 1950s – to uncontrolled expansion. The politicians were less interested in preserving the past than in building for the future. They envisioned a new, attractive 20th century capital whose skyline was filled with skyscrapers made of glass, steel and marble.

Statistical Data

Today, some 325,000 people live in the city of San José. When the area surrounding the capital, the *Area Capitalina* in the Meseta Central (Central Valley), is included, the number of inhabitants increases to 900,000.

The province of San José has 1.3 million inhabitants, making up nearly 40 percent of the population of Costa Rica. People who live in the city like to call themselves *Josefinos*. Their city is located at 1,150 meters above sea level, in a broad, fertile high plateau that has a comfortable average temperature of 20°C throughout the year and a recorded average annual rainfall of 2,000 mm.

As in virtually every Latin American city founded by the Spaniards, the streets in San José are laid out in a grid pattern

Above: The lively center of San José, with its shops and crowded streets, bustles with colorul activity. Right: Many Ticos regularly try their luck at the lottery.

resembling a chess board. The old center, which is only partially preserved, is surrounded by newly-constructed housing, industrial areas, sprawling parks, sports facilities, rich and poor neighborhoods, and the lush green hillsides of the highland plateau.

THE HISTORIC CENTER

Orientation

All streets in the city center – *calles* and *avenidas* – are numbered. The usually broader avenidas run from east to west, the calles from north to south. The Avenida Central cuts through the city and forms its east-west axis. North of the Avenida Central, the avenidas bear uneven numbers; to the south, the numbers are even.

Similarly, the Calle Central intersects the Avenida Central from north to south at a right angle. All calles east of the Calle Central bear uneven numbers; those west of it have even numbers.

When asking one of the local residents for directions in San José – or in any other Costa Rican city – the answer is likely to sound something like this: "Go three blocks to the west and then four blocks south." Or they will count the distance in 100-meter blocks, meaning housing blocks, even when these are less than 100 meters long. Half a block translates into 50 meters.

Addresses in Costa Rica seldom contain house numbers. An address is given citing the nearest intersection. For example, Mercado Central at Avenida Central between Calles 6 and 8 would be entered in the address registry as Av. Ctl, C. 6/8 or Av. 0, C. 6/8.

When giving their addresses, Ticos prefer referring to a famous building, monument or similar landmark near their residence. "Two blocks south of the old whatever-it's-called bar," is a typical address – even long after the bar has closed. A number of years ago, the popular newspaper *Tico Times* reported that San José taxi drivers, in all earnestness, frequently gave directions containing information such as: "Three hundred meters east of the spot where, way back when, they burned the dog that was run over," or "turn right at the meadow where the cows once grazed." For travelers, such directions don't necessarily guarantee they will reach their destination in Costa Rica.

Costa Rica's drivers also fail to inspire much confidence. Once behind the wheel of a car, they often seem to forget their good manners and their motto, "*quedar bien.*" Pedestrians are often made to feel like wild game in season when crossing a busy street, which can turn into a harrowing adventure.

A constant concert of horns and shouting matches between drivers discussing the right-of-way can increase the noise level to a fever pitch. Far too few parking spaces, too many one-way streets and – to put it mildly – an extremely modest use of street signs convince many travelers to take the first opportunity to exchange the chaos of the big city jungle

for the relative peace and quiet of the rain forest.

The most important sights in the center of San José can be easily reached on foot. The Central Park is the ideal place to start your walking tour.

Parque Central

The Parque Central (Avenida 2, between Calles Central and 2) is the oldest park in the city. Laid out in 1885, the park has meanwhile lost its reputation as the cultural center of San José to the Plaza de la Cultura. The uninviting music pavilion made out of concrete, the **El Quiosco**, was a gift to Costa Rica in the late 1940s from Nicaragua's notorious dictator Anastasio Somoza. The pavilion is set in the heart of the park. Sunday concerts played by the city orchestra take place under its roof.

Above: The city center is characterized by colorful activity. Right: Folklore from the Andes on the Plaza de la Cultura.

On weekdays, the shabby pavilion, which is badly in need of repair, is surrounded by peddlers and beggars who hang out there and at the **Carmen Lyra Children's Library** located next door. The library was named after a successful Costa Rican author children's books. The streets south of the palm tree bordered park contain many of San José's more popular bars and night clubs (see pages 63 and 64).

La Cathedral Metropolitana

San José's cathedral lives up to its magnificent name. It is the most important church in the city. Following the destruction of the original cathedral in the earthquake of 1821, construction on the present structure was begun in 1871. The impressive house of worship was built in the then preferred neoclassical style, with countless white columns, white walls and a blue roof. To the right of the entrance is a monument to the memory of Monseñor Bernardo Augusto Thiel, a German priest

whom Costa Rica's clergy raised to the office of the country's second bishop in 1880. With the help of the Catholic Party, a religious political party he founded, Monseñor Thiel managed to increase the influence of the Catholic Church in Costa Rica.

The interior of the cathedral is surprisingly unspectacular. The wooden construction is typical of 19th-century Costa Rican architecture. The double columns are made of solid wood and painted. Even the huge filigree chandelier is carved of wood. Leaded stained-glass windows show scenes from the Bible and portraits of the saints. They are similar to windows found throughout Latin American churches.

The impressive and valuable main altar is under the painted cupola. It is where high mass has been celebrated for more than a century. One of the side-chapels merits closer inspection. The ceiling and inner walls of the **Capilla de Santissimo Sacramento** are lavishly decorated with flowers and leaves.

Teatro Melico Salazar

Two blocks west of the Plaza de la Cultura (Avenida 2, Calle Central) is another national monument, the **Melico Salazar Theater**, built in the 1920s. It was named after Costa Rica's famous opera singer, Manuel Salazar Zuñigas, who came to San José in 1929 from the Scala in Milan. His triumph in the capital convinced him to move to Costa Rica in 1937. He remain there until his death in 1950. The imposing building, with its Corinthian columns and high balconies, is now the home of the *Orquestra Sinfónica Nacional* (National Symphony Orchestra). International orchestras and ballet companies perform there from March through November. On Tuesday evenings there is a weekly folklore show especially for tourists.

Plaza de la Cultura

The square known as the Plaza of Culture (Avenidas Central and 2, and Calles

47

3 and 5) is little more than an elevated concrete construction similar to an un-roofed terrace. Because of the many young people (often unemployed) and tourists who frequent the square, it has become one of the most popular places in the capital.

Artisan stalls selling jewelry, paintings, hammocks, maps and all kinds of colorful knick-knacks line the west side of the Plaza de la Cultura. For a couple of dollars (or colones) marimba bands and other strolling musicians play international melodies or local folk songs. Street performers and magicians entertain the crowd with magic tricks, and acrobats defy gravity.

The imposing facade of the Teatro Nacional forms the south side of the Plaza. **The Tourist Office** (ICT) is on the lower level of the Plaza, next door to the Gold

Above: East come, easy go – public games of chance are popular throughout Costa Rica. Right: The Teatro Nacional, the largest building in the capital.

Museum. On most sunny afternoons the Plaza de la Cultura presents the ideal place to observe the local inhabitants as they rush by.

Teatro Nacional

Many Josefinos and foreign visitors rank the **National Theater** as the city's most important building. The theater was begun following the total destruction by an earthquake of the building that occupied the site until 1888. The new theater was meant to be an imposing construction that could adequately represent Costa Rica's new wealth. According to an often repeated story, the international prima donna Adelina Patti had refused to sing in the old theater because members of the audience sitting in the orchestra section had to bring their own folding chairs to the performances. The Josefinos were not about to tolerate such criticism, and the newly rich banana and coffee barons donated large sums of money for a new theater. The city also contributed a

large sum, and Costa Rica engaged an illustrious international team of experts composed of Belgian architects and Spanish and Italian painters and wood carvers, along with local engineers who sought inspiration from the opera houses of Paris, Vienna and La Scala of Milan. Shortly after its completion, in 1894, the Teatro Nacional was inaugurated by a performance featuring stars from Paris in Charles-François Gounod's opera *Faust*.

For the façade of the building, which is now used mainly for concerts, the architects chose the neoclassical style. They placed statues of Beethoven and Spanish dramatist Calderón de la Barca at the entrance. No cost was spared in the construction. A large number of magnificent, valuable Italian marble columns support the roof over the lobby.

The charming Viennese-style café has a painted ceiling by Ferrario Carlo Milano. It is the perfect spot to take a rest while touring the building. The café also features changing exhibits of art by young local artists.

The tour of the theater continues with the grand staircase, constructed of solid marble steps. A look skyward reveals *Una Alegoría*, Costa Rica's most famous artwork, painted in 1897 by Milanese artist Aleardo Villa. It shows an idealized view of the coffee harvest in Costa Rica. The pickers wear colorful traditional skirts. In the background the planters bargain with buyers before the sacks of "black gold" are loaded onto waiting flag-bedecked sailing ships in Puerto Limón. *Una Alegoría* was reproduced on the back of the five-colones bank note, which is no longer in circulation, but which can still be found in stalls at the souvenir markets.

Neither gold leaf nor velvet were spared in the decoration of the foyer of the National Theater. The theme is set by the gigantic triptych, painted by Bespasiano Bignami and entitled *Twilight, Day and Night*. The auditorium can accommodate more than 1,000 viewers. Milanese painter Roberto Fontana painted the slightly vaulted ceiling with a work

entitled, *In Memory of the Muse of Music.* Since 1965, the theater has been under historic protection as a national monument. The damage caused by the 1991 earthquake has been repaired, and now the National Symphony Orchestra is again able to play in the theater. Operas, ballets and plays are once again performed on its famous stage.

La Casona Souvenir Market

La Casona means " the big house," and the San Jose souvenir market occupies just such a building, now unfortunately sadly dilapidated. The once imposing colonial style house (Calle Central, Avenida Central) features a great variety of souvenirs of all kinds. Dozens of stands fill two floors on which every type of handicraft ever made by Costa Rica's artisans can be found. *Artesanía* (handi-

Above and right: Filigree gods made of gold and silver; modern stone sculpture (National Museum).

crafts), especially items made of wood and fabric, are sold here. Coffee and coffee liqueurs are also available. The "mobile" handicraft market, formerly on the Plaza de la Cultura, has now moved further east to the Plaza de la Independencia.

Museo de Oro

On the lower level of the Tourist Office, almost hidden in the busy bustle of the big city, is the small but wonderful **Museum of Pre-Columbian Gold** at the Plaza de la Cultura (Calle 5, Avenida Central and 2). The building, provided by the Banco Central, also houses a coin collection. Like so many of San José's buildings, it also suffered serious damage in the 1991 earthquake, but remained open, displaying its numerous gold objects and Costa Rican art.

The **Museo Numismático**, on the first subterranean level, reveals the development of Costa Rica's monetary system, which is explained with the help of draw-

ings, maps, photographs and texts. Behind a gallery dedicated to contemporary art, an ethnological exhibit gives a glimpse into the lives of the original native inhabitants of Costa Rica, the Huetar, Boruca and Chorotega Indians.

The **Museo de Oro** is Costa Rica's most valuable museum, both for the precious objects it displays and for the wealth of historic information it offers. It has 70 glass cases full of religious, military and decorative gold objects, such as bracelets, headbands, and bangles and bands worn on the ankles. The explanation of how the Indians produced such objects is also fascinating and helps to understand their highly evolved culture.

They created gold figures by using what we call the lost-wax process, in which a model is formed out of wax and embedded into clay, forming a mold in which there is one small opening. Once the clay hardens it is heated until the wax melts and runs out, producing a mold for the molten gold. The Indians made jewelry by melting the gold ore in a small

fireproof clay mold and producing a ball (*tejuelo*). They beat this with smooth rounded stones, then heated the gold a second time and plunged it into cold water before working the metal further. On some days (not on a regular schedule) the Gold Musuem offers organized tours in English or Spanish, free of charge.

While visiting the museum, for security reasons, all visitors are required to check their cameras, purses, umbrellas and jackets in the attended cloakroom.

Museo Nacional

The **National Museum**, the pride of Costa Rica, is housed in the old Fuerte Bellavista (Calle 17 and Avenida Central/2), on the eastern side of the Plaza de la Democracía, which was only laid out in 1989. The fort, originally named Bellavista (Beautiful View), was constructed in 1887 and served as the headquarters for Costa Rica's military until it was abolished in 1948. President José Figueres Ferrer announced the abolition

of the military from the steps in front of the building. The museum that now occupies the building is divided into four separate exhibition halls. In the **Sala de Arqueología**, also known as Sala Doris Stone, stone artifacts, such as blades, scrapers, knives and gimlets made of flint and obsidian, ceramic pots, sculpture hewed from volcanic stone and superbly crafted *metates*, sacrificial altars formed of volcanic stone, are on display. Researchers trained in prehistoric art have assembled an important collection of pre-Columbian art and objects, spanning a period from 20,000 years ago to the beginning of the Spanish conquest. A collection of jade collars and amulets, used for rituals, enhances this exhibit.

The **Sala de Oro**, in the northeastern corner of the fort, contains a collection of humanoid figures made of gold, which the early Mesoamerican Indians wor-

shiped as gods. The religious symbols demonstrate fine workmanship. Only the best artisans of the tribe were allowed to work on such holy figures.

The **Sala Colonial** features colonial objects, such as paintings, simple furniture from the time of the first Spanish settlements, clothing from those "good old days," certificates, religious pictures and statues of saints. These afford visitors and the many school children who visit the museum in groups a glimpse into the sometimes difficult and often less than comfortable life of the Spanish conquerors. It is not possible to enter the Sala Colonial, though; you have to view the exhibits from the gallery.

The **Sala de la Historia**, the fourth and final section of the National Museum, is dedicated to Costa Rica's more recent history, which begins with its independence. Historic photographs, yellowing newspaper clippings, weapons, 19th-century uniforms and old agricultural implements illustrate the development of the country following its rebirth as a

Above: An attractive Tica in the Parque Nacional. Right: An out-of-service steam locomotive in the Railroad Museum.

sovereign state at the beginning of the coffee era. A sugar mill (*trapiche*) and an old but still usable ox cart in the inner courtyard of the museum complete the exhibition.

Most of the exhibits are explained only in Spanish; a few are translated into English. Back outside, it is worth taking time to examine the outside walls of the National Museum. The towers and walls of the former army headquarters still bear the traces of shots fired during the civil war of 1948. Heavy cannon from colonial times line the carefully-groomed courtyard of the museum, a reminder of the "powerful reasons" behind the Spanish conquistadors' success in conquering the Indian population. The tiny museum souvenir shop sells postcards and books on this theme.

Parque Nacional

The National Park, on a slightly raised bluff south of the National Library (between Avenidas 1 and 3, and Calles 15 and 19), claims to be the largest and quietest park in the city. The pride of this shady place is the **National Warrior Monument** erected in 1856. The statue, cast at the Rodin studio in Paris, shows a victorious Costa Rican soldier fighting against soldier of fortune and slave trader William Walker. The former presidential palace, today the home of the Costa Rican **Congress**, is on the south side of the park. In the southwest corner, opposite the warrior monument, is a statue of Costa Rica's national hero, **Juan Santamaría**, whose heroic act ended the siege of Santa Rosa. The Parque Nacional is surrounded by other important sights. To the northwest the former liquor distillery, built in 1856 to produce delicious fiery drinks, is today a museum. In the north is the **National Library**, a place for those in search of spiritual sustenance.

Museo Nacional de Ferrocarril

The **National Railroad Museum** is in the former Atlantico Railway Station

53

(Avenida 3, Calle 17 and 23) – out of necessity rather than design, because the station was no longer needed following the destruction of the Atlantic Railroad in the 1991 earthquake. In the museum, which opened in 1993, you can see the first locomotive that traveled between San José and Puerto Limón. Railroad buffs will be thrilled with the old Northern Railways locomotives, model railroads, historic photos of old railway stations and exhibits documenting the construction of the railway.

Parque España

Spanish Park (Avenida 3 and Avenida 7 at Calles 9 and 11) is planted with giant trees and bamboo which reach high into the smog-filled sky. In 1992, the park made headlines when a monument entitled **El Conquistador**, showing

Above: "La Familia" in front of the Central Bank. Right: A pre-Columbian cult cornmeal trough in the Jade Museum.

a Spanish conqueror, was erected in its western section in commemoration of the 500th anniversary of the European discovery of America. Controversy over the statue raged, and pro and con groups argued for the removal or the retention of the armored knight. The issue was decided at a high political level and calculated to be very diplomatic toward Spain. In the end the decision favored the land of the conquistadors, and city leaders decided to keep the statue in the park.

The chirping of thousands of birds fills Spanish Park in the early morning and late evening hours. It is as if all the city's birds chose this particular place to meet and hold their nocturnal symphony before turning in for the night. On Sundays, Josefinos and tourists gather at the colorful open-air market held in Spanish Park. The INS building and the **Jade Museum** are at its northern end. The statue in front of the museum is called **La Familia** and honors the family as the basis of society.

The **Edifício Metálico**, an imposing steel building, rises in the north. The foreign ministry overlooks the northeastern section of the Parque España and adds a touch of color to the concrete gray of the surrounding buildings.

The **Casa Amarilla**, or "Yellow House," is familiar to everyone in Costa Rica. The small nearby chapel, with its red-brown *azulejos* (tiles) and pretty Andelusian fountain in its courtyard, is not as well known. Among its treasures is a piece of the Berlin Wall, which was donated to Costa Rica by Germany.

Jade Museum

Two streets south of the zoo (Avenida 7, Calle 9 and 11), across from the Parque España, is the famous **Jade Museum**, on the 11th floor of the **Instituto Nacional de Seguros**. The museum was opened in 1984 and affords an excellent panoramic view of the city along with the world's largest collection of American jade. The

glass cases are filled with 6,000 jewel-like pieces of green, blue and black jade – the pre-Columbian heritage of various regional cultures of Central America. In addition to examples of superb workmanship showing the highly developed technique employed by ancient Costa Ricans, the museum possesses works by the Olmecs, the prehistoric Mesoamerican people from whom all other Indian cultures developed. It also displays 2,000-year-old treasures from the Mayan civilization of the Yucatan Peninsula in Mexico. The first works of high quality were made following the development of the thread-saw technique, around 300 A.D. The necklaces, earrings, pendants and carved monkeys, crocodiles and jaguars (animals important in fertility rites because of their mystical powers) exhibit superb craftsmanship.

Casa Amarilla

One block east of the Jade Museum (Avenida 7) is an old mansion with bright yellow walls – the **Casa Amarilla**, or "Yellow House," occupied by the foreign ministry. Fortunately, the building was spared by the earthquakes that plague the Meseta Central and by the rebuilding madness of the 1950s.

Centro Nacional de la Cultura

The former coffee liqueur factory, built in 1856, which is opposite the Casa Amarilla, makes it clear that coffee is not the only stimulating brew made from "black gold." The founder of the factory was president and coffee baron Juan Rafael Mora, who was the first to produce coffee liqueur in Costa Rica. Other alcoholic beverages, including *Guaro*, a high proof spirit distilled from sugar cane, and rum were also produced at the factory under government control. A few years ago the city rebuilt the factory with a great deal of taste, and reopened it as the **Centro Nacional de la Cultura**, a cultural center with ample room for exhibits, performances and space for the

Museo de Arte y Diseño Contemporáneo (Museum of Contemporary Art and Design). The center has lecture rooms along with dance and graphic arts studios. In the evenings there are often performances which are open to the public. Presses, a kettle, a furnace and other machinery formerly used in the old distillery are displayed in the courtyard.

Parque Zoológico Simón Bolívar

San José, like just about every capital in the world, has a zoo. The entrance to the small national **Simón Bolívar Zoo**, located in a park of the same name on the shore of the Río Torres, is on Avenida 11, Calle 7 and 9.

In cages that are too small, native animals, such as agoutis, peccaries, opossums, wildcats, tapirs, sloths, monkeys,

armadillos and anteaters live alongside exotic animals from Africa and Asia. The zoo is especially heavily frequented on weekends when families from the city and the suburbs come to spend the day. The children create a steady and astoundingly high level of noise and cause constant excitement, which is not limited to the popular monkey house. Classes of school children visit the zoo on weekdays, further aggravating the animals' already jangled nerves.

The Simón Bolívar Zoo compares poorly to the country's grandiose national parks. The shortage of funds and the sorry conditions under which the animals are kept stand in sharp contrast to the government's exemplary protection of flora and fauna in Costa Rica's national parks.

Fortunately, plans already exist to move the zoo to larger quarters near Garitas, where it will be possible to improve conditions for the animals. The accommodations for snakes and frogs are more up to modern standards.

Above: A peccary with its characteristic long coarse-haired coat. Right: The Edificio Metálico was made in Belgium and shipped to San José where it was assembled.

Edificio Metálico

The ocher-colored building made of cast iron known as the Edificio Metálico, or "Metal Building," is part of the architectural variety of San José, just as the few preserved cast iron houses from the turn of the century enrich New York's SoHo neighborhood. Designed by French architect Victor Baltard, who also planned Les Halles in Paris, the Edificio Metállico was produced in Belgium in 1892 and shipped in pieces to Costa Rica, where it was welded together on the site it occupies to this day. A school is now housed in the famous building at the northwest corner of the Parque España (Avenida 5 and Avenica 7).

Parque Morazán

The Morazán Park, one of four parks in the central city (Avenida 7, Calle 3), occupies four city blocks. In its center is a rather unusual building topped by a cupola, the **Templo de La Musica**. The architect found his inspiration in the Trianon in the park surrounding the palace of Versailles. Concerts are held under the cupola on Sunday afternoons. Historic statues surround the music temple. There is a popular children's playground in the northeastern corner of the park along with a small **Japanese Garden**, which was completed in 1992. The tiny garden is indeed a sight for sore eyes in the jungle of the big city. The park is named in honor of General Francisco Morazán Quesada, who was president in 1842 and remained in office for only five months. A number of better hotels, including the modern glass skyscraper of the Aurola Holiday Inn, which is directly on the park, have sprung up north of the park in the neighborhoods of Amon, Morazán and Otoya.

Museo del Niño

The hill at the north end of Calle 4 is crowned by a yellow fort that served as a jail for many years. In 1994, this spacious

building – some of the cells have been left in their original condition – was converted into the **Museum of Children**. Technical developments, from the exploration of space to the latest improvements in Costa Rican agriculture, are beautifully explained with the help of computers, videos and animation.

Many of the exhibits are designed to be touched, and children are allowed to carry out small experiments. Adults can gain an overview of Costa Rica's history and learn about every day living conditions in the country. Certain rooms are reserved for visiting art exhibitions.

Museo Postal, Telegráfico y Filatelico

Passionate stamp collectors are delighted by San José. **The Post, Telegraph and Postage Stamp Museum** on the first floor of the main post office on

Above and right: Avocados, guavas and pigs' heads – on sale at the Mercado Central where the choice of items is enormous.

Calle 2, Avenida 1-3, displays exquisite stamps that illustrate the complete history of Costa Rica. Many are exotically colored showing fascinating subjects. Historical documents relating to stamps, and special stamps illustrating the seasons or showing colorful animals and plants are sure to make the heart of any true collector beat a little bit faster. Current series of beautifully illustrated special stamps may be purchased at the museum.

Iglesia de la Merced

Like numerous other large buildings in the capital city, the Church of Mercy, five blocks west of the Cathedral, also suffered damage in the 1991 earthquake. After restoration, which took years to complete, the church with its red pointed towers and gold leaf decorated wooden altars is once again in superb condition. The main altar is made of Italian marble and decorated with gilded wood carving. In addition to the beautifully executed stained glass windows portraying saints,

you should also glance upward at the marvelous wooden ceiling. The figure of a black Christ, behind the western portal, also deserves closer inspection.

Mercado Central

Anyone who has traveled through Central America and visited the markets of Chiapas in Mexico or the towns of Guatemala should be prepared for a slight disappointment when visiting San José's market. The **Central Market**, between Calle 6 and Avenida 1, is not as colorful as the Indian markets in Costa Rica's neighboring countries to the north, but it is still the most original and colorful market in Costa Rica.

The variety of goods on sale seems endless: baskets, flowers, hammocks, spices, vegetables, poultry, gifts, fish, saddles, spurs, riding whips, medicinal herbs, leather belts and much, much more. Street vendors, who never seem to get hoarse, advertise their wares by shouting, adding to the deafening din.

Hard bargaining is obligatory – but keep an eye on your wallet! As in most markets, pickpockets mingle with the crowd.

SIGHTSEEING OUTSIDE THE CITY CENTER

Museo de Arte Costaricense

On San José's west side, at the end of the long and broad shopping avenue called the **Paseo Colón**, next to the entrance to the Sabana Grande Park, is the **Museum of Costa Rican Art**. In 1978, the museum moved into the former airport building with its decorated tower. Native architects adapted the building with a great deal of taste, taking pains to assure that the new museum had plenty of natural light and additional artificial lighting, essential for viewing and enjoying the paintings on exhibit.

Oil paintings and water colors, including works by Fausto Pacheco, Francisco Amighetti, Teodorico Quirós and Max Jiménez – the most famous of Costa

Rica's first generation of painters – are displayed. More recently, following World War II, abstract artists Manuel de la Cruz Gonzalez and Juan Luis Rodriguez brought modern art to the country. Interesting bronze, marble, granite and wood sculptures by Juan Rafael Chacón and Olger Villegas represent Costa Rica's contemporary art scene. Rudi Espinoza's lithographs and Fabio Herrera's canvases in acrylic paint give a comprehensive view of Costa Rican art.

The museum's most important work, the **Salon Dorado** by French artist Luis Ferrón, is on the first floor. His bronze-like relief covers 150 square meters and shows scenes from Costa Rica's turbulent history. The four walls of the salon graphically depict the slow and difficult development of the country from the first settlements, through the Spanish conquest of the Indians, the struggle for independence and all the way through to the construction of the first airport in 1940 – in this very building.

Museo de Ciencias Naturales La Salle

Natural history fans can discover a wealth of information about Central America's fauna at the **Natural History Museum**, located southwest of Sabana Grande Park (laid out on land formerly used by the old airport). The collection in Carretera 167, in the old Colegio La Salle, includes displays of the country's mammals, reptiles, birds and insects (the butterflies are especially interesting). A visit to the museum is a must for anyone planning to explore the country's national parks.

The animals at the museum can be observed and studied without fear of their running or flying away. The museum also has paleontological and archeological exhibits which illustrate Costa Rica's prehistoric development.

Above: Boa constrictors find mice delicious.
Right: A poison arrow frog (both on display at the Serpentario).

Serpentario

On the second floor of the building (Avenida 1, Calle 9-11) is the **Serpentarium**, a snake zoo, with many terrariums containing tropical reptiles and amphibians. Small signs in Spanish and English provide the most important information about the animals, including their names and natural habitats.

Costa Rica can claim about 140 different types of snakes, 17 of which are poisonous. Because snakes are rarer in the national parks than on Costa Rica's banana plantations, anyone who wants to see rare specimens should visit the Snake Zoo to discover venomous snakes, such as various sea snakes, coral snakes, the dreaded fer-de-lance (*terciopelo*) and the more than three-meter-long bushmaster.

The Serpentarium also has examples of the poison arrow frog found in national parks in the Caribbean area, and the weather frog, also known as the tree-climbing frog. Even the gar, the rare prehistoric fish still found in the Tortuguero National Park, is represented in the museum as a living fossil.

The Serpentarium's piranhas are fed on Thursdays at 5 p.m., but please observe them from a comfortable distance!

Museo de Insectos

The entrance to the **Insect Museum**, which is in the San Pedro section of the city, is through the main entrance of the faculty of musical arts. The inevitable and unanswered question is what do musicians and insects have in common? The museum has an excellent video showing superb close-up photographs and an explanation of the various phases of metamorphosis in the life of a caterpillar, from cocoon to butterfly, ending in spectacular colorful butterflies in all their variety. Afterwards, you can visit the collection of *mariposas* (butterflies) one floor below and learn more about these extraordinary creatures. A trip to the museum should include a walk through the extensive neighboring park.

Spirogyra Jardín de Mariposas

After visiting Costa Rica's many national parks and the Insect Museum, anyone who still hasn't seen enough butterflies should not miss the opportunity of visiting the small **Spirogyra Butterfly Garden**, 150 meters southeast of the El Pueblo shopping center. Spirogyra, a half-hour walk from the Parque Central, displays Costa Rican butterflies up close and alive rather than pinned upon a board.

Museo Criminológico

The Chamber of Horrors in the London Wax Museum is the only thing even remotely comparable to the somewhat shocking displays at the **Criminological Museum** in the High Court of San José. The enormous building (Avenida 6, Calle 17 and 19) contains gory displays which

Above: A rare tropical butterfly at the Spirogyra Butterfly Garden.

are meant to shock and to discourage would-be criminals. The methods employed by Costa Rica's law enforcement officials are anything but subtle.

The displays include military-looking machetes, pistols which tear through bone and tissue, razor-sharp knives, and even preserved human body parts which have been severed by these weapons. It is a macabre collection in a category entirely of its own.

Even the history of criminality in Costa Rica and the driest of criminal statistics are exhibited with the intention of producing a powerful impression on the spectator.

Gruesome examples bring their point home: an illegal abortion is illustrated by a preserved fetus in a glass jar – a graphic example of the bitter controversy over legalized abortion which has raged in Costa Rica for decades.

Tabloid journalists and authors of criminal pulp fiction may find inspiration in the department dedicated to "the country's most spectacular crimes."

Cemeterio Central

The **Central Cemetery** (southern side of Avenida 10, between Calles 20 and 36) is full of impressive Italian-style mausoleums, often bearing photographs of the departed and sentimental poetry or biblical quotations.

A visit on November 1 and 2, All Saints Day and All Souls Day, is recommended. Family members spend hours preparing the graves of their departed relatives and decorating them with flowers and candles. Visitors should conduct themselves with decorum and keep a respectful distance from the mourners.

Parque Sabana Grande

The **Football Stadium** (Estadio Nacional) is in the **Parque La Sabana Padre Chapui**, in the western section of the capital. In the stadium, which can accommodate tens of thousands of spectators, semi-professional and amateur league soccer games are held from May to October.

A visit to one of the championship games held on Sundays is an unforgettable experience. In Costa Rica around 600 semi-professional players, from 28 registered soccer clubs, fight to assemble points for the championship. Home games in the qualifying round for the 1990 World Championship in Italy, in which Costa Rica did surprisingly well, took place in the Sabana Stadium.

Sabana Park also has facilities for volleyball and basketball, tennis courts, jogging trails and a swimming stadium.

For the official visit of the Spanish King Juan Carlos and his wife in 1992, Josefinos converted a part of the park into the **Plaza V Centenario**. The name given this part of the park and the statue of **Christopher Columbus** at its center are meant to commemorate the 500th anniversary of the accidental discovery of America.

Art Galleries

Two galleries are recommended for visitors who want to buy paintings by Costa Rican artists: the **Galería de Arte Amir**, on Avenida Central, Calle 1 and 3, and the **Galería Contemporanea**, Avenida Central 1, Calle 1. Experts may find many of the works unexceptional, but modern masterpieces frequently come up for sale in these galleries.

SAN JOSÉ NIGHTLIFE

Anyone who has spent a number of nights visiting the national parks and enjoying their peace and quite, disturbed only by the nocturnal chirping of cicadas, is sure to find a welcome change in the "Saturday Night Fever" of the capital. The variety of nightlife is almost endless and goes well beyond Saturday night. A magazine entitled *Info Spectacles* comes out every Tuesday and contains information about live concerts, shows, night clubs and other evening diversions.

The music bar known as **El Cuartel de la Boca del Monte** – a reminder of the original name of the village that eventually became San José – (Avenida 1, Calle 21 and 23) attracts a particularly young crowd. On Wednesdays there is a program of live music, providing a good opportunity to mingle with attractive *Josefinas* or handsome *Josefinos* and to indulge in some dance floor gymnastics, which is a good way to get into condition for climbing Mt. Cerro Chirripó.

The San Pedro section of town, one block south of the Banco Popular, has lots of bars, such as **Coyote**, frequented by students. The more sophisticated **Crocodrilo** (see next page) also serves excellent food.

La Esmeralda (Avenida 2, Calle 5 and 7) is the city's mariachi center. This type of music, originally from Guadalajara in Mexico, was played at Mexico's lively wedding celebrations (the word

mariachi comes from the French word *mariage*). Mariachi is played throughout the day and night at La Esmeralda, but late evening is the best time to attend because the music is at its liveliest.

At the **Soda Palace** (Avenida 2, Calle 2) *bocas*, Spanish-style appetizers, are served around the clock – free of charge when you order a beer. Around midnight it becomes the favorite place for musicians to gather for jam sessions. Anyone with a guitar, harmonica, keyboard or any other musical instrument is welcome to join in.

The Costa Rican version of **Key Largo** (Calle 7, Avenida 3) is in a beautifully-restored colonial villa. Key Largo attracts a somewhat more sophisticated clientele. Live bands perform in its small casino, and many couples take to the dance floor. Well-heeled guests often attract the attention of young women who sometimes

Above: Dance clubs and discos attract both young and old. Right: The Teatro Nacional, a fine example of Costa Rican baroque.

have to work very hard to "animate" their clients to have a good time. In any case, they do their job very discretely.

Josephine's (Avenida 9, Calle 2-4) is San José's answer to the famous Moulin Rouge in Paris. Other popular striptease shows are available at **Olympus** (Calle Central, Avenida 5-7), **Alcazar** (Calle Central, Avenida 7) and **Hollywood**, in the part of the city called Sabana Sur.

The best **discotheques** usually bear fanciful names like the **Club Crocodrilo**, in the university section of San Pedro (Calle Central). Despite its name and the stuffed crocodile above the long bar – the disco admits no crocodiles! The club, with its dance floor and video clips accompanying recorded music, mainly attracts students and young singles. It is a good place for tourists and Ticos to meet and mingle.

Caution is to be observed when asking an apparently unattached young lady to dance; be sure she really is single, or you may encounter the more unpleasant side of the word *macho*. The name of the dis-

cotheque **Salsa 54** (Calle 3, Avenida 3) is an attempt to evoke the memory of the famous and trendy Studio 54 in New York City. But here, near the Parque Morazán, the dancers swing to the rhythm of Latin American music. The gaudy spotlights and the music blasting from ear-numbing speakers soon send the dancers into a sort of trance. The insistent thumping sends a collective shiver through the sweating bodies on the dance floor, and they jerk in unison at each sharply felt beat.

Further variations on the same theme are found at the popular discotheques **Zachadas** (Calle 3, Avenida Central and 1), **Casa Blanca** (Calle 3, Avenida 1-3), and **Aloha** (Calle 6-8, Avenida 12).

The Theater Scene – A Choice

The most coveted tickets in San José are to symphony concerts, opera and ballet performances at the **Teatro Nacional**, (Avenida 2, Calle 3-5). The National Theater holds performances from April to November. There are no scheduled performances outside of these months. The **Teatro Melico Salazar** (Avenida 2, Calle Central 2) also features a large choice of music, dance and stage performances in an architecturally interesting theater building.

The **Teatro La Máscara** (Calle 13, Avenida 2-6) is famous for performances of modern dance and alternative theater.

As you would expect, the **Teatro Chaplin** (Avenida 12, Calle 11-13) specializes in pantomime performances.

The **Teatro Eugene O'Neill** (Calle Los Negritos) in the Barrio Escalante presents international theater productions and is financed by the North American-Costa Rican Culture Institute.

The **Teatro Laurence Olivier** (Avenida 2, Calle 28) is more than just a theater; it is a social and cultural center, as well as an international meeting place where San José's English-speaking community gathers. It includes the English-language *Little Theater Group*, a cozy coffee shop, an art gallery, a jazz club and a small movie theater.

SAN JOSÉ
Accommodation

LUXURY: **Grano de Oro Hotel** (C. 30, Av. 2-4, west of the center, two streets south of the Paseo Colón), tel. 255-3322, fax. 221-2782. Opened in 1992, built in turn-of-the-century style, luxuriously and tastefully furnished, excellent service, beautiful garden setting, acceptable prices. **Aurola Holiday Inn** (C. 5, Av. 5 on the Parque Morazán), tel. 233-7233. Extremely modern both inside and out. Its glass facade is a point of orientation for the inner city. **Alóki Hotel** (in the Barrio Otoya), tel. 222-6702. Colonial style with a Spanish-style inner courtyard, excellent cuisine.
Don Carlos Hotel (C. 9, Av. 7-9), tel. 221-6707, fax. 255-0828. Beautiful reconstructed villa with 36 comfortable rooms, marimba music in the evenings.
La Casa Verde de Amón (C. 7, Av. 9), tel./fax. 223-0969. Nine comfortable rooms in a Victorian building, with sauna and cafeteria, surrounded by a beautiful garden.
MODERATE: **Fortuna Hotel** (Av. 6, C. 2 and 4), tel. 223-5344. Budget rooms with baths. **Gran Hotel de Costa Rica** (Av. 2 , C. 3), tel. 221-4000, fax. 221-3501. Faded elegance, large rooms, casino.
Casa 429 Hotel (C. 5, Av. 4-6), tel. 222-1708, fax. 233-5785. Two blocks south of the Plaza de la Cultura. Small, in a house from the 1940s, comfortable furnishings, a notable exhibition of paintings. **Kekoldi Hotel** (Av. 9, C. 3 in the Barrio Amon), tel. 223-3244, fax. 257-5476. Attractive and good value.
Hemingway Inn (Av. 9, C. 9), tel./fax. 221-1804; old, well-cared-for building with a beautiful inner courtyard. **Mesón del Angel Hotel** (C. 20, Av. 3), tel. 223-7747, fax. 233-2007, near the Coca Cola bus station, well-furnished rooms, inner courtyard. **La Amistad Inn** (Av. 11, C. 15), tel. 221-1597, a reasonably-priced bed & breakfast, all rooms with baths.
BUDGET: **Ritz Hotel**, Apartado 6783-1000, (C. Ctl., Av. 8 and 10), tel. 222-4103, fax. 222-8849. Managed by a friendly and experienced Swiss couple, three blocks south of the Parque Central. **Johnson Hotel** (C. 8, Av. Ctl. 2), across from the Mercado Central, very good value. **Hotel Central** (Av. 3. C. 6), tel. 222-3509, fax. 221-2767. **Hotel La Aurora** (C. 8, Av. 2), tel. 222-1463. **Pensión Otoya** (C. 1, Av. 3-5), tel. 221-3925, popular travelers' meeting place, inexpensive.
Hotel Av. Segunda (Av. 2, C. 9-11), tel. 222-0260. **Gran Hotel Centroamericano** (Av. 2, C. 6-8), tel. 221-3362. **Bella Vista Hotel** (Av. Ctl., C. 19-21), tel. 223-0095, budget rooms, restaurant. **Diplomat Hotel** (C. 6, Av. Ctl.2), tel. 221-8133, with restaurant and bar. **Casa Hilda B&B** (Av. 11, C. 3), tel. 221-0037, 6 rooms, nice family atmosphere.

Compostela Hotel (C. 6, Av. 3-5), tel. 221-0694, simply-furnished rooms, under Spanish management. **Crucero Hotel** (C.4, Av. 7-9), tel. 233-3124, 8 budget rooms. **Boruca Hotel** (C. 14, Av. 1-3), tel. 233-0016, near the Coca Cola bus station. **Amón Hotel** (Av. 7, C. 3-5), tel. 233-0315, communal showers and breakfast. **Hotel Ritmo del Caribe** (Paseo Colón, Calle 32), tel./fax. 256-1636.

Restaurants

International variety is the key to San José's eating places. Here is a selection:
TYPICAL NATIONAL DISHES include steaks and fish along with tamales, corn on the cob and *gallo pinto* with créme fraîche – which, along with other specialties, are available at the **Mercado Central**, but it may be advisable to wait until accustomed to the new cuisine.
Tiquicia Restaurant, in an old farmhouse in Escazú, features a beautiful view of the valley. The Tiquicia is not open daily, so it is best to call first (tel. 222-0468). Strolling musicians sometimes entertain diners.
La Esmeralda Restaurant, traditional restaurant, first opened at the end of the 19th century. It is also the union headquarters of mariachi musicians in the capital city and makes appointments for mariachis to play at private parties. Telphone orders are accepted. It is open until 4 a.m. – just the place for a late-night attack of hunger.
Choza del Indio Restaurant, in the suburb of Sabanilla, one block east of the village church, features rural atmosphere and inexpensive dishes.
La Cocina de Leña Restaurant ("The Wood Stove"), located in the El Pueblo Shopping Center, is famous in San José for traditional highly flavored corn soup with pork, delicious fluffy refried beans (*frijoles refritos*), spicy guacamole, tamales, beef asado and hot and spicy *chilies rellenos* (stuffed peppers).
For those who prefer to dine al fresco, the place to go is **Lukas Restaurant** in the El Pueblo section of the city. Delicious appetizers, fresh fish and hefty meat dishes are served to sounds of soft jazz and romantic Latin American music.
ITALIAN: High quality Italian cuisine is available at **Fellini** (Av. 4a, C. 36), west of the center, and at **La Piazetta** (Paseo Colon, C. 40).
The most famous *Ristorante* in San José is **Balcon de Europa** (C. 9, Av. Ctl.). It has been in existence since the beginning of the century and has moved and expanded several times. Historic photos documenting the early days of the restaurant decorate the walls and give a vivid picture of San José during its golden age.

CHINESE food is available in several San José restaurants. Recommended are **Tin-jo**, serving Sichuan and Canton specialities, and **Dong Wang**, featuring the tastes of Taiwan. Both are on C. 11, Av. 6-8.

MEXICAN: Mexico has had a great influence on Costa Rican cuisine. **Antojitos Restaurant** in the Rohrmos on the road to Pavas, west of the Parque Sabana, serves exquisite specialities from the land of the sombrero. There is Mariachi music on Fridays and Sundays. Also good and inexpensive is **La Hacienda de Pancho Restaurant**, two blocks east of La Rotonda del Zapote.

VEGETARIAN: Vegetarian means Indian in Costa Rica. We recommend the two **Vishnu Restaurants** (C. 3, Av. 1 and Av. 1, C. 1-3).

Museums

Museo de Oro, Plaza de la Cultura, tel. 223-0528, Tue.-Sun., 10 a.m. to 4:30 p.m. **Museo Nacional** (C. 17, Av. C-2), tel. 257-1433, Tue.-Sat., 8:30 a.m. to 4:30 p.m. Sun., 9 a.m. to 4:30 p.m. **Museo de Arte y Diseño Contemporáneo** (C. 15, Av.3), tel. 222-7155, Tue.-Fri., 10 a.m to 5 p.m. **Museo Nacional de Ferrocarril** (Av. 3, C. 19-23), tel. 222-8542, Mon.-Thu. 9 a.m. to 4 p.m., Fri. 9 a.m. to 3:30 p.m. **Museo de Jade** (Av. 7, C. 9-11, INS-skyscraper, 11th Floor), tel. 287-6034, Mon.-Sat. 8:30 a.m. to 4 p.m.

Car Rental

ADA, tel. 222-2188; **Adobe**, tel. 221-5425; **Avis**, tel. 232-9922; **Budget**, tel. 223-3284; **Dollar**, Paseo Colón, Calle 32, tel. 257-1585, fax. 222-1765; **Elegante**, tel. 231-0066; **Hertz**, Paseo Colón, Calle 38, tel. 221-1818, fax. 233-7254; **Hola**, tel. 231-5666, fax. 296-2562; **National**, Paseo Colón, tel. 290-8787, fax. 290-0431; **Thrifty**, tel. 257-3434. Most agencies have a branch at the airport.

Book Stores

Librería Lehmann (Av. C., C. 1), **Librería Universal** (same address), **Casey's Book Shop** (C. C.l, Av. 7 and 9) and **American Book Shop** (Av. 1/C. 1). **The Spanish newspapers**, *La Nación, La República, La Prensa Libre* and *La Extra*, along with *The Tico Times*, an English-language weekly (Fridays) newspaper for North Americans living in Costa Rica, are sold in the above book stores. International newspapers: *The New York Times*, *The Miami Herald*, *USA Today* and the *Wall Street Journal* usually appear two days late in San José. Important for hikers: Topographic maps are also available here. **7th Street Book** (C.7, v. Ctl.-1), well-stocked book store with travel and nature guides. **Mora Books** (Av. 1, C.3-5), used books and CDs bought and sold.

Buses

The terminal of most city buses is on Av. 2 between the Parque Central and the Plaza de la Cultura. From there buses also go to San Pedro (east). Most regional buses leave from the Coca Cola secton of the city (between C. 10 and 22 and Av. Ctl, Paseo Colon and Av. 9).

Movies

Going to the movies is an inexpensive pastime (tickets cost US $2). Newly released international films are usually shown in their original version, i.e., English, French and German with Spanish subtitles. Cinemas showing new releases are: **Cine Colón** (Paseo Colón, C. 38 and 40), **Cine Universal**, (Paseo Colón, C. 26 and 28) and **Cine Capri** (Av. Central, C. 9).

Hospitals

Clinica Americana (C. Central-1, Av. 14), tel. 222-1010. **Clinica Bíblica** (C. Central-1, Av. 14), tel. 223-6422. **Hospital Nacional de Niños** (C. 18-20, Paseo Colón), tel. 222-0122. **Hospital San Juan de Diós** (C. 14, Paseo Colón), tel. 222-0166.

Emergency Numbers

Police: 117. **Fire**: 118. **Emergency**: 911.

Spanish Courses

Instituto Universal de Idiomas (Moravia, Av. 2 / C. 9), tel. 223-9662, fax. 223-9917. From intensive courses in small groups lasting several days to four weeks of instruction, including accommodations with a local family.

Central American Institute for International Affairs (ICAI) (Apartado 10302), tel. 233-8571, fax. 221-5238. Four-week-long intensive course, including accommodations with a family, excursions and lectures.

American Institute for Language and Culture (Apartado 200-1001), tel. 225-4313, fax. 224-4244. Located in the university section of San Pedro, individual instruction and small groups, four hours per day, plus group activities. **Instituto Interamericano de Idiomas** (C. 33, Av. 5, Barrio Escalante), tel. 221-7649, intensive courses from several days to several weeks, or individual instruction.

Tourist Information

Instituto Costarricense de Turismo (ICT), Plaza de la Cultura (C. 5, Av. Central), tel. 222-1090 and at the Juan Santamaría airport. Hotline in the country: 800-012-3456. The ICT supplies maps, bus schedules, addresses of embassies and medical doctors. The staff speaks English. Open Mon.-Fri. 9 a.m. to 5 p.m.

EASTERN MESETA CENTRAL

CARTAGO
OROSÍ
TURRIALBA
VOLCÁN IRAZÚ N. P.
VOLCÁN TURRIALBA N. P.
BRAULIO CARRILLO N. P.

CARTAGO

Cartago, with its 100,000 inhabitants, is Costa Rica's third largest city and the best starting point for trips into the eastern section of the central highlands. Cartago, just 22 kilometers southeast of San José, is located at an altitude of 1,440 meters above sea level. It is easy to reach the city along the toll highway, called the **Autopista Florencio del Castillo**.

Cartago is known for two famous sights: a church ruin and a basilica. But most travelers go there because it is the ideal place to start excursions to the spectacular Volcán Irazú and to the Valle Orosí.

Spanish Governor Juan Vásquez de Coronado founded Cartago, the first city in the new colony, in 1563. Shortly afterwards he wrote the King that he had never seen a more beautiful valley. The place he chose for his city lay between two rivers. Why he named the idyllic place after the mighty ancient city of Carthage in North Africa, a city destroyed by the Romans, is unclear. Perhaps he foresaw the many powerful earthquakes that would plague the city in the future.

Previous pages: Coffee plantation and corn-fields, Meseta Central. Left: Basilica de Nuestra Señora de Los Angeles, Cartago.

Until the war of 1823 against San José, Alajuela and Heredia for the honor of becoming the capital of Costa Rica, Cartago was the undisputed trading center, capital and bishopric of the "Rich Coast." The two extremely destructive earthquakes of 1841 and 1910 crippled the growth of the city and destroyed nearly all of the old colonial structures. Today, Cartago is almost bereft of historical buildings, except for a church ruin.

The **Volcán Irazú** is the closest mountain to Cartago and symbolizes the threat that has held the city in its thrall since its founding days. Even today the volcano occasionally makes the earth under the city tremble, and sprinkles ash on its streets and roofs.

The **Basílica de Nuestra Señora de Los Angeles**, the Church of Our Lady of the Angels, a few hundred meters east of the city center, remains the religious heart of Costa Rica. It is the home of the country's holiest relic, *La Negrita*, or the "Little Negress." The blue-white Byzantine church with its cupola is famous throughout the country, not only for its architecture but also for its impressive interior. The basilica is decorated with intricate wood carving, leaded-glass windows and painted flower motifs that cover its walls and columns. Hundreds of votive candles flicker, sending up wisps

of smoke, and incense wafts through the immense interior, making a visit to the Basilica a special experience. Every year on August 2 thousands of worshipers from all over Costa Rica and neighboring countries gather at the basilica for a procession, sometimes lasting days, in honor of the Negrita of Cartago. On the saint's feast day many believers crawl the last kilometer to the church on their knees, fervently praying all the way. The object of so much piety is the 15-centimeter-high black statuette that sits on a jeweled throne of gold above the main altar.

The reason for the continued popularity of La Negrita is buried in legend. According to legend, in 1634 a young mulatto woman named Juana Pereira found a small stone statue of the Virgin with the infant Jesus in her arms. She took the statue home and placed it in a

Above: The Cartago basilica, one of the most beautiful churches in the country.
Right: Orchids have been grown in Lankester Garden since 1917.

box. Then the miracle occurred: the statue mysteriously returned to the place where it had been found. This happened twice. Church elders were consulted and concluded that the Virgin Mary wanted a church to be built on the spot where the statue was found, and so the cathedral was built a short time later. When it was destroyed in the earthquake of 1926, the basilica in the Neo-Byzantine style of the 19th century replaced it. Reportedly, the Virgin reappeared in 1950, which the faithful took to be a sign of her gratitude for the new church.

If you follow the steps behind the gilded altar down into the **Cripta de Piedra**, you can observe firsthand the stone upon which Juana Pereira is believed to have found the miracle-working statue. In an adjacent room are the offerings from petitioners whose prayers have been answered and promises fulfilled, giving silent testimony to the miracles worked by the statue. Countless people have left symbols of miraculous cures worked by the Negrita on various parts of their

bodies. The room even contains sports trophies for games and tournaments won with the help of the Negrita.

A small spring near the basilica is said to have healing powers. The miracle-working water, bottled and blessed, is on sale, along with other devotional items, in the small shop across the street.

The basilica does not, however, symbolize Cartago. That honor goes to the ruins of the large church known as **La Parroquia**.

The residents of Cartago dedicated the church to the Apostle John the Baptist in 1575. Not long afterwards, it was destroyed by an earthquake. In 1910 it was rebuilt, only to be destroyed by yet another powerful earthquake. This was taken to be a sign not to try to rebuild the parish church again. That is why only the massive granite-block ruins of the church's outer walls remain on the Plaza Central. The statue that stands in front of the ruin represents the "immortal" tenor, Manuel Salazar Zuñigas, much beloved by Costa Rican opera fans.

Lankester Garden

Just six kilometers east of Cartago, on the road to Paraíso, is the **Lankester Garden**, which is internationally famous through the number and variety of its orchids. The original owner was a British orchid fancier named Charles (*Carlos*) Lancaster, who laid out the garden on approximately 10 hectares of land in 1917 in order to plant, catalogue and breed new forms of Costa Rican orchids. By the time of his death at the age of 90 in 1969, Lancaster had created 110 new hybrids and catalogued another 80 species up to that time unknown in Costa Rica. After 1969 the jungle threatened to reclaim the garden until the University of Costa Rica took over its care.

Fortunately, Lankester Garden is now open to the public throughout the year. The best time to visit it is between March and May, when most of the 800 different types of orchids (from 1,200 species known to exist) are in bloom. Some are epiphytes, growing on host trees and tak-

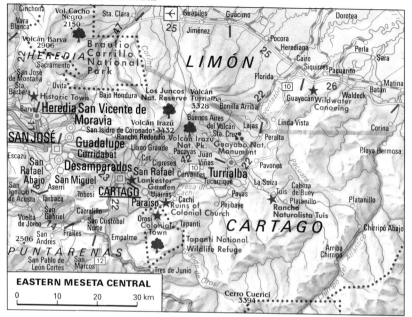

EASTERN MESETA CENTRAL
0   10   20   30 km

ing their nourishment from the air and rain. Every half hour there is an hour-long guided tour which is included in the price of admission.

The average temperature is 20°C, and the garden is watered by an underground sprinkler system, creating ideal conditions for growing orchids. A greenhouse contains more delicate species. The pink *Cattleya skinnerii* and the national flower of Costa Rica, better known by its Spanish name *la guaria morada*, are found here, along with countless orchids from all over the world. They are surrounded by birds and butterflies.

Ujarrás

From Lankester Garden the road continues to Paraíso, and seven kilometers further comes to Ujarrás. The main attraction here is the church ruin, 1.5 kilometers south of the main road in what

Right: The idyllic ruins of Ujarrás, surrounded by a groomed garden.

was once the center of the village. Only the massive outer walls of the village church remain standing. Formerly known as **La Iglesia de Nuestra Señora de la Limpia Concepción** (Church of Our Lady of the Immaculate Conception), it was built on the spot where the Virgin Mary miraculously appeared on a tree trunk to a young Indian fisherman. When the fisherman, with the help of his friends, tried to move the trunk to Ujarrás, he discovered it was so heavy that all of the fishermen together were unable to budge it. They took that to be a heavenly sign to build a church dedicated to the Virgin Mary on that very spot.

The church was built of native limestone between 1681 and 1693, in classic Spanish Colonial style. For many years it housed the miracle-working picture of the Virgin. The picture was subsequently moved to the parish church in Paraíso. When threatened by the notorious English pirate Morgan in 1666, the villagers took the likeness into battle with them and believe it helped them vanquish Mor-

gan and his not-so-merry men. In 1725, the picture was credited with another miracle, and is believed to have saved the village when church bells began inexplicably to ring, warning the inhabitants of a flood. When a second flood occurred in 1833, the power of the Virgin was apparently exhausted, and the village and its church were inundated and later abandoned. The village was eventually rebuilt on higher ground.

The ruin was declared a national monument in 1920. A short time later, a lovely garden containing coffee plants, banana trees, flowers and other exotic plants was laid out around it.

Ujarrás also has two *balnearios* (swimming pools). One – with a smaller pool – is directly opposite the entrance to the church. The other, with a larger pool, is on the banks of a lake one kilometer from the church ruin. The amusement area in which the pool is located is called **Paradero Lagustre Charrara** and is popular for its picnic grounds, restaurants and boat rentals.

Cachí

The road from Ujarrás to Cachí features a *mirador* (a viewpoint) that is comfortably furnished with barbecue grills, picnic benches and tables offering a splendid panoramic view of the lake and surrounding countryside.

Some 10,000 years ago, streams of lava from the volcano blocked off the Reventazón and Orosí rivers, forming a natural dam that eventually created a natural floodwater lake.

The water soon sought a new exit. Today it is closed with modern, manmade floodgates. The wall of the dam, the *represa de Cachí*, is just three kilometers outside of Ujarrás on the northeastern bank of Lake Cachí. The dam provides vital electricity to the Valle Central Oriente. Lake Cachí, 1,000-meters above sea level, is the source of the **Río Reventazón**, a popular river for rafting and kayaking. After a relatively short stretch, the river plunges rapidly down to the Caribbean lowlands.

OROSÍ

South of Paraíso the road drops steeply for six kilometers to the Valle Orosí, through which the Río Orosí flows past coffee plantations and warm-water springs. The idyllic village of Orosí lies snugly tucked into the valley. It was founded in 1561 by Franciscan monks and merits a longer stop.

In 1699, the plague broke out in Orosí and the village was abandoned for decades to come. In 1735, the former inhabitants returned and founded a new church, the **Iglesia de San José de Orosí**, complete with attached cloister symbolizing a new and better beginning. The church, which is still in use today, is a very simple adobe brick construction, in part covered with limestone mortar, at the foot of the **Cerro de Santa Lucia**. Its massive wooden roof, terra cotta floor

Above: The Valle Orosí – created by volcanic forces. Right: Tapirs find a perfect habitat in Tapantí.

and heavy church pews impressively portray the lifestyle prevalent in rural Costa Rica two hundred years ago. The recently renovated interior of the church is paneled with dark wood, a perfect background for paintings by 18th-century Mexican artist Miguel Cabrera.

In 1980, the **Museo de Arte Religioso**, a religious museum, was established in the former Franciscan cloister near the church. It contains 120 items including furniture from the old cloister, paintings, icons, holy pictures, crucifixes, silver censers, containers for myrrh and a complete monk's cell, showing how members of the religious order lived.

The hot mineral-water spa one kilometer south of the Orosí, **Balnearios Agua Caliente Los Patios**, offers a different sort of pleasure. The well maintained facility with its mineral thermal springs features 50°C water for bathing, showers, dressing rooms, a bar and a restaurant, and provides a welcome diversion in warm as well as cool weather. Orosí has one further attraction: right

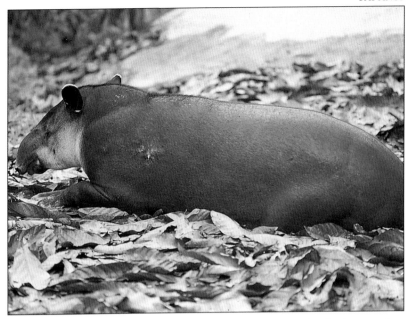

next to Los Patios is a **coffee mill** (*beneficio*). A tour called Orosí Coffee Adventure takes visitors on three-hour guided tours through the finca and the surrounding countryside. If you happen to work up an appetite during the tour, the **Hotel Río Palomo**, four kilometers away on the road to Palomo, is the place to stop. It is famous for its excellent fresh fish and has a large swimming pool.

Parque Nacional Tapantí

A barely-used road leads from Orosí to the 5,100-hectare **Tapantí** game preserve, which has now been officially designated a national park. Tapantí still harbors several hectares of virgin evergreen forest at an altitude between 1,200 and 2,500 meters above sea level. Tapantí has the highest average rate of precipitation in the region, 3,000 mm, providing an ideal environment for epiphytes such as orchids and bromeliads. Rainfall of up to 7,000 mm has been recorded in its higher reaches. This mass of water has to flow

somewhere, accounting for the more than 100 streams and rivers that amble through the park. During the rainy season countless waterfalls appear and the hiking trails turn into rivers of mud.

Tapantí is also the name that Huetar Indians, who live in the area, gave to the tapir. The park also harbors jaguars, ocelots and tiger cats, but they are very difficult to spot in the heavy vegetation. Howler monkeys, raccoons and agoutis also inhabit the jungle.

More than 250 different kinds of birds, including toucans, quetzals, parrots and antbirds inhabit the tree tops, along with butterflies of every possible color combination. Frogs, snakes and toads hop or slither along the permanently humid forest floor.

On sunny days it is possible to spot one of the apparently permanently busy hummingbirds that make the park their home. Many of the 51 species of hummingbird native to Costa Rica live in Tapantí. They come in all imaginable colors: iridescent green, dark blue and glit-

tering violet. Some have an orange-colored throat, others sport glowing sapphire-blue crowns on their heads. With up to 100 wing beats per second, they flit amongst the flowering plants sucking the sweet nectar, along with any small insects hiding in the cups of blossoms, with their long, fine-pointed beaks. Because their front and back wings are separate, they are able to fly backwards – the only species of bird able to do so.

Hummingbirds are phenomenal creatures for many other reasons: their hearts beat up to 1,200 times per minute, and they require eight times their body weight in food and water every day. They are also loners, spending only enough time with a mate to accomplish the sexual act, which lasts only a few seconds. The female hummingbird is a single parent, taking over the hatching and the feeding of the fledglings on her own.

Above: Bromeliads and vines spread uncontrollably in Guayabo, where the humidity and warm climate produce lush vegetation.

A very useful information center is at the entrance to the park. Several well-maintained trails head off in various directions. The four-kilometer-long **Sendero Oropendola** leads to a natural basin filled with cool water and offers beautiful views as well as picnic tables.

The administration office has an interesting collection of fossilized seashells from the Eocene period (40-45 million years ago). Most of the shells were found in the area.

The best time to travel to Tapantí National Park is in the dry season between January and April.

TURRIALBA

After a visit to the deserted wilderness of the national park, many visitors are ready to return to civilization and the company of other human beings. If that is the case, take the road to **Turrialba**, a town of 30,000 inhabitants. It is an important regional center for producing, packing and shipping coffee, sugar cane and bananas, which are harvested in the eastern Meseta Central.

The town is located 65 kilometers east of San José, at 650 meters above sea level. It nestles at the bottom of a valley that was once covered by a lake. For most of its existence, Turrialba has served as the gateway to the Atlantic. Until 1978 it lay on the only route between the capital and the Caribbean coast. Turrialba served as an important railway junction until the powerful 1991 earthquake destroyed the Atlantic Railroad.

Turrialba has few tourist sights to recommend it. The **Parque La Dominica** (a city park), six blocks west of the church, is a popular meeting place for young and old. Swimming is possible at **Balneario Las Americas** on the city's east side on the road leading to CATIE.

CATIE, the Centro Agronómico Tropical y Enseñanza, is just four kilometers east of Turrialba. It is the world's most important research facility for tropical agriculture. For the casual visitor, the center offers a pond inhabited by rare waterfowl.

Visitors with a professional interest in agriculture can explore the 1,000-hectare complex more thoroughly, and use the library. Overnight accommodations are also available.

The road continues eastward (a fork veers off to Casa Turire), crossing the Río Reventazón, Costa Rica's most important white-water river, before beginning to climb toward a small pass.

The Hotel Turrialtico offers a superb view. The entrance to the **Parque Viborana** is a few kilometers from the hotel. This new snake farm is open to visitors and features 26 species of snake native to Costa Rica.

The Parque Viborana is 40 kilometers from the town of Siquirres (see page 194), along a seldom used road that winds through the mountains and reveals incredibly beautiful vistas which never cease to amaze drivers.

Monumento Nacional Guayabo

The road from Turrialba passes the village of **Colonia Guayabo**, 20 kilometers to the northeast on the northern slope of the Volcán Turrialba. The entrance to Guayabo National Monument (officially named a national monument in 1973) is just beyond. The ruins cover 218 hectares and are the most important archeological site in Costa Rica. Although smaller and less spectacular than the Mayan ruins in Chiapas, Yucatan and Guatemala, Guayabo is an important key to Costa Rica's pre-Columbian past.

Anthropologists estimate that the site was inhabited before 1000 B.C. Around that time, the 10,000 people who lived in the city left for reasons that still remain unclear. Perhaps they were driven away by a natural catastrophe or they left because of war with a rival city in the neighboring Talamanca area.

Naturalist Anastasio Alfaro discovered the ruins at the end of the 19th century, but systematic excavation only began in 1968. Until then, white governments had tried to repress the Indian heritage in many Latin American countries. Dr. Carlos Aguilar Piedra, archeologist at the University of Costa Rica, has taken charge of the excavations; about 10 percent of the area has been cleared so far.

A path that is easy to climb leads to a lookout which offers a panoramic view of the old Indian settlement built between two rivers. From this vantage point it is easy to pick out the large rounded cross-shaped formations made of stones smoothed by the river. These *montículos* probably served as foundations for wooden huts.

A broad, paved ceremonial avenue (*calzada*) points, straight as an arrow, toward the summit of the Volcán Turrialba. This amazing road is similar to the famous *Calzada de los Muertos* in Teotihuacan near Mexico City. In many places sacrificial altars and pottery jars are still

79

to be found. Most were religious. Unfortunately, the artifacts that remain represent only a small part of what the original inhabitants left behind. As in most Latin American countries, *huaceros*, or grave robbers, got to the site long before the archeologists.

An aqueduct that still functions carried water to a cleverly-designed reservoir, assuring that the inhabitants had plenty of water throughout the dry season. How many people did the water serve? And for how long? Perhaps Guayabo served as a ceremonial center rather than a permanent settlement.

The massive stone graves, overgrown with moss and vines, and petroglyphs on a monolithic structure depicting a jaguar and a crocodile give researchers yet another mystery to solve.

A visit to Guayabo becomes an unforgettable experience when you observe

the symbiosis between the ruins and the unstoppable forces of nature. The jungle vegetation that has encroached and nearly obliterated the ruins, and the bird world, with its toucans, hummingbirds, oropendolas and other exotic creatures, create an incomparable backdrop for this symbol of an Indian culture that has long since disappeared.

Rancho Naturalista Tuís

The 50-hectare **Rancho Naturalista Tuís** is a true paradise for nature lovers. It is located 20 kilometers south of Turrialba, near the village of Tuís, 900 meters above sea level.

The rancho is surrounded by rain forest and humid jungle, and features a small inn called the Albergue de Montaña. Its North American owners are dedicated hobby ornithologists who organize birdwatching tours and excursions into the region. More than 300 different species of birds have been observed on the grounds of the ranch.

Above: Working in the fields in the thick fog of the Volcán Irazú. Right: The main crater of Irazú is 300 meters deep.

VOLCÁN IRAZÚ
NATIONAL PARK

Two mighty volcanoes, Irazú and Turrialba, both more than 3,000 meters high, dominate the eastern highlands between the cities of Cartago and Turrialba. On a clear day they are visible from far and wide.

Volcán Irazú (3,432 m), the higher of the two mountains, was declared a national park in 1955 by the Costa Rican government. The Turrialba volcano became a national park in 1996. The name *Irazú* stems from two Indian words; *ara*, meaning point and *tzu*, meaning thunder. The aptly-named "Thunder Point" is Costa Rica's most active volcano.

The first eruption recorded by white settlers was in 1723. Further eruptions followed irregularly with occasional long periods of inactivity. When then U.S. President Kennedy visited Costa Rica on March 13, 1963, the volcano woke from its 20-year Rip Van Winkle sleep and spewed ashes and smoke for two full years. The eruption covered an area of 300 square kilometers with ash. Another 100 square kilometers were buried under rock and volcanic mud. The eruption damaged the grain harvest in the regions surrounding Cartago and San José, and blocked water pipes, gutters and sewers. The ash, when it comes into contact with water, solidifies into a kind of cement that is virtually impossible to remove.

Presently, it is possible to see four craters from the lookout point. The active main crater in the middle of the park has a diameter of 1,050 meters at the top of its cone and is 300 meters deep. The crater is filled with a yellow-green sulfurous fluid. Its eastern neighbor has an aristocratic name, Diego de la Haya. Its crater measures 100 meters in depth and has a diameter of 700 meters. Two more extinct craters rise nearby.

The frosty temperatures at the edge of the crater of Irazú, which Ticos also call "The Powder Keg of Nature," range between 11° and -3°C, depending on the season. A warm sweater or jacket is ad-

81

visable for anyone planning to make the trip to the crater. The harsh conditions at the summit have limited vegetation to a sparse covering of dwarf oak, sturdy vines and ferns.

Frequent cloud bursts occur throughout the year at the summit of the volcano. The masses of rainwater stream down the lava slopes to regularly irrigate the fertile fields below. There is a paved road leading all the way from Cartago to the edge of the crater, a distance of 34 kilometers. Visitors are advised to make the trip as early as possible because, generally, at around 10 o'clock in the morning thick rain clouds begin to gather over the peak, obscuring the view.

The edge of the crater has been developed for tourists, and features convenient picnic tables as well as a small *soda restaurant* that sells snacks and cold drinks.

Above: Fog in the forest of the Braulio Carrillo National Park. Right: Bird watching in Braulio Carrillo National Park.

VOLCÁN TURRIALBA NATIONAL PARK

The easternmost volcano in the country is the 3,328-meter-high Volcán Turrialba, which was active in the first half of the 19th century but has remained quiet since 1866. The Spanish named it *Torre Alba* (Tower of the Dawn) for the towering column of smoke that it sometimes emitted.

From **Santa Cruz** (12 kilometers north of Turrialba) a winding cross-country road leads to the summit, passing Bar Canada and winding through the cloud forest. The last 12 kilometers are only passable on foot or horseback. The three craters of Turrialba are visible from the summit. The middle one occasionally spews steam and sulfur.

Los Juncos Cloud Forest Nature Preserve

On a clear day, from the summit of Turrialba you can see the private, 1,400-

hectare Los Juncos Cloud Forest Nature Preserve, which crosses the continental divide with its towering stands of virgin forest. *Senderos Iberoamerica*, the company that manages the property, organizes full-day trips into the forest, which offer ideal conditions for bird watching. The company also maintains a biological observatory with simple accommodations consisting of approximately 20 beds that visitors can use. Los Juncos is just a few kilometers south of Braulio Carrillo National Park and is connected to the park by hiking trails.

BRAULIO CARRILLO NATIONAL PARK

A significant part of the Cordillera Central was set aside as a national park following the opening of the now heavily traveled Autopista Braulio Carrillo (Carretera 32) in 1978. The highway starts in the northeast highlands and cuts through tropical vegetation to the Caribbean lowland plains. This economically vital road to Puerto Limón made it possible for small farmers and lumber companies to reach and clear formerly untouched areas of virgin forest. The creation of national parks was meant to stop such incursion.

The first unsuccessful attempt to build a road between San José and the Caribbean coast was begun by President Braulio Carrillo Colina in 1840. It is in his honor that the national park is named.

Today the park, with its more than 45,000 hectares, contains the most varied and best preserved rain forest in Costa Rica. It is also the least developed touristically. Rivers – the **Guácimo** in the northeast, **Corinto** in the southeast and **Peje** in the west – enclose the area. **Volcán Barva** (2,906 m) is the highest point in the park. The descent into the Caribbean lowlands begins at the **Cacho Negro** volcano (2,150 m). Hikers can marvel at the virgin jungle with wool trees (*ceibo*), noble mahoganies (*caoba*)

and palms (*palmito*), beloved for their edible interior, better known as hearts of palm. Smaller plants, colorful mushrooms, pastel orchids, thick moss, delicate vines and blooming bromeliads lend unbelievable variety to the jungle. Costa Ricans call the *gunnera*, also known as the giant elephant ear plant or *sombrilla del pobre*, the "poor man's parasol."

More than 140 different animal species live in this biotope, including capuchin (*Cebus capucinus*) monkeys, and howler monkeys which are easy to spot thanks to the noise they make. Jaguars, ocelots and pumas, on the other hand, are harder to discover.

The jungle is also home to the tapir, raccoon, red deer, peccary and many other animals usually seen only in zoos. The venomous bushmaster (*Lacheses mutus*) snake is also found here. The tree tops are full of quetzals, toucans, hummingbirds, parrots, Montezuma oropendolas and hooded eagles. The Braulio Carrillo National Park offers sturdy nature lovers, who don't shy away from the

occasional unexpected cloudburst or fear getting their feet wet fording countless streams, a variety of hiking adventures. A warning: Cases of theft from cars parked at the entrance to the park and instances of armed robbers attacking hikers are on the rise.

A trip through the Braulio Carrillo National Park aboard the jungle **Aerial Tram** (see page 193) is more expensive than hiking but keeps your feet dry. The tram travels a short stretch (1.3 kilometers) in one direction at tree-top level, then drops to ground level for the return journey. The entrance is near Carretera 32, five kilometers beyond the Sucio Bridge.

A private nature preserve, **Rara Avis** (see page 209), offers another unique experience in ecologically sound tourism. The park is world renowned for its incredible variety of native and migratory birds.

Above: A quetzal – unfortunately an ever rarer sight in the rain forest.

San Vicente de Moravia

On the road from the Braulio Carrillo National Park back to San José, it is a good idea to take a short detour via the village of San Vicente de Moravia, seven kilometers northeast of the capital city. The village, formerly serving the large coffee plantations in the area, is now famous for its handicrafts; leather articles such as belts, hair clips, leather boxes, wood carvings, costume jewelry, ceramic pots and figures. The workshop called Caballo Blanco (White Horse) is especially well known for the goods it sells at the corner of the Parque Central. Other shops worth a visit are La Rueda, La Tinaja, Ceramics Buchanan and Artesanía Bribri. The latter sells handicrafts produced by the Bribrí Indians on their reservations.

San Isidro de Coronado

Another side trip from Moravia takes the visitor to the six-kilometer-distant village of San Isidro de Coronado, situated at 1,500 meters above sea level. This quiet rural town was built thanks to the profits of its milk industry. The residents are especially proud of their Neo-Gothic **church** built in the 1930s. Local architect Teodorico Quirós used steel girders – an unusual but useful departure from tradition, which can only be applauded in this region so often plagued by earthquakes. The church is also worth visiting on account of its rich interior decorations.

San Isidro de Coronado has an additional attraction, the **Instituto Clodomiro Picado Snake Farm**. The University of Costa Rica carries out its research here on harmless and venomous snakes, such as the fer-de-lance (*Terciopelo*). You can watch the scientists as they "milk" the snakes in order to obtain the substance needed to produce antidotes to the poisonous venom, and observe the feeding of the reptiles.

CARTAGO
Accommodation
BUDGET: Only budget hotels are available in the city. The best is **Los Angeles Lodge** (Av. 4, C. 16-18), across from the Basilica, simple but clean rooms with baths, tel./fax. 551-0957. **Motel Casa Blanca** (Barrio Asís), tel. 551-2833. **Pensión El Brumoso**.
Restaurants
COSTA RICAN: **Puerta del Sol** (Av. 4, C. 16), near the Basilica. **Salón Paris** (Av. 2), good local cuisine. **Pastelería El Nido** (Av. 4, C. 12), specializing in delicious pastry. *CHINESE:* **City Garden** (Av. 4, C. 2 and 4), very large and very busy.
Arrival
Buses from San José (C. 5, Av. 18) run every 10 minutes from 5 a.m. to 7 p.m., then every 40 minutes until 11 p.m.

RANCHO REDONDO
Accommodation
MODERATE: **Hacienda San Miguel**, tel. 291-094, beautiful villa with swimming pool, whirlpool, sauna and fireplaces. Guided tours into the surrounding rain forest are possible.

LANKESTER GARDEN
Open 8:30 a.m. to 3:30 p.m. It is reachable by bus from Cartago, direction Paraíso, tel. 551-9877.

OROSÍ
Accommodation
MODERATE: **Hotel Río Palomo**, 7 cottages (accommodating up to 6 persons), large pool, tel. 533-3128, fax. 533-3057. *BUDGET:* **Montaña Linda**, tel. 533-3640. **Reventazón de Orosi**, family atmosphere, Spanish courses.
Restaurants
Centro Social Reventazón, simple, one block east of the football field, usually quite lively.
Balneario Termal Orosí, large restaurant with bar and several thermal pools. It is very popular with families with children.
Balneario Motel Río Palomo (tel./fax. see above), directly on the river, elegant bamboo furnishings, free coffee tasting, two large pools. Reservations are necessary for dinner.
Sightseeing / Tours
Museo de Arte Religioso, next to the Iglesia San José de Orosí, tel. 533-3051. Opening times: 9 a.m. to 5 p.m. **Orosí Coffee Adventure**, 1 km south of Orosí, next to the Balnearios Los Patios, tel. 533-3030. The *beneficio* offers four different types of tour with lunch at the hot springs, excursions to the Tapantí region, and visits to the coffee plantations.
Balnearios Los Patios, 2 km south of Orosí, well-maintained, 37°C thermal pools, changing rooms,

showers, restaurant. Open from 8 a.m. to 4 p.m. Closed Mondays.

TAPANTÍ
Accommodations
Cabañas Los Maestras (800 meters from park entrance), friendly service, rooms with baths, camping possible.
Restaurants
Las Encinas (1 km south of Paraíso), open dining room surrounded by pines. **Parque Doña Anacleto**, nearby, beautiful view of the valley.

TURRIALBA
Accommodation
LUXURY: **Casa Turire Hotel,** ca. 12 km from town, luxury lodge in a beautiful location, with swimming pool, tel. 531-1111. *MODERATE:* **Pochotel Lodge**, tel. 556-0111, rustic rooms with baths, 10 km in the direction of Siquirres. **Wagelia** (Av. 4, C. 2-4), tel. 556-1566, nice air-conditioned rooms. **Hotel Turrialtico**, tel. 556-1111. *BUDGET:* **Laroche Hotel** (C. 4, Av. 2), tel. 556-1621, shared bathrooms.

LOS JUNCOS
South of the Braulio Carrillo National Park. The observation station contains 20 beds. Guided tours are held three times a week to the private cloud forest preserve and include lunch at a farm.

MONUMENTO NACIONAL GUAYABO
Open Tue.-Sun., 8 a.m. to 3:30 p.m. Buses leave from the station in Turrialba at 10:30 a.m. to the village of La Teresita (15 km) and return at 1:30 p.m. It is then another 4 km on foot to Guayabo.

BRAULIO CARRILLO NATIONAL PARK
Tours
Day hikes to the Barva volcano and ornithological tours: Costa Rica Expeditions, tel. 257-0766, Los Caminos La Selva, tel. 255-3486, Horizontes, tel. 222-2022. **Visiting Volcán Barva**: Arrive via San José de la Montaña, take hiking path that begins at this route to the 2,906 m summit. The 9 km Paso Llano takes 4 to 6 hours. The path is clear and well marked. Tents are allowed and fresh water is available in the streams and waterfalls.

SAN ISIDRO DE CORONADO
Instituto Clodomiro Picado Snake Farm, 1 km outside the town on the road to Moravia, open Mon.-Fri. 8 a.m. to noon and 1 p.m. to 4 p.m. Removal of venom only on Fri. at 2 p.m., feeding daily, tel. 229-0344.

WESTERN MESETA CENTRAL

HEREDIA
ALAJUELA
FROM ALAJUELA TO
CIUDAD QUESADA
VOLCÁN POÁS N. P.

The mountainous landscape of western Meseta Central is characterized by high volcanoes, small lagoon-like lakes, idyllic villages, old churches and narrow winding streets. This densely populated region of Costa Rica has only two major cities, Heredia and Alajuela.

The most interesting tourist attractions in the western Meseta Central lie to the north of the capital city, making Heredia the most logical starting point for excursions into this unique area.

HEREDIA

Once you have escaped the traffic jams of San José and are happily cruising along on the **Autopista General Cañas**, continue in the direction of Alajuela. The exit for Heredia is just before the airport. Heredia, considered a major city by its inhabitants, is just 10 kilometers away.

The city was founded in 1706 and was first known by its Huetar Indian name, Cubujuquí. The white settlers who moved there were not content to keep this Indian name for long and soon changed it to Heredia in honor of Fernandez de Heredia, the president of the neighboring

Previous pages: Birds-eye view of the mighty Poás. Left: Coffee harvest on a highland plantation near Heredia.

colony in Guatemala. In the 18th century some 30,000 people lived in Heredia, and when its suburbs were included the new city numbered an impressive 70,000 inhabitants.

Like most Costa Rican cities, Heredia was laid out in a grid pattern and included a central park, **Parque Central**, which forms the heart of the city. To the east is the imposing **Iglesia de la Inmaculada Concepción** (Church of the Immaculate Conception), which took more than 30 years to build and was only completed in 1797. Its massive walls and the heavy four-sided towers that flank the main entrance create a powerful facade. Thanks to its massive construction, it is one of the few buildings in the highlands to have survived the many earthquakes that have plagued the region. Now it has been justly accorded the honor of being named a national monument.

The **Casa de la Cultura**, a large building dating from the turn of the century, is on the northeast side of the Parque Central. Concerts and plays are held in its glass-roofed atrium. **El Fortín**, the ruin of a colonial fort, is right next door. It has also been raised to the status of a historic site. A pavilion, called the *Palacio Municipal*, has been built in the middle of the ruin. Occasional performances by visiting cultural groups are held there.

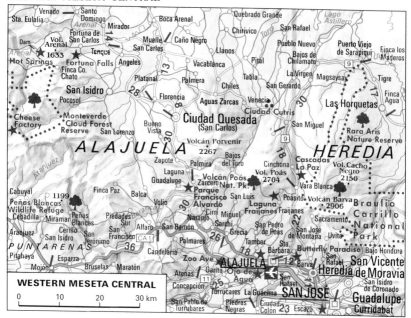

The area around the Parque Central also features a neoclassical building from 1915. Behind the beautiful ornate facade, which many travelers stop to admire, is the **post office** (*correos*).

San Rafael

The area around Heredia is characterized by numerous coffee fincas, or plantations, which take advantage of the ideal conditions in the highlands to grow the valuable bean. San Rafael is a typical village in this coffee-growing area. It has an impressive Neo-Gothic church with soaring steeples that are a landmark, visible from miles away.

The church, which was completed in 1962, has beautiful leaded stained-glass windows and an intricate stone-work façade, which apparently took its inspiration from the Gothic cathedral of Notre Dame in Paris.

Right: The Iglesia de la Inmaculada Concepción in the center of Heredia.

Barva

One of the oldest settlements in Costa Rica is **Barva**, founded in 1561. The historic town lies just two kilometers north of Heredia. Today the entire town is historically protected. Its most imposing structure is the **Basílica de Barva**, which was built in the 18th century and sets the style for this delightful colonial town.

A relaxing walk through Barva's shady, peaceful streets and alleys leads to the **Café Britt**, a large coffee finca southwest of the town center. A visit to the coffee plantation (*Aventura de Café Tour*) begins with a multi-media-show which demonstrates the lengthy and complicated process of planting, harvesting and processing Costa Rican coffee. Afterwards, visitors are given a chance to sample a variety of coffees under the guidance of a professional coffee taster. At the end of the tour – what else would you expect – you can buy coffee and accessories at the plantation's souvenir shop.

Refreshed by the strong aromatic coffee, continue your walk. About three kilometers to the northwest is the village of **San Pedro de Barva**. Its main attraction is the coffee research station (*Instituto de Café*) and coffee museum, which is 400 meters north of the village church. The research station is involved in developing new varieties of coffee.

Other excursions are possible from Heredia. The idyllic mountain village of **San José de la Montaña**, for example, is located at 1,500 meters above sea level on the southern slope of the Barva volcano. This health resort with its elegant 18th-century houses is extremely charming. The winding road from the little town leads to Sacramento, nine kilometers away. The town functions as the gateway to the former Volcán Barva National Park, which is now part of Braulio Carrillo National Park.

Northeast of Heredia, about three kilometers away, is San Rafael, and another eight kilometers further, the park of **Monte de la Cruz**. The view from the mountainside presents a panorama of the western highlands. The small privately-owned forest preserve has a well-maintained network of trails which leads through imposing pine woods with ferns that reach up to the height of a man, wild orchids and countless epiphytes. The refreshing walk in the crisp mountain air provides a fascinating glimpse into the flora of the highlands. The park also has picnic areas with barbecue grills where visitors who have packed themselves a picnic lunch can satisfy their appetites.

ALAJUELA

The famous Panamerican Highway leads from San José to **Alajuela**, the second largest city of Costa Rica. Alajuela is 20 kilometers northeast of the capital and three kilometers from its international airport. The city on the lower slopes of Volcán Poas is home to 50,000 people. Located at 950 meters above sea level, it has a warmer climate than the 200-meter-higher capital of San José. Alajuela is

quieter and has less traffic, noise and commotion than the hectic capital. For many residents, especially retired people, this is reason enough to leave San José for the nearby "suburb" of Alajuela.

The city was founded in 1782 at the insistence of the Catholic Church, which ordered missionaries to built a church to spare the widely scattered farmers the long trip to Heredia. Finding a name for the new settlement proved difficult. The inhabitants tried out several before settling on the city's current name. Originally it was called La Lajuela. Later, for quite a few years, it had the name Villa Hermosa before being once again renamed San Juan de Nepomuceno. Only in 1825 did the city finally get its present name of Alajuela.

On Sunday mornings Alajuela reveals its rural character when farmers from the surrounding areas bring fresh vegetables,

Above: Alajuela is proud of its national hero Juan Santamaría. Right: Sloths in the Parque Central.

fruit and poultry to the market. Alajuela has few tourist attractions, but its inhabitants are very proud of its museum, the **Museo Histórico Cultural Juan Santamaría**. The building, which served as a city jail in colonial times, is on Calle 2, Avenida 2. The small collection vividly retells the story of Costa Rica's defense against soldier of fortune William Walker, the former slave trader who tried to invade Costa Rica from his base in neighboring Nicaragua in 1856.

Costa Rica's hastily assembled and inadequately equipped army managed to surround Walker in La Casona, in what is today the Santa Rosa National Park. Juan Santamaría, a drummer boy who may in fact have been drunk, set fire to the fort where Walker's troops had barricaded themselves. The brave drummer and two of his companions were killed, but they gave Costa Rica's troops the chance they needed to win the battle and force Walker to retreat.

Santamaría is now celebrated as the country's greatest hero. The two rooms

of the museum contain historic paintings, maps, sketches, illustrations and weapons from the time of the battle. A video retells the story of the battle of Santa Rosa in several languages. The museum also has an auditorium and a small but well-stocked library containing history books. There is also a section featuring native handicrafts.

The **Parque Juan Santamaría**, two blocks south of the Parque Central, also honors the memory of Alajuela's best-known resident. A statue group on a high pedestal shows soldiers armed with torches and rifles storming William Walker's headquarters.

Such heroism gives ample grounds for celebrating, and Ticos are more than prepared to do so. In Alajuela, where the hero was born, the celebrations are especially festive. Every year on April 11 the city celebrates its most famous son on *Juan Santamaría Day*, with colorful parades, brass bands, lively dancing that fills the streets and wild parties in the bars of the city.

The handicraft markets that are set up as part of the festivities open one week before the holiday. But Juan Santamaría Day is not Alajuela's only big holiday: the inhabitants also celebrate the city's nine-day-long *Mango Festival* each year in July, in honor of the tropical fruit.

West of the cathedral, which was severely damaged in an earthquake in 1990, lies the Parque Central, which is officially named **Plaza del General Tomás Guardia** after the former president of the country who was also a native son of Alajuela. The park is the perfect place to rest on a shady bench and observe young people, couples who have just fallen in love and pretty girls taking their afternoon walk.

This is also the favorite occupation of the city's retired citizens, who while away the hours in the shade of the park's huge mango trees. Some of the park benches include tables with chess boards, and the game of kings can be played under the watchful eyes of the sloths and tanagers that live in the trees.

93

Balneario Ojo de Agua

Numerous small villages and amusement facilities surround Alajuela and provide popular diversions for its citizens on weekends and holidays. Thousands of Ticos, many of them Josefinos, leave their city homes to make excursions into the countryside. One of the most popular destinations is just five kilometers outside of Alajuela, directly at the entrance to the village of San Antonio de Belén. It is the **Balneario Ojo de Agua**, the "Eye of Water." The natural spring, rebuilt to resemble the pupil of an eye, delivers almost 20,000 liters of water per minute. The 20°C water flows via a man-made waterfall into several swimming pools which seem to be filled, no matter what time of day, with splashing children. The amusement facility, first opened in 1937, draws around half a million visitors each

Above: Ojo de Agua – aqautic amusement not just for children. Right: The national flower, guaria morada, in La Garita.

year. The water is piped all the way to Puntarenas, in the northwest, where it flows into the city's reservoirs.

La Guácima

The **Butterfly Farm** is a few kilometers southwest of Alajuela, near La Guácima. Various kinds of tropical butterflies are on sale as caterpillars or cocoons, and are sold mostly to foreign collectors and businesses, but the farm appeals to anyone interested in butterflies. Visitors get detailed information about species native to Costa Rica, their life cycles and existence in the country's various environments. With luck, early morning visitors may even witness the emergence of a colorful butterfly from its cocoon. In the "bee garden" (bees were kept by the Maya), visitors can observe stinger-free bees or take a tour of the park, with its variety of tropical birds, in richly-decorated ox carts. On weekends La Guácima has a noisier attraction: car and motorcycle races.

Butterfly Paradise

The growing interest in butterflies has greatly benefitted the recently established Butterfly Paradise, one kilometer north of San Joaquín on the road to Santa Barbara. The park organizes informative guided tours and provides countless colorful subjects for photographs.

Ave Zoo

The Ave Zoo features a far larger choice of animals. It is on the well-constructed road to San Ramón. Ave Zoo belongs to the National Zoo in San José and is famous for the many native birds in its large aviaries. Toucans, cranes, parrots, curassows, vultures, bright red New World parakeets and macaws (*lapas rojas*), and peacocks live there. Many birds, such as red macaws, fly freely through the park.

In addition to the bird collection, an excellent selection of Costa Rican wild animals has been given temporary quarters here – deer, red-faced spider monkeys, turtles and crocodiles – which children especially love. The goal of the Ave Zoo is to provide a good habitat for endangered species of animals which will later be returned to live in Costa Rica's national parks and game preserves.

FROM ALAJUELA TO CIUDAD QUESADA

La Garita

After a few kilometers the road from Alajuela, in the direction of Atenas, reaches the little village of **La Garita**. The settlement consists of a loose collection of pretty houses, farms and many small *sodas* serving visitors. Most of the inhabitants of the village make their living planting bananas and citrus fruit. The pleasant year-round temperature remains between 20 and 25°C.

A superb display of flowers, especially bougainvilleas, decorates the houses. The fields of the nearby nursery, **Orchid Alley**, contain more than 100,000 orchids, including Costa Rica's national flower, the *guaria morada*. It is well worth spending a little time at Orchid Alley and taking a closer look at the fascinating world of orchids. The park, with its more than 1,200 varieties, is famous throughout the area and contains the largest collection of orchids in Central America.

Flowering varieties are found regardless of the season. There is a variety native to the scorching heat of the coast and the type found in the frosty elevations of volcano craters. Some kinds of orchids bloom only for one day, others remain in flower for weeks. The most varied are found in the humid shade of the cloud forest where conditions for orchids approach the absolute ideal.

Corn is one of the most important products for the economy of the region. The high point of a visit to the area around La

Garita is a meal at the **Fiesta del Maíz restaurant**, which is arranged like a cozy covered beer garden. It serves the delicious corn grown in the highlands, prepared in a mouth-watering variety of recipes. Corn is sauteed, grilled with butter, salt and pepper, served as corn on the cob or in kernels, and eaten as a tasty accompaniment to meat dishes. Mariachi bands entertain on weekends, going from table to table singing lovely *rancheras* for the appreciative crowd.

Atenas

West of La Garita the road narrows and begins its steep climb toward **Atenas**, a small rural town dependent on agriculture. Atenas is famous for its excellent fruit. A statue of the Virgin Mary crowns a hill about one kilometer east of

Above and right: Cornfields and wooden-wheeled carts, drawn by zebu oxen, are typical sights in the fertile agricultural region surrounding Sarchí.

the city and is visible from the street. There is a handicrafts shop on the outskirts of the town. It is especially popular with Josefinos who like to drive out to the lovely town on weekends.

A small, pretty church, surrounded by palm trees, marks the center of the town. Its cool interior rewards the visitor with an insight into the religious practices of rural Costa Rican communities.

Grecia

In the middle of the Costa Rican highlands, a few kilometers north of Atenas, is another town with a remarkable name, Grecia (Greece). Although the inhabitants are all Costa Ricans, they call themselves *Griegos* (Greeks) in accordance with the name of their town.

Grecia's skyline is dominated by the bright red metal **Cathedral de la Mercedes**. With its white painted Neo-Gothic window frames, the church seems to be an apparition straight out of Disneyland. The Griegos imported the building elements, made of plates of thin metal welded together, from Belgium in 1897 – much as their neighbors the Josefinos did with their Edifício Metálico in San José. They also did themselves proud with the interior, which boasts a white wooden vaulted ceiling, marble altars, fine wood carvings, an original brick floor, a crystal chandelier and intricate leaded stained-glass windows.

In the pretty **Palm Park** in front of the cathedral, with its little fountain and music pavilion, stands an obelisk commemorating Grecia's founding in July 1864.

The nearby **Casa de la Cultura** is used for cultural events, and houses a small regional museum documenting the history and development of the area around Grecia in the course of the past 200 years. Incidentally – in case you missed the news – Grecia was awarded a prize several years ago for being the cleanest town

in Latin America, and the town is busily sweeping and trimming in the hope of winning the prize a second time.

Sarchí

Just 30 kilometers northwest of Alajuela, in a steep-walled valley whose slopes are richly planted with coffee trees, is the village of Sarchí. The Río Trojas separates it into two parts: Sarchí Norte (north) is the larger of the two and was built at a lower elevation; Sarchí Sur (south), one kilometer east of its big brother, is smaller but noticeably livelier. Its name is believed to date back to the early Aztecs and their word for "under the volcano," *xalachi*.

Sarchí has been famous for decades in Costa Rica for its fine handicrafts. The tradition has its roots at the beginning of the 19th century, when the first colorfully-painted ox carts (*carretas*), with their large wooden wheels, were developed in the village. They are still to be seen in the fields of the Costa Rican high-lands – usually drawn by boney but tough zebu oxen and driven by old men whose faces are tanned to the color of leather.

Shops in Sarchí Sur, the higher-lying part of town, sell handicrafts made of exotic tropical wood (often, unfortunately, from trees felled in virgin rain forest). The items range from musical instruments, chess boards and pieces, letter openers and jewelry boxes to salad bowls, rocking chairs, serving platters, miniature ox carts, statuettes and carved figures.

Leather goods are also sold and include belts, sandals, vests, hats and wallets. On weekends, Ticos who come up from the cities mingle with the crowds, creating a mass of local and foreign visitors and filling Sarchí's streets and shops to the point of bursting.

There is no problem when the comfortable rocking chair or colorful ox cart is too big to fit into a traveler's luggage. Most shops offer a special service, packing and shipping bulky souvenirs to the buyer's home address.

Naranjo

To the west, after approximately five kilometers, the road reaches the sleepy rural village of **Naranjo**. Its snow-white church, constructed in 1923, is an adventurous cocktail of neoclassical and Neo-Baroque design elements. But even here, the 1991 earthquake left a path of destruction, still visible in the Parque Central with its towering mango trees.

Palmares

Anyone visiting Costa Rica in January should get on the Panamericana and make a detour to the village of **Palmares**. The exit is halfway between San Ramón and Naranjo. Every year the village celebrates its now-famous fiesta, which has become known all over the country. The fiesta, which lasts for ten days, is a kind

Above: The painted ox cart is a labor of love.
Right: Young farm workers on their way to the weekly market.

of Central American carnival featuring bull fights, exhibitions and circus attractions. It presents an excellent opportunity to discover how Ticos celebrate and to take part in a genuine highland fiesta.

San Ramón

The next interesting village on the road from Alajuela to Zarcero and Ciudad Quesada is **San Ramón**. Its most important building is the **Catedral de San Ramón**, which is on the eastern side of the park. The **Parque Central** is also called Parque Alberto Manuel Brenes in honor of a local botanist.

The supporting frame of the rather recently built church is made of Krupp steel, imported from Germany and welded into place at San Ramón. Elements of pseudo-Baroque architecture, superimposed on the relatively new structure, make it appear far older and grander than it actually is. The interior of the cathedral also seems to have been designed largely for show.

The **Palacio Municipal** is on the northern side of the Parque Central. It was built in 1893 in the style of a feudal mansion and features a lovely inner courtyard and airy rooms with high ceilings. In 1983 it was made a national monument. Some of its rooms are now used by the University of Costa Rica as lecture halls. Next to the main entrance of the Palacio Municipal is the **Museo de San Ramón**. Students created the museum and manage it very effectively. Its collection of historic photographs, prints, sketches and drawings give the visitor an excellent insight into the history, culture and society of the town. One room of the exhibit demonstrates how simply the *campesinos* lived around the turn of the century. In addition, the museum is a good place to get more information about San Ramón, the "home of presidents and poets" and its famous native sons.

On Saturdays the **Feria del Agricultor**, the weekly agricultural market, takes place in the center of town. Buyers and sellers from all over the Meseta Central, including the capital, gather in San Ramón, turning it into a busy, colorful marketplace.

Zarcero

Taking the road to Zarcero to the north, you arrive in a region that enjoys a climate called *primavera eterna* (eternal spring) by local farmers. Set at an altitude of 1,700 meters, here you can enjoy refreshing mountain air and escape the summer-like heat of the lower-lying areas. Sparkling white houses with red roofs present a picturesque view against the lush green vegetation. Coffee plantations and pine forests cover the slopes of the mountains.

In front of Zarcero's church is the very unusual **Parque Francisco Alvardo**. In 1960, gardener Evangelisto Blanco began to trim and form the bushes here into bizarre shapes. In time he and his successors created arcades, elephants, birds, rabbits, corkscrews, snakes, dancing couples, oxen – even a bull fight.

Zarcero is also famous throughout the land for its peach jam and homemade cheese, which you should definitely try.

Ciudad Quesada

Refreshed after a snack of peach jam and cheese sandwiches, you are ready for the beautiful trip through the northern part of the western highlands, via Ciudad Quesada and Volcán Poas, back to Alajuela. Ciudad Quesada lies north of Zarceros, at the relatively low altitude of 650 meters above sea level. The city is Costa Rica's undisputed cheese capital. Its name, however, does not come from the Spanish word *queso* (cheese), but from the poet Napoleon Quesada, in whose honor the city was named. The town, with its 30,000 inhabitants, is better known in Costa Rica under its former name, San Carlos.

Above: Living art in the Parque Francisco Alvardo in Zarcero. Right: The fertile landscape of the central highlands.

The soil and topography of this region, which descends to the lowlands, is superbly well suited for grazing and breeding cattle. The lush green meadows get an average annual rainfall of almost 5,000 mm, and grass grows throughout the year. The economic center of this extremely fertile region, and the initial market for its abundant products, is Ciudad Quesada. The popular Parque Central with its music pavilion, a large church and a swimming pool (*balneario*) are located in the northwest part of town. There are also numerous movie theaters, banks and several hotels here.

VOLCÁN POÁS NATIONAL PARK

The 5,600-hectare national park, with its 2,704-meter-high Volcán Poás, is one of the most popular places for excursions in Costa Rica. Some 200,000 people visit the dormant volcano each year.

The road to the 2,300-meter-high crater rim passes the ranger station and proceeds through dense cloud forest, filled with moss, vines, bromeliads and many other sorts of epiphytes.

The forest is home to at least 80 bird species, including the magnificent quetzal and a variety of toucan.

A trip to Poás is best undertaken (the same is true of all of Costa Rica's volcanoes) in the early morning hours, when the summit is still free of clouds. Later in the day heavy clouds often obscure the sun and it becomes bitterly cold.

The 1.5-meter-wide crater rim descends steeply to a lake with a hill made up of volcanic rubble that constantly emits foul-smelling steam. Until 1968 it was known to spray jets of hot water 100 meters into the air. The volcano is part of the continental divide, marking the point at which water descends to the Caribbean lowlands. The volcano was formerly very active. Its most powerful eruption on record was in 1910. Numerous other erup-

tions occurred between 1952 and 1954. Poás' last eruption of any consequence was in 1989.

A recently constructed path, the *Sendero Boto*, leads from the rim of the crater to a small crater lake, *Laguna Boto*, which is in the ancient crater formed by the Poás volcano approximately 7,500 years ago.

Río La Paz Waterfall

A few kilometers north of the village of Vara Blanca, nature puts on a first-class show. The Río La Paz plunges down an especially steep slope of the Volcán Poás and forms a spectacular waterfall. In the course of eight kilometers, it tumbles through various levels and falls a total of 1,380 meters.

Local people tell many tales about the wonderful power of the waterfall. Its spray is said to be negatively electrically charged and is said to reduce stress. Only by trying it yourself can you find out if what they say is true.

Laguna Fraijanes

Traveling from the entrance of Volcán Poás National Park toward Alajuela, after about eight kilometers you reach a small volcanic lake with icy cold water. Ticos have named it Laguna Fraijanes. It lies within an 18-hectare recreation area which is very popular among the local population, and which attracts week-enders from San José and other cities in the Meseta Central.

Ticos come to spend the entire day and enjoy an ever-popular Costa Rican picnic. Their children never seem to tire of the playground. Adults spend the day singing, dancing or playing basketball or volleyball on the courts. They enthusiastically indulge in the national sport of soccer, or simply disappear into the forest, where many paths and hiking trails provide relaxing encounters with nature. Those who prefer less exercise can ride horses or do a little fishing. From the lake it is just 15 kilometers back to Alajuela.

HEREDIA
Getting There
By bus from San José: *Microbuses Rapidos Heredianos*, from 5 a.m. to 10 p.m. without interruption, departing from C. 2, Av. 7-9.

Accommodation
LUXURY: **Valladolid** (Av. 7, C. 7), tel. 260-2905, fax. 260-2912. Luxurious apartments with whirlpool, sauna, air-conditioning, kitchenette. **Hotel América** (C. C., Av. 2.4), tel. 260-9292, fax. 260-9293, new 3-star-hotel with restaurant, nice rooms with bath, TV.

MODERATE: **La Posada de la Montaña**, in the mountains near San Isidro de Heredia, tel. 268-8096, large garden, beautiful view of San José. **Apartotel Vargas**, 1 km north of Colégio Santa Cecilia, tel. 237-8526, romantic location, surrounded by coffee fields.

BUDGET: **Hotel Verano** (C. 4, Av. 6), tel. 237-1616. On the western side of the marketplace, on the top floor of the building, clean rooms, shared showers. **Hotel Colonial** (C. 4-6, Av. 4), tel. 237-5258. **Pensión Herediana,** (C. Ctl., Av. 4-6), tel. 237-3217.

Restaurants
Fresas (C. 7, Av. 1), young people meet here to enjoy local dishes at reasonable prices.

San Antonio (C. 6, Av. 4), something for every taste, good inexpensive Costa Rican and international dishes.

The Cowboy (C. 9, Av. 5), steak house serving everything from the grill.

El Príncipe (Av. C., C.7), extensive menu, good, but not exactly cheap.

Museums
Museo de la Cultura Popular: Take the road to Barva and follow the signs. Restored farmhouse in turn-of-the-century style. Folklore shows on weekends. Open Tue.-Sun. 10 a.m. to 6 p,m , tel. 260-1619.

BARVA
Finca Café Britt, *Aventura de Café Tour*, tel. 260-2748. Open from 9 a.m. to 3 p.m.

ALAJUELA
Getting There
By bus from San José, between 6 a.m. and 7 p.m., leaves every 10 minutes, via the airport.

Accommodation
LUXURY: **Apartotel Villas de Cariari**, on the road from the airport to San José, tel. 239-1003. Next door, **Hotel Cariari**, tel. 239-0022. Nearby, **Apartotel Residencias del Golfo**, tel. 239-1020. **Buena Vista Hotel**, Las Pailas (5 km, direction Poás), tel. 442-8595, fax. 442-8701, new hotel in

great location, nice rooms, restaurant, pool. **Orquídeas Inn Resort Hotel**, 5 km northwest of Alajuelas on the road to Poás, tel. 433-9346. Hotel in the style of a Spanish hacienda, garden, large rooms, elegantly furnished.

MODERATE: **Hotel Alajuela** (C. 2, Av. Ctl), tel. 441-6595, often booked solid. **Apartotel El Erizo** (Av. 1, on the road to Grecia), tel./fax. 442-6879.

BUDGET: **La Guaria Inn**, (Av. 2, C. 1-3), tel./fax. 441-9573, small inn, friendly service. **Islands B&B** (Av. 1, C. 7-9), tel. 442-0573, neat rooms with baths. **La Rana Holandesa B&B**, in the village of Carrizal, tel./fax. 483-0816, friendly private inn under Dutch management.

Museums
Museo Histórico Cultural Juan Santamaría (C. Ctl. and 2, Av. 3), tel. 441-4775, open Tue.-Sun. 8 a.m. to 4.30 p.m., free admission.

OJO DE AGUA
Getting There: By bus from the Alajuela bus station, (Av. 1, C. 18-20), every hour weekdays, more often on weekends; from Heredia (C. 6, Av. 6). Open daily 8 a.m. to 5 p.m.

BUTTERFLY FARM
Getting There: By bus from San José (C. 20-22, Av. 1), departure at 11 a.m. and 2 p.m. Open daily from 9 a.m. to 5 p.m., tel. 438-0400.

BUTTERFLY PARADISE
Getting There: By bus difficult to impossible. By car go to San Joaquín or Santa Barabara and follow the signs from there, tel. 265-6694, open daily 9 a.m. to 4 p.m.

ZOO AVE
Getting There: By bus, it has its own stop in Alajuela; by car, on the Alajuela-Atenas road. Open daily 9 a.m. to 5 p.m., tel. 433-8989.

LA GARITA
Accommodation
MODERATE: **Hotel La Pina Dorada**, south of the village school, large garden and pool, tel. 487-7220. **Hotel Chatelle Country Resort**, 1 km south of Fiesta del Maíz restaurant, tel. 487-7781, rustic rooms and suites, swimming pool, restaurant. **Hotel Río Real**, tel. 487-7022.

BUDGET: **Villa Raquel** (Bed and Breakfast), 2 km south of the village, near Turrúcares, tel. 433-8926.

Restaurants
Fiesta del Maíz, tel. 487-7057; large bistro serving corn specialities such as *tamales*, *chorreadas* and grilled corn on the cob. Open daily until late in the

evening. **Las Campañas**, tel. 487-7021; fine international cuisine. **La Casita** (steak house), on the road to Atenas, tel. 487-7408. This is a great restaurant for meat lovers with big appetites, serving hearty side dishes.

ATENAS
Accommodation

MODERATE: **Apartementos Athenas**, tel./fax. 446-5792, beautiful property with pool. **El Cafetal Inn**, tel. 446-5785, bed & breakfast in nice location. **Villa de la Colina**, bed & breakfast, tel. 446-5057, rustic wooden houses with terrace and beautiful view. **Anas Place**, tel. 446-5019, friendly privately-owned inn.

Restaurant

Don Tadeo Restaurant Parrilla, tel. 446-5161; delicious dishes featuring specialties from the grill, cozy atmosphere.

SARCHÍ
Accommodation

Villa Sarchí Lodge, Sarchí Norte, tel./fax. 454-4006, new lodge, beautifully located with restaurant and swimming pool.

Restaurants

Cafeteria Helechos, Plaza de Artesanía, light dishes and delicious ice cream. **Baco Steak House**, on the southwest corner of the Plaza Central, Sarchí Norte, tel. 454-4121; known for its hearty meat dishes and Costa Rican cuisine. **Super Mariscos**, next to the Banco Nacional, Sarchí Norte, tel. 454-4330, excellent fish.

Handicrafts

Cooperativa de Artesanos Coopearsa, tel. 454-4050, good value for money. **Mueblería La Orquídea**, tel. 454-4035, specializing in small wooden furniture. **Fábrica de Carretas Joaquín Chaverrí**, Sarchí Sur. Here you can watch artists and artisans at work sawing, planing, carving and painting traditional ox carts.

SAN RAMÓN
Accommodation

LUXURY: **Villablanca Hotel**, arrival via San Juan and Angeles Norte, tel. 661-1600, large complex with its own nature preserve, nice house with fireplace.
BUDGET: **Hotel El Viajero, Hotel Gran**.
Museums

Museo de San Ramon, open Mon.-Fri., 1 p.m. to 5 p.m.

CIUDAD QUESADA
Accommodation

LUXURY: **El Túcano Resort y Spa**, 9 km east of the city, in the direction of Aguas Zarcas, tel. 460-

1822. Luxurious hotel complex with spa, pool, sauna, etc.
MODERATE: **Hotel La Central**, on the west side of the Parque Central, tel. 460-0301, older rooms with bath. **Hotel La Mirada**, 4 km north of Quesada, nice view, tel. 460-2222. **Hotel Don Goyo** (C. 2, Av. 4), tel. 460-1780, neat rooms in a relatively quiet location.
BUDGET: **Hotel Axel Alberto**, one block north of the Parque Central, tel. 460-1423. **Hotel Terminal**, at the bus station, tel. 460-2158.
Restaurants

Marisquería Tonjibe, on the south side of the Parque Central, known for its fish.
La Jarra, on the southeast corner of the main square, good local cooking, serves breakfast.
Los Parados, 50 meters from the road to Aguas Zarcas, original post-modern decor, specializing in grilled dishes, especially fresh *pollo* (chicken).
Asia Restaurant and Bar (Av. 1, C. 2-4), Chinese cuisine, only open evenings.
Hospitals

Hospital Carlos Luís Valverde, tel. 445-5852. **Red Cross**, tel. 445-5484.

VOLCAN POÁS
NATIONAL PARK
Accommodation

MODERATE: **Poás Volcano Lodge**, on the road to Vara Blanca (800 meters west of the village), tel./fax. 482-2194, quiet, idyllic location.
BUDGET: **Cabinas Quetzal**, 4 km beyond Poasito, great view. **Albergue Ecológico La Providencia**, 500 meters in front of the park entrance, tel. 231-7804, rustic houses without electricity, beautiful location but cold (2,500 meter altitude).

CASCADAS LA PAZ

Getting There: From the turnoff to the volcano, direction Puerto Viejo de Sarapiquí, 8 km north, past Vara Blanca.

LAGUNA FRAIJANES

Getting There: By bus from Alajuela, four times daily between 9 a.m. and 6 p.m., Sundays, every hour between 9 a.m. and 5 p.m. Open Tue.-Sun. 9 a.m. to 3:30 p.m.
Buses leave three blocks west of the Mercado Central.
Restaurants

Las Fresas, west of the lake on the road to San Pedro de Poás, surrounded by strawberry and blackberry fields.
Chubascos, just north of the lake, serves Costa Rican dishes.

PUNTARENAS REGION

PUNTARENAS
NATURE PRESERVES
MONTEVERDE
VOLCÁN ARENAL
NORTHERN LOWLANDS
NICOYA EAST COAST

PUNTARENAS

The port city of Puntarenas is the ideal starting point for trips to the tropical rain forest region of Monteverde and to the beaches of the southern Nicoya Peninsula. Puntarenas, with its unusual oval shape, is located on a six-kilometer-long, 70 to 600-meter-wide spit of land in the Gulf of Nicoya. With roughly 40,000 inhabitants, it is no longer the vital seaport it once was. With the opening of the modern harbor facilities of Puerto Caldera, further to the south, many jobs have left Puntarenas.

Its founding fathers named the city Puntarenas (Sandy Point) after the many kilometers of sandy Pacific coast surrounding it. The city can look back on a long and eventful history. The Spanish conquistadors who colonized the region in 1522 named it Puerto Major de Puntarenas. The major obstacle to its development was its distance from San José.

It would take another three centuries before merchants and traders could reach Puntarenas over land. The road between the central highlands and Puntarenas was not completed until 1846. After that the

Previous pages: Mountain bike versus thoroughbreds – who will win? (Arenal Region). Left: White-shouldered capuchin monkey.

harbor city grew rapidly and was declared a free port in 1847. At that time planters had to transport their coffee from the highlands to the port in ox carts. It was then shipped first to Chile, then around Cape Horn to Europe. The far shorter route from Costa Rica's Caribbean ports was still only a theoretical possibility as neither roads nor railways had been built.

Puntarenas remained Costa Rica's most important harbor until 1890, when the Atlantic Railroad from San José to Puerto Limó was completed. Once rail transportation to the Caribbean was available, Puntarenas lost much of its importance. That changed once again in 1910, when the railroad from San José to Puntarenas was finished. The port city once again prospered. By the turn of the century, streetcars were in operation on the narrow spit of land.

In 1927, the city had 6,700 inhabitants. Numerous bordellos were opened to satisfy the needs of sailors in the large mother-of-pearl fleet that operated from the port. These establishments give Puntarenas its unique ambience, which it retains to this day.

In 1981, the government began construction of a new harbor facility, approximately 20 kilometers further south at Puerto Calderato, to accommodate

107

large freighters and cruise ships because the facilities in Puntarenas were no longer sufficient. The move resulted in an economic setback from which the city has still not recovered. To this day, Puntarenas has the highest rate of unemployment in Costa Rica. Those who do have jobs still live, directly or indirectly, from the sea. They fish or work in the canneries processing *corvina* (corbina), shrimp, lobster or tuna fish.

A city tour of Puntarenas can be best begun at Avenida Central, Calles 5/7. This is the site of the historic **church** built in 1902 out of sandstone. It's walls are massive enough for a fort and only the main portal and windows have been modernized. The old Catholic house of worship is the only church in Costa Rica that faces east.

Next to the church is a small **park** with narrow paths paved with crushed seashells. Nearby is the **Teatro de Pun-**

Above: Sandstone church in the historic center of Puntarenas.

tarenas and the **Casa de la Cultura** with its library, art gallery and museum. The cultural center holds concert and theater performances.

Another popular attraction is the **Museo de Historia Marina** in the same building (entrance on Avenida Central), with exhibits relating to the history of the city and the development of seafaring. Nearby is the **market**, where Tico, Chinese and Arab merchants sell fresh fish, fruit and vegetables.

Bamboo bushes ring the **music pavilion**, one block north of the church, between Calles 5 and 7. In summer concerts are held there.

The business area is on the **Paseo de los Turistas**. This boulevard runs parallel to the Gulf of Nicoya and attracts more than just tourists and weekend visitors from the highlands. Street peddlers cry out their wares and try to tempt strollers with *maté*, a kind of milk shake, creamy *pinolillo* made from roasted corn, and sweet *granizado*, a local form of ice cream. After strolling up and down the Paseo twice, you are ready to take a break in one of the many *sodas* or restaurants that line the boulevard.

The Paseo de los Turistas is a good place to study the habits of the *Porteños*, as the inhabitants of Puntarenas call themselves.

Porteños, wearing shorts and T-shirts, stroll the boulevard in small groups. Old ladies sit at their windows or bend over their balconies watching the strollers out of boredom or curiosity. Old men spend their days in the shade of the park discussing politics and the latest news. Drunken sailors weave their way home, and garishly dressed prostitutes pace the sidewalks in front of the brightly painted wooden houses.

The tropical heat, the exotic smells of spices, tropical flowers, coconut oil and – above all – the penetrating scent of the sea lend Puntarenas its unique charm and a very special kind of character.

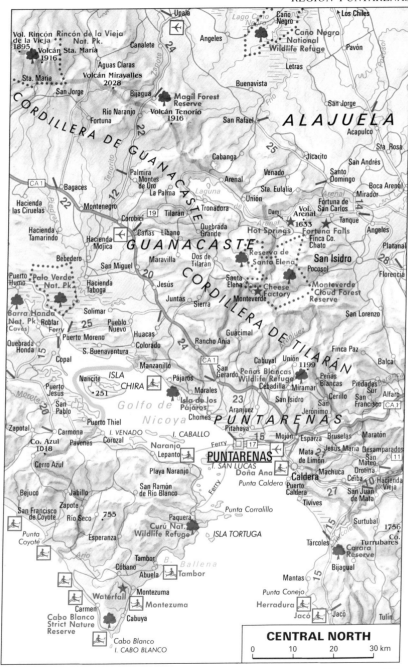

Upala

Vol. Rincón Rincón de la Vieja
de la Vieja Nat. Pk.
1895
Volcán Sta. María
1916
Sta. Maria
San Jorge

Canalete

Lago Caño Negro

Caño Negro
Caño Negro
National
Wildlife Refuge

Los Chiles

Pavón

Angeles

Aguas Claras
Volcán Miravalles
2028
Bijagua
Magil Forest
Reserve
Río Naranjo Volcán Tenorio
Fortuna 1916

Buenavista

San Jorge

Letras

San Rafael

A L A J U E L A

Acapulco

Sta. Rosa

C O R D I L L E R A   D E   G U A N A C A S T E

Cabanga

Arenal

Venado

Jicarito

Santo
Domingo

San Andrés

CA 1

Bagaces

Palmira
Montes
de Oro
La Palma

Sta. Eulalia

Fortuna de
San Carlos

Boca Arenal
Mirador

Hacienda
las Ciruelas

Montenegro

Laguna

Tronadora

Unión

Dam

Vol.
Arenal
1633

Tanque

Angeles

Hacienda
Tamarindo

Corobicí

Tilarán

Quebrada
Grande

Hot Springs

Fortuna Falls
Finca Co.
Chato

Platanal

G U A N A C A S T E

Cañas Líbano

Reserva de
Santa Elena

San Isidro

Florencia

Bebedero

San Miguel

Maravilla

Dos de
Tilarán

Pocosol

Hacienda
Mojica

Jesús

Santa
Elena

Cheese
Factory

Monteverde
Cloud Forest
Reserve

Puerto
Humo

Palo Verde
Nat. Pk.

Hacienda
Taboga

Juntás

Sierra

Monteverde

Barra Honda
Nat. Pk.
(Caves)

Solimar

Roblar
Ferry

Pueblo
Nuevo

San Lorenzo

C O R D I L L E R A   D E   T I L A R Á N

Quebrada
Honda

Puerto Moreno

Huacas

Guácimal

Finca Paz

Copal

S. Buenaventura

Colorado

Rancho Ania

Puerto
Jesús

Manzanillo

CA 1

Balca

San
Gerardo

Peñas Blancas
Wildlife Refuge

Unión
1199

Cabuyal

Peñas
Blancas

Piedades
Sur

Nancite

ISLA
CHIRA

251

Pájaros

Morales

Cebadilla

Miramar

Cerillo

Alfaro

CA 1

San
Pablo

Isla de los
Pájaros

San Isidro

San
Jerónimo

San
Francisco

Golfo de
Nicoya

Chomes

Aranjuez

P U N T A R E N A S

Puerto Thiel

I. VENADO

I. CABALLO

Pitahaya

Zapotal

Carmona

Corozal

Naranjo

Ferry
17

Mojón

Esparza Bruselas

Maratón

Co. Azul
1018

Pavones

Lepanto

15

PUNTARENAS
I. SAN LUCAS

Jesús María

Mata
de Limón

Desamparados
San
Mateo
Orotina

11

Cerro Azul

Playa Naranjo

Doña Ana
Punta Caldera

Caldera
Puerto
Caldera

Machuca

Ceiba

Hacienda
Vieja

Bejuco

Jabillo

San Ramón
de Río Blanco

Punta Corralillo

Tivives

San Juan
de Mata

San Francisco
de Coyote

Zapote
Río Seco

755

Paquera

Punta
Coyote

Esperanza

Curú Nat.
Wildlife Refuge

ISLA TORTUGA

Surtubal

Tárcoles

1756
Co.
Turrubares

Carara
Reserve

Tambor

B. Ballena

Cóbano

Abuela

Tambor

Mantas

Bijagual

Waterfall

Montezuma

Montezuma

Punta Conejo

Carmen

Herradura

Jacó

Jacó

Cabo Blanco
Strict Nature
Reserve

Cabuya

Tulín

Cabo Blanco
I. CABO BLANCO

CENTRAL NORTH

0   10   20   30 km

It is a mistake to dwell too long on the city's romantic aspects. Unemployment, poverty and disillusionment scar the lives of many of the people who live here. Young jobless Porteños, much like the unemployed in other cities, often resort to petty crime to eke out a living. It pays to be careful and watch out for pickpockets, especially at night.

Every year the city blossoms on the Sunday that falls nearest to July 16. That is the day set aside for the **Fiesta del Virgin del Mar**, honoring St. Carmen, the Virgin of the Sea. The fiesta has its origin in a local legend. In 1913, four fishermen from Puntarenas sailing a small boat encountered a violent storm at sea. In fear for their lives one of the *pescadores* asked St. Carmen to save them, promising he would organize a feast in her honor, involving all the boats, if he and his companions were saved.

Above: Fishing boats and ferries in the harbor of Puntarenas. Right: Playa Doña Ana, one of the many beaches in the area.

110

The saint obliged, and fisherman hold an annual procession to this day. All the boats, from fishing scows to luxury sailing yachts are decked out with lights, flags and colorful pennants. Even the Chinese residents of Puntarenas participate, sailing their dragon boat in honor of St. Carmen.

In the evening the sailing regattas and bicycle races give way to a sort of carnival, which usually ends with dancing in the streets and alleys. In the bars, the celebrants toast the holy Virgin of the Sea until they fall off their bar stools.

Puntarenas offers a variety of day and nighttime entertainment. Two discos, El Primero and Mar, feature international and Caribbean music. Strangers become friends in packed bars that vibrate with the sounds of salsa. The outdoor cafés are quieter and cozier, and young couples dash off to the **Cinema del Pacifico** where, in the dark, they pay more attention to each other than they do to the movie. In addition to national and international restaurants, Puntarenas also has

many other tourist attractions. The **Balneario Municipal** (public swimming pool) is located at the end of the spit of land. There are numerous banks, water-taxis, car rental companies and a medical facility, the Monseñor Sanabria Hospital. Calypso Cruises offers excursions to the Isla de Tortuga and cruises of the Gulf from Nicoya to the Isla de Pájaros. Several sailing clubs organize deep-sea fishing tours.

Playa Doña Ana, Mata de Limón and Tivives

Before heading off again into the interior of northern Costa Rica, you should make an excursion to **Playa Doña Ana**. The beach is 13 kilometers south of Puntarenas, at the southern end of the **Bahía de Caldera**. Huge waves make it an ideal place for surfing, and its fine sandy beach is appreciated by sun worshipers. To be more exact, there are actually two beaches in the small bay enclosed by cliffs: **Boca Barranca** and Playa Doña

Ana. Playa Doña Ana is the only one that has been developed for public use. It is also where the annual Costa Rican surfing championship is held. To get there, take the road south from Puntarenas and turn off at the Soda Doña Ana restaurant. At the entrance to the beach there is a car park that charges a fee. A small fee is also charged for use of the beach. The facilities include snack bars, changing cabins and lavatories.

Puerto Caldera, Costa Rica's new Pacific coast central freight harbor, is four kilometers south of Doña Ana. Construction began in 1981, and was completed with the help of international development funds from Japan and Venezuela. The giant complex was only finished in 1991. A pleasant restaurant and two banks are in the modern harbor building.

Mata de Limón, a small village with simple hotels, has a number of restaurants specializing in *mariscos* (seafood). It is in the **Boca de Caldera**, surrounded by mangrove swamps, and has a beach suitable for surfing. Its most interesting

111

tourist attraction, however, is south of the river estuary, where boats can be rented for day trips into the swamps to observe alligators and tropical birds in their natural habitat. Mata de Limón is also popular with highland city residents who often drive out on weekends to watch the sunset and dine at the elegant Costa del Mar restaurant.

Vacation cottages line the four-kilometer-long beach of **Tivives** at the mouth of the Río Jesús María. Behind the beach is a 670-hectare area of white mangroves, which grow up to 35 meters high and provide nesting places for tropical birds. Howler and capuchin monkeys keep up an appropriate level of noise, and jaguarundis and ocelots make the forest their habitat.

A paved road leads inland from Tivives to the town of Orotina.

Above: Traveling through the still reaches of the Carara Preserve. Right: Brown pelicans are a common sight on the coast of the Isla de los Pájaros.

NATURE PRESERVES

Carara Biological Preserve

Reachable from San José or Puntarenas, the **Carara Preserve** is to the left, directly beyond the bridge over the Río Tárcoles. Carara means "crocodile" in the language of the Huetar Indians who originally lived in the area. With a bit of luck and patience you may be able to spot a crocodile from the bridge as it suns itself on the muddy river bank.

The popular Carara Preserve, with an area of 4,700 hectares, contains five vegetation zones. The zone at the mouth of the **Río Tárcoles** is characterized by meadows and fields that average 3,000 mm of rain annually and register an average temperature of 27°C throughout the year. Many exotic animal species live in this protected environment: giant anteaters, ocelots, red-faced spider monkeys and poison arrow frogs. Birds also find this an ideal nesting area: spoonbills, storks, darters, trogons, motmots, tou-

cans, and many pairs of bright red macaws search the mangrove swamps and rain forest for food and provide exotic subjects for visiting photographers.

The park also contains 15 different archeological sites that record nearly 2,000 years of Indian history and make the Carara a favorite destination of historians. The best time to visit is during the dry season, especially in the months of March and April.

Isla de los Pájaros

The Costa Rican National Park Administration has set aside another *reserva biológica* 15 kilometers northwest of Puntarenas: the Isla de los Pájaros. The four-hectare island, just 600 meters from the costal village of Punta Morales in the Gulf of Nicoya, is easy to reach by boat from Puntarenas. Visitors have to get a permit to visit this bird island, as is the case in the nature preserves of Guayabo and Negritos. Permission is only granted to scientists and visitors with special interests. Numerous colonies of sea birds, including brown pelicans, seagulls and frigate birds, nest on Isla de los Pájaros. There are no tourist facilities and camping is not allowed.

MONTEVERDE

The Monteverde (Green Mountain) Nature Preserve is an excellent example of responsible, ecologically sound tourism in Costa Rica. The farm village also named **Monteverde**, located at 1,400 meters above sea level, was founded in 1951 by Quakers from the U.S. state of Alabama. In the ensuing years it became famous throughout Costa Rica. Four young men, who refused military service out of religious reasons, chose Costa Rica as their home in exile in 1949, following their release from prison. They chose the country because it had abolished its military in 1948. In 1951, they packed their few worldly goods into a truck and drove from Alabama to Monteverde. The trip took three months. They bought 1,500 hectares of inexpensive land, and with financial help from the native inhabitants they established a cheese factory called **Productores de Monteverde**, which now employs nearly 400 people and produces a ton of cheese every day.

From the very beginning, the founders insisted that the Río Guacimal, vital to their drinking water supply and necessary for the factory, be kept free of pollution. Although it had no official status, they treated the basin of the Río Guacimal as if it were a nature preserve.

Monteverde was made into a preserve thanks to a natural phenomenon. In 1964, scientists visiting the area discovered the very rare deaf and dumb brightly-colored "Golden Toad" at Monteverde. In 1972, they established a small wildlife refuge here. Three years later, with financial help from the World Wildlife Fund (WWF), the small park was expanded to include the basin of the Río Guacimal.

Today the **Reserva Biológica Bosque Nuboso Monteverde** covers 10,500 hectares. The preserve is privately owned but is administered by Costa Rica's center for tropical research. Its fame and the many possibilities for observing nature that it offers make it a very popular park, which attracts more than 30,000 visitors each year.

Some 30 hotels and inns serve the park, but the preserve remains a peaceful, friendly and quiet place. In the evenings it is completely dead. Nonetheless, Monteverde remains a place of superlatives. The protected area reaches from the Pacific coast to the Caribbean and includes eight distinct ecological zones ranging from windswept scrubland to sunny tropical forests with towering trees. Swampy forest gives way to zones of philodendron, bamboo groves and fern thickets.

Above and right: In the Monteverde Nature Preserve – exotic plants and threatened species (jaguar).

The animals that inhabit Monteverde are equally varied: 100 species of mammal are found here, along with 400 bird species (above all toucans, hummingbirds and bellbirds), 1,200 amphibian and reptile species and 5,000 different kinds of insect. A visit to Monteverde is worth the effort for its wildcats alone. Jaguars, pumas, margays, jaguarundis and ocelots stalk the jungle but keep a safe distance from the tourist paths.

Hiking trails (*senderos*) that wind through the rain forest are elevated in swampy places and covered by boardwalks, but waterproof boots or high-topped hiking shoes are recommended. No more than 120 people are allowed into the preserve at any one time.

Sendero Chomogo leads up a steep hillside to a clearing with a view of the continental divide. On a clear day it is possible to see both oceans. The road leads downhill toward the Pacific for a short way before intersecting with the **Sendero Río**, which returns to the starting point.

The **Sendero Bosque Nuboso** winds through the upper reaches of the tropical rain forest. A brochure at the park entrance shows the way and helps with orientation. Hikes along the **Sendero Tranquilo Reserva** take three to four hours. These tours are only possible in the company of a guide, who assures that no more than six people are on any path at one time.

The hike up the 1,842-meter-high **Cerro Amigos** rewards the effort on a clear day with a view of the Volcán Arenal, 20 kilometers away.

The residents of Monteverde hold an annual music festival (between December and March) featuring a program of classical and jazz concerts.

The best time to go, considering the annual rainfall of 2,500 mm which guarantees high humidity, is between December and April. Quetzals are usually to be seen in the higher elevations of the cloud forest between February and May, especially in the early evening hours following the sunset. Those who want to avoid crowds should visit Monteverde during the rainy season.

Reserva de Santa Elena

Another cloud forest preserve was opened in 1992 near the town of Santa Elena. The **Reserva de Bosque Nuboso Santa Elena** is administered by a foundation, and the land is the property of the state. Well-maintained trails lead through the forest, and reveal a wealth of flora and fauna. When the weather is good, it is sometimes possible to find a vantage point from which the Arenal volcano is visible. The latest innovation in the area is the so-called **Sky Walk**, which is directly off the approach road. It consists of a two-kilometer-long elevated path through a new private 228-hectare preserve. Visitors walk through the forest across five hanging bridges that are up to 120 meters long and swing up to 37 meters over the forest floor. The Sky Walk affords a rare glimpse into the usually unreachable treetops of the rain

115

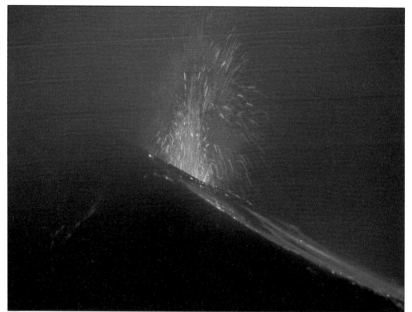

forest, at a far more reasonable price than the aerial tram (see page 193).

The new **Orchid Garden**, with more than 380 species of this fascinating plant, is on the road to Monteverde, about 850 meters beyond the town limits of Santa Elena. The garden is also an orchid research project (*Proyecto de Investigación de Orquídeas de Monteverde*) and is open daily from 8 a.m. to 5 p.m. For additonal information, call 645-5510.

VOLCÁN ARENAL

The small town of **Fortuna de San Carlos**, with its approximately 5,000 residents, is located 250 meters above sea level at the foot of the six-kilometer-distant Arenal volcano, which is best viewed at sunset from a bench on the plaza. Until the 1980s, there were hardly any tourist accommodations in the vil-

Above: Nightly eruption of Arenal – a very special fireworks display. Right: Windsurfing on Lake Arenal.

lage. Today it has some 20 hotels and inns, and virtually every private home rents rooms during the peak season.

The **Cataratas de Fortuna**, a waterfall, plunges off the mountain about five kilometers from the town. Signs along the marked path which begins at the village church show the way. By car the waterfall is reachable along a rocky road that is not exactly a pleasure to drive. From the road a steep trail (10 minutes on foot) leads to the bottom of the idyllic, narrow waterfall.

Less than six kilometers away, on the road to Arenal, is the Los Lagos Preserve. It has a **crocodile farm** where young alligators and crocodiles are raised – not for commercial purposes – but to be released into the wild when they are fully grown.

An excursion to the rim of the 1,633-meter-high **Volcán Arenal** is part of the reason for going to Fortuna. Tours organized by hotels in the area usual begin at dusk (around 7 p.m.). On clear nights it is possible to see streams of red-hot lava as they shoot into the air and roll down

the mountain. The local residents are happy to show off their volcano, which has been the earth's most active since its violent eruption on July 29, 1968. That eruption buried the town of Tabacon under molten lava, and the volcano has continued spewing lava ever since. Before 1968, Arenal had been dormant for 500 years. Small explosions from within the mountain, audible as far away as Fortuna, can be heard almost every day. A particularly violent eruption in 1998 once again won Mount Arenal a place in news headlines.

The **Cavern of Venado** is a day's excursion from Fortuna. It was first discovered in 1945 by local residents, and lie 15 kilometers north of Lake Arenal, near the village of Venado. The entrance to the limestone grotto is 300 meters high. A small stream flows through the two-kilometer-long cave, which is only open to visitors with guides and which cannot be explored for more than a couple of hundred meters. Here you will see stalagmites and stalactites, as well as

salas (hollow chambers) and small *cascadas* (waterfalls), limestone "curtains," and openings in the cavern's ceiling in which bats make their home.

Lago Arenal

Lago Arenal, Costa Rica's largest lake, is 538 meters above sea level. It is equally popular with swimmers, anglers and windsurfers. The lake was created some three million years ago by tectonic movements of the earths crust. The Indians who lived around the lake found it an inexhaustible source of fish. In 1973, Costa Rica's electrical authority built a dam at the eastern edge of the valley, raising the level of the lake and inundating the ancient villages of Arenal and Tronador. The water of the 32-kilometer-long narrow lake is an important source of electricity for the area.

The west side of the lake is swept by strong winds, especially during the dry period from December to February when up to 30-knot winds give windsurfers the

ride of their life on waves that sometimes reach one meter in height. The water temperature remains about 21°C all year round, encouraging even the most timid surfers to do without their neoprene suits. The surfers share the lake with anglers who come to hook *mojarras* (lake bass), *guapotes* (rainbow perch) and *machacas* (related to piranhas). Most of Fortuna's hotels can arrange fishing excursions.

The **Hot Springs of Tabacón** are 13 kilometers from Fortuna. The volcano's lava fields heat the water of the Río Tabacón, creating hot mineral springs believed to heal skin disease and ease pains from arthritis and muscular disorders. The colonial-style spa provides relaxing baths in 30-35°C water from five natural mineral springs. The gardens and panoramic view provide absolute pleasure, which can only be topped by a warm shower under a mineral spring waterfall.

Above: On the last weekend of April rodeo fever breaks out in Tilarán. Right: Just wait till I grow up... (caiman at Río Frío).

The village of **Tilarán**, which is also within a few hours of Fortuna, is located at 550 meters above sea level, five kilometers from Lago Arenal. The village marks the beginning of the 40- kilometer-long access road into the Monteverde region (see page 113).

Tilarán, however, is best known to both domestic and foreign visitors for its *Fiesta de Días Cívicas*, a famous rodeo and country fair, which is held every year on the last weekend of April. Tilarán's 10 hotels are almost always fully booked during the rodeo, and anyone who wants to attend should make reservations well in advance.

THE NORTHERN LOWLANDS

The town of **San Rafael** on the banks of the Río Frío is often simply called Guatuso by its 6,000 inhabitants. It offers little in the way of tourist attractions but is a good place to go to rent a boat or hire a guide for excursions into the Caño Negro Nature Preserve.

Caño Negro Nature Preserve

The nearly 10,000-hectare preserve is set aside for the protection of Costa Rica's native animals. It is of special interest to ornithologists, who come to study the storks, pink spoon-billed herons, darters, common herons and cormorants that inhabit this lowland preserve near Costa Rica's northern border. Large flocks of migrating birds fly through Caño Negro between January and March. Small groups of birds are also visible the rest of the year. Because Caño Negro is thinly inhabited and off the beaten track, rare animals such as pumas, tapirs and jaguars are still to be found in its thickets.

During the rainy season the Río Frío often overflows its banks forming a lake that extends for several square kilometers. This is a good place to observe waterfowl. The lake completely disappears during the dry season.

There is a forest station in the small village of Caño Negro, 25 kilometers to the southwest, where simple accommodations are available. Forest station employees are also armed with information about fishing trips (except in the months from April to June), excursions on horseback and guided hikes.

Excursions into this unique animal paradise by boat on the Río Frío can be arranged at the small border town of Los Chiles, which is also the point of departure for Nicaragua. It is also possible to take the rough road through incredibly beautiful scenery from Caño Negro via Angeles and Upala southward to the Nicoya peninsula.

NICOYA EAST COAST

Isla San Lucas

The approximately 700-hectare former prison island of San Lucas is three kilometers east of the long white beach of **Playa Naranjo**, where ferries from Puntarenas dock. Formerly the island was also known as the "Island of Indescribable Fear," "Island of Eternal Silence"

and "Devils Island." The Spanish conquistador Gonzalo Fernandez Oviedo first used it when he banished hundreds of Chara Indians to the forlorn place.

Japanese pearl divers used the island for a short time in the 19th century. The government of Costa Rica turned the it into a penitentiary for political prisoners in 1862. The prison was closed in 1991 leaving only its torture chamber and a small chapel to slowly rot away.

Curú Game Preserve

The 1,214-hectare **Hacienda Curú** – still another attraction on the Nicoya peninsula – lies between Pochote and Paquera, the ferry harbor from which it is possible to sail to Puntarenas. The Hacienda is the private property of Doña Julieta Schutz. A part of the Hacienda has been turned over to the 84-hectare **Curú**

Above: Cabo Blanco on the Nicoya peninsula. Right: Snorkeling in the crystal clear waters of the Pacific.

Game Preserve, which includes five kilometers of coastline, combining deciduous forest, palm-lined beaches and mangrove swamps.

The preserve is home to some 120 bird species, iguanas, lobsters, crabs, chitons, large clams and turtles, all of which find the environment north of the bay hospitable. Whales can be seen in the bay, too, especially in January. The forests are home to monkeys (howler and capuchin), sloths, pumas, ocelots, agoutis and anteaters. Curú's beaches are perfect for snorkeling and swimming.

Playa Tambor

The fishing village of **Tambor** on **Bahía Ballena** (Whale Bay) has a narrow gray sand beach, often visited by monkeys, and a small church – attractions hardly worth mentioning – but it is the area itself that draws tourists; especially for, as its name implies, the possibility of sighting whales. Tambor has two famous luxury resorts. The **Hotel Playa Tam-**

bor, with 2,400 hectares, is Costa Rica's largest resort. It has swimming pools and its own airport. More attractive is **Tango Mar**, five kilometers west of Tambor. Guests can spend tropical nights in Polynesian-style huts built on stilts and enjoy romantic white sand beaches and a golf course.

Montezuma

The former fishing village bearing the noble name of the Aztec's last emperor now attracts backpackers, hippies and dropouts. East of **Montezuma** there are a number of beautiful white sand beaches: **Playa Cocal**, **Playa Cocalito** and **Playa Quizales**. The uncontrolled cutting of forests on the mountain slopes has resulted in water shortages for tourists and locals during the dry season. In addition to swimming and relaxing on the beaches, visitors can rent fishing boats, dive, snorkel or take organized tours on horseback.

A day trip to **Isla Tortuga**, a 320-hectare island 14 kilometers from the mainland, offers a change of scenery and crystal-clear water for snorkeling.

Cabo Blanco

Cabo Blanco (White Cape) has an interesting history. A Swedish couple who emigrated to Costa Rica, Karen Morgenson and Nils Olof Wessberg, bought a piece of land on the southern tip of the Peninsula de Nicoya in 1955 and started a fruit plantation. They soon realized neighboring farmers were systematically destroying the rain forest by clearing land to win new pastures for their animals. In order to save at least a part of the forest, the couple obtained international support and founded an 1,100-hectare preserve in 1963, which they subsequently gave to the state. With this act the idea of national parks in Costa Rica was born, and Wessberg became its initiator. In 1975, he was

murdered by opponents to his conservation policies.

A ranger station, south of **Cabuya** at the entrance to the protected area, has very good detailed maps of the preserve. With a bit of luck you may spot one of the countless animals that live there: tiger cats, agoutis, sloths, raccoons, snakes, and howler, capuchin and red-faced spider monkeys.

Near the Pacific are brooding grounds for many kinds of sea birds. Some 500 brooding pairs have been recorded along with the country's largest colony of brown boobies, laughing gulls, terns, frigate birds, brown pelicans and other species that have become rare elsewhere. Cabo Blanco can be explored on foot or on horseback. **Sendero Sueco** leads to the beaches of Playa Balsita and Playa Cabo Blanco. **Sendero El Barco** goes from Playa Balsita to the park's western boundary. From the sea, Cabo Blanco is instantly recognizable because of the thick coating of white bird excrement that has given it its name.

121

PUNTARENAS
Getting There
Buses leave daily, almost every hour, from San José; twice daily to Santa Elena and five times daily to Tilarán and Liberia. Buses return to San José from the Puntarenas station (Paseo de los Turistas, C. 2).
Accommodation
LUXURY: **Hotel Yadrá** (C. 35-37, Paseo de los Turistas), tel. 661-2662.
MODERATE: **Las Brisas** (Paseo de los Turistas, C. 31-33), tel. 661-4040. **Hotel Porto Bello**, 3 km east of the center near Cocal, tel. 661-1322.
Hotel La Punta, near the balneario (Av. 1), tel. 661-0696, relatively quiet with a restaurant and pool.
Hotel Tioga (Paseo de los Turistas, C. 17-19), tel. 661-0271.
BUDGET: **Hotel Chorotega** (C. 1, Av. 3), tel. 661-0998, cheap but good. **El Jorón** (Paseo de los Turistas, C. 25), tel. 661-0467. **Pensión Cabezas** (Av. 1, C. 2-4), tel. 661-1045. **Cabinas Central** (C. 7, Av. 2-4), tel. 661-1484. **Gran Hotel Imperial**, (Paseo de los Turistas, C. Central), tel. 661-0579.
Restaurants
Many restaurants on the Paseo de los Turistas serve international food. Chinese restaurants are on Avenida 1.
Paseo de los Turistas: **Taberna Cerveceria**, tel. 661-0330, a Munich-style beer hall in the tropics. **Miramar** (C. 17-19), Italian dishes and seafood.
La Mazorca has a cozy bamboo bar.
La Casa de los Mariscos, seafood.
Aloha, al fresco dining with local and Caribbean dishes.
La Caravelle (Paseo de los Turistas, C. 23).
Kahite Blanco (Av. 1, C. 19), tel. 661-2093, large popular seafood restaurant, dancing on weekends.

PLAYA DOÑA ANA
Accommodation
LUXURY: **Hotel Fiesta**, 11 km east of Puntarenas, tel. 663-0808. Large oceanfront hotel complex (310 air-conditioned rooms) with restaurants and pool, all inclusive.
MODERATE: **Hotel Río Mar**, 600 meters from the beach, tel. 663-0158, simple but clean.

MATA DE LIMÓN
Accommodation
BUDGET: **Hotel Casablanca**, tel. 222-2921. **Hotel Viña del Mar**, tel. 663-4030. **Cabinas Las Santas**, tel. 441-0510.
Restaurants
Puerto Nuevo, at the entrance to the town near the railroad tracks, Costa Rican food.
Costa del Sol, on the main street, tel. 6544008, good fish dishes.

CARARA BIOLOGICAL PRESERVE
Opening Times
Daily 7 a.m. to 5 p.m. (May-Oct. 8 a.m. to 6 p.m.). Follow the signs to the entrance. No overnight accommodations in park.
Accommodation
MODERATE: **Villa Lapas Hotel**, tel. 288-1611, quiet location with swimming pool.

SANTA ELENA / MONTEVERDE
Getting There
Buses twice daily from San José (C. 14, Av. 9-11), once daily from Puntarenas. Buses run between Santa Elena and the Monteverde preserve.
Opening Times
Monteverde, daily 7a.m. to 4 p.m. **Santa Elena**, daily 7 a.m. to 4 p.m. **Sky Walk**, daily 6 a.m. to 5 p.m., tel./fax. 645-5238.
Accommodation
Most hotels are on the road between Santa Elena and Monteverde (the distance from Santa Elena is in parenthesis).
MODERATE: **Arco Iris Lodge** (in Santa Elena), tel. 645-5153, clean cabins for up to 6 persons, central location, quiet. **Sunset Hotel** (north of St. Elena, on the road to the St. Elena Preserve), tel. 645-5048, nice view of the Gulf de Nicoya. **Hotel Sapo Dorado** (750 meters), tel. 645-5010, nice bungalows, quiet location. **Hotel Belmar** (1.7 km), tel. 645-5046. Swiss-style wooden building, rooms with views. **Hotel Fonda Vela** (3.7 km), tel./fax. 645-5152, beautiful location, nice rooms.
BUDGET: **Pensión Sta. Elena** (in St. Elena), tel. 645-5156, restaurant. **Pensión La Flor de Monteverde** (650 meters), tel. 645-5236, clean rooms, shared baths, inexpensive. **Pensión Manakin** (1.3 km), tel. 645-5080, cheap but good.
Restaurants
Restaurant Don Miguel (100 meters), typical local dishes. **Restaurante de Lucia** (1.1 km, turn-off to the right), tel./fax. 645-5537, nice place, good meat dishes, expensive. Reservations are necessary in peak season. Many simple inexpensive restaurants are found in center of Santa Elena.

FORTUNA
Getting There
From San José three times daily from the Coca Cola-bus station (takes about 4 hours). Mornings and afternoons from Tilarán (3 hours).
Accommodation
MODERATE: **Hotel Las Cabañitas**, at entrance to the town, tel. 479-9400. Nice wooden cottages at the edge of town. **Hotel San Bosco**, north of the soccer field, tel. 479-9050, large hotel. The better rooms are in the new building.

BUDGET: Private inns (*cabinas*) are found all over town. **Cabinas Rolopz**, tel. 479-9058, **Cabinas Grijalba**, tel. 479-9129, **Cabinas Carmela**, tel. 479-9364, **Cabinas Oriuma**, tel. 479-9111. **Cabinas Rossi**, 2 km, in the direction of the volcano, tel. 479-9023, neat rooms with baths

Restaurants
La Choza del Laurel, end of town, in the direction of the volcano, excellent local cuisine at reasonable prices. **Pizzería Vagabondo**, 2.2 km in the direction of the volcano, nice place with very good pizza and pasta, rather expensive. **Restaurant La Pradera**, 2.4 km in the direction of the volcano, good restaurant with typical local dishes.

VOLCÁN ARENAL / LAGO ARENAL
Accommodation / Restaurants
The distance from Fortuna in the direction of Tilarán is given in km in parenthesis.
LUXURY: **Tabacon Resort Hotel** (12 km), new hotel near thermal springs. **Arenal Lodge** (16 km), tel. 220-1712, beautiful view of the volcano.
MODERATE: **Cabañas Montaña de Fuego** (8.5 km), tel. 479-9106. nice cabins with volcano view. **Arenal Vista Lodge** (16 km left + 11 km), tel. 220-1712, view of lake and volcano. **Hotel Los Heroes** (ca. 18 km), tel./fax. 441.4193, Swiss-style hotel on the lake, good restaurant. **Marina Club Hotel** (ca. 20 km), tel./fax. 479-9178, nice complex with lake view. **Mystica Lake Lodge** (ca. 45 km, on northwest end of lake), tel. 382-1499, comfortable rooms, Italian restaurant.
BUDGET: **Cabinas La Alondra** (ca. 25 km), basic rooms near lake. **Cabinas Rodriguez** (34 km, in Nuevo Arenal), tel. 694-4237, clean, simple, inexpensive. **Los Lagos Lodge** (ca. 43 km), tel. 694-4227, no-frills rooms in a good location.

CAÑO NEGRO / LOS CHILES
Getting There
Buses to Los Chiles leave San José twice daily (Av. 3, C.16) and take ca. 5 hrs. Frp, Quesada, ca. every 1.5 hrs. and take ca. 2.5 hrs. In Los Chiles there are boat rentals on the Río Frio to Caño Negro Preserve.
Accommodation
BUDGET: **Cabinas Jaribú**, northwest of soccer field, tel./fax. 471-1116, clean and inexpensive. **Guajipal Lodge**, 2 km south, tel./fax. 471-1242, clean rooms with baths. **Centro Turistico El Gaspar**, next door, tel. 382-1266, new complex with a restaurant and swimming pool.

MONTEZUMA
Accommodation
MODERATE: **Cabinas El Jardin**, at entrance to town, tel. 642-0074, good rooms with baths. **Hotel**

Horizontes, 2 km from Montezuma, tel./fax. 642-0259, new hotel with swimming pool, ocean view and language courses. **Hotel Amor de Mar**, at the end of town near Cabo Blanco, tel./fax. 642-0262, children-friendly oceanfront hotel. **Bungalows El Sano Banano**, on the Playa Grande, check-in at restaurant, tel./fax. 642-0068, new bungalows on the ocean.
BUDGET: Many budget and inexpensive accommodations are found throughout the town. **Hotel Montezuma Pacific**, west of the church, tel. 642-0204. Some rooms have air-conditioning. **Hotel La Aurora**, next door, tel./fax 642-0051, neat rooms with or without baths. **Hotel Lucy**, at the edge of town, direction Cabo Blanco, on ocean, tel. 642-0273, renovated rooms, good restaurant.
Restaurants
La Frescura, **El Parque**, **Tucan** and **Soda La Gemelas** feature Costa Rican cuisine.
Restaurant Sano Banano has good milk shakes, fruit salad, yogurt and vegetarian dishes.
El Pargo Feliz, famous for fresh fish and lobster.

CABO BLANCO NATURE PRESERVE
Getting There
Approximately 10 km south of Montezuma
Opening Times
Wednesday through Sunday, 8 a.m. to 1 p.m.

PLAYA TAMBOR
Accommodation
LUXURY: **Hotel Playa Tambor**, gigantic hotel complex, tel. 661-2039. **Hotel Tango Mar**, tel. 661-2798.
MODERATE: **La Hacienda**, tel. 661-2980.
BUDGET: **Hotel Dos Lagartos**, tel. 683-0236. **Hotel Zorba's Place**, Playa Pochote, tel. 661-3233.

CURÚ GAME PRESERVE
Opening Times
Daily 8 a.m. to 4 p.m., tel. 661-2392. Visitors no longer need to call ahead.
Accommodation
Budget cabins, mostly for researchers and special interest travelers, on the beach, with board. **Cruceros del Sur** arranges admission and excursions lasting several days from Puntarenas to Curú by yacht, tel. San José 220-1679.

PLAYA NARANJO
Accommodation
MODERATE: **Hotel Oasis del Pacifico**, tel. 661-1555, older vacation complex with pool and park.
BUDGET: **Hotel el Paso**, tel. 661-2610, rooms with baths, small pool.

THE NORTHWEST

LIBERIA
RINCÓN DE LA VIEJA N. P.
GUANACASTE N. P.
SANTA ROSA N. P.
NICOYA PENINSULA
BARRA HONDA N. P.
PALO VERDE N. P.

The northwest of Costa Rica presents a landscape of contrasts and offers visitors a large variety of tourist attractions. The Cordillera de Guanacaste, with its volcanoes and spectacular national parks, is the source of endless fascination. The Nicoya Peninsula has always been popular with travelers for its idyllic beaches and colorful traditional villages.

Liberia, in the heart of the northwest, is the largest city of the region. Located directly on the Panamericana, it is the perfect starting point for trips into this circa 10,000-square-kilometer region.

LIBERIA

Liberia, the capital of the Guanacaste province, is located further north than any other Costa Rican city of any size. It is situated 140 meters above sea level and is surrounded by farms. Most of its 30,000 inhabitants make their living from agriculture. For nature lovers, Liberia is the gateway to the Santa Rosa, Guanacaste and Palo Verde National Parks, as well as to the Lomas Barbudal Nature Preserve.

Previous pages: Sabañeros (cowboys) in the northwest have a very dusty job. Left: The entire family helps collect eggs laid by sea turtles.

Liberia was founded in 1769 as *Pueblo de Guanacaste* and renamed *Liberia* in 1854 because of its location near the Río Liberia. Ticos also call Liberia "White City" (*Ciudad Blanca*). The reason for this appellation is instantly apparent to every visitor. The brilliant white coral limestone, of which much of the city is built, contains quartzite which makes it sparkle in the sunshine. The walls of all the older buildings are made of this material, especially those neighboring the **Casa de Cultura**. Many of the residential structures are made of adobe, sun-dried mud bricks. The spacious houses, with their high rooms, stucco decoration and elegant furnishings, are delightful. Often they are built around a flower-filled inner courtyard, completing the colonial atmosphere.

Many of the old corner houses have unusual double doors placed at the corner of the building. In the winter they can be opened on both sides to let in the morning as well as the evening sunlight. In the summer one side can be closed to avoid the heat, while the other remains open, letting in the light. Ticos call this sophisticated innovation, *puertas del sol* (sun doors).

The small **Museo de Sabañero** (Cowboy Museum) in the Casa de Cultura exhibits the agricultural implements and tools typical of the area. Ox yokes, milking stools, scythes, wagon wheels, handmade saddles, spurs and riding whips now seem romantic reminders of the past. They show how important animal breeding and ranching has always been in this remote region.

In another fitting tribute to the province's cowboys, the inhabitants have erected a **statue of a sabañero** to commemorate the city's 200th anniversary. The monument occupies a place of honor between Calles 10 and 12.

Costa Rican towns and cities all possess a **Parque Central**, which is to this country what the *Zócalo* is to Mexico and the *Plaza de Armas* to Peru. It is a carefully-groomed city park with benches, flower beds and the inevitable music pavilion for marimba band concerts. The park is especially popular on Saturday evenings and Sunday afternoons, when it becomes the meeting point for the city's young singles and attracts cliques of giggling school girls and maids looking for prospective mates.

About six blocks northeast of the park, on Avenida Central, is Liberia's oldest church, the **Iglesia de la Ermita de la Resurección** (Church of the Hermit of the Resurrection), a mouthful usually shortened by parishioners simply to *La Agonía* (The Throes of Death). It remains to the visitor's imagination to decide if the popular name questions the miracle of the resurrection as it seems to imply. The church is made of adobe with a simple exterior, and an interior artfully decorated with stucco. Its style seems far more colonial than the date of its founding in 1852 would allow.

Liberia's long hot evenings are chiefly spent at the **Cine Olímpia** movie house watching U.S. action thrillers or Latin American romantic comedies. More interesting is a dance encounter with young Ticos and Ticas at the **Discotheque Kurú** on Avenida Central next to the Pókopí restaurant.

Liberia holds a festival each year on July 25. The important celebration commemorates a plebiscite held in 1812 that decided the fate of the province and separated it from Nicaragua. During the city fiesta, strutting cowboys demonstrate their courage in countless rodeos and bloodless bull fights. The spectators are endlessly entertained and only take a break from the action to stroll among the stands serving typical local foods. There are parades, animal auctions, fireworks and mariachi bands playing heart-rending music while marimba concerts get the ecstatic audiences moving. In short, there is something for everyone.

The first week of September is set aside as the *Semana Cultural*. It is a repetition of the city festival on a smaller scale, but lasts a full week. A recently added attraction is called **Fiesta Brava**. It takes place daily on the Hacienda La Cueva, a 3,000-hectare cattle ranch whose main building dates back to 1824, Visitors have an opportunity to mingle with traditionally-dressed *sabuñeros* and attractive *sabañeras* (cowgirls), can taste the delicious foods of Guanacaste and try their hand (or other parts of their anatomy) at the wild local sport of riding on the back of a bucking steer (admission is charged).

The airport is 13 kilometers west of the city. Since the end of 1996, the **Tomás Guardia Airport** is also open to international flights. So far only a few North American charter flights have taken advantage of the opportunity.

RINCÓN DE LA VIEJA NATIONAL PARK

The **Rincón de la Vieja National Park** is in Liberia's backyard. It begins just a few kilometers northeast of the city limits. The national park (its name means "corner of the old") spreads out over 14,000 hectares, at altitudes ranging from 600 to just under 2,000 meters above sea

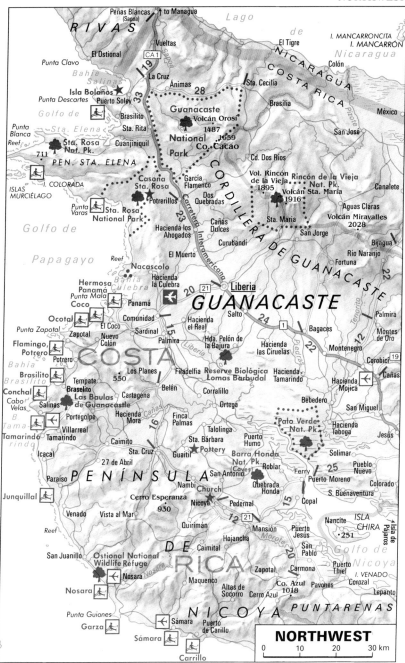

NORTHWEST

0   10   20   30 km

level. The volcano of the same name (1,806 m) and the Volcán Santa Maria (1916 m) are visible from far and wide.

The Rincón National Park is famous in Costa Rica for the unusual cone of its volcano, its yawning crater, small lakes and volcanic steam vents. Smoke curls from crevices in the earth and bubbling mud springs emit sulfurous fumes.

The last eruption of the Volcán Rincón was in 1991. The corrosive gas accompanying the lava that streamed down the mountain significantly damaged the forest vegetation, especially on the southeastern slopes.

The national park is divided into various vegetation zones, determined by altitude and the average annual amount of rainfall they receive. The Caribbean side of the continental divide experiences significantly higher precipitation than the Pacific side (up to 5,000 mm annually).

Above: The dry Pacific side of the Rincón de la Vieja. Right: Volcanic hot spot – a bubbling mud spring.

The more than 30 rivers and streams that flow through the park assure that it has ample water throughout the year.

The humid environment supports a large number of creatures. More than 300 tropical bird species live in the park. Quetzals, exquisite hummingbirds, trogons, parrots, toucans, bellbirds, woodpeckers and wild doves nest in the tropical rain forest. Peccaries, armadillos, sloths, coatis, monkeys, skunks, squirrels and tapirs inhabit the park.

Hikers have spotted pumas, jaguars, margays and ocelots, which stalk the jungle and quickly disappear on spotting human intruders. Insects can be dangerous, especially ticks, which are known to spread meningitis.

A short path leads around the forest station of Santa Maria. The path from Santa Maria extends three kilometers further to the sulfurous springs, and farther still to the boiling mud pond of **Las Pailas** near the forest station of Las Espuelas. Another hiking path winds to the summit of Mt. Rincón and to its vast crater. The trail begins at the Santa Maria ranger station, passes the Las Hornillas and Las Espuelas stations, snakes through the high grass-covered slopes, and steeply ascends through clouds and thick fog to the summit. A few signs mark the path, but it is easy to get disoriented, and it is advisable for anyone planning to climb to the summit to hire a local guide.

Volcán Miravalles

A few kilometers east of Rincón de la Vieja, another volcano soars out of the Cordillera de Guanacaste. It is the Volcán Miravalles, the highest peak (2,028 m) of the mountain chain. Although currently dormant, geothermal activity visible around the village of Las Hornillas (700 meters above sea level) are a strong indication that, with little warning, the sleeping giant could at any time become active again.

A research and observation station is located south of the volcano near the village of La Fortuna on the Río Pizote. The station, called *Proyecto Geotérmico Miravalles*, was established to find ways of harnessing the volcano's energy to produce electricity.

GUANACASTE NATIONAL PARK

This national park was first established in 1989 in order to protect the region's wildlife during seasonal migrations through the grasslands at the foot of the Volcán Orosí. Many rare and endangered species live in the area, and make their seasonal trek from the upper reaches of the cloud forest on the slopes of the volcanoes to the deciduous forests of the Santa Rosa National Park on the Santa Elena Peninsula.

Although the Panamerican Highway divides the two parks, they still serve a useful function. Only through consistent

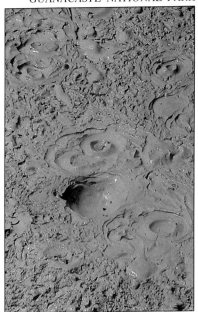

protection of such migratory routes – as in the Serengeti National Park in Tansania – can the future of endemic fauna be guaranteed in this region.   .

The two volcanoes, **Orosí** (1,487 m) and **Cacao** (1,659 m) crown the 36,000-hectare **Guanacaste National Park**, which begins about 20 kilometers north of Liberia. Four biological research stations are located in the park and have incredible views. The **Maritza**, **Pitilla**, **Mengo** and **Cacao** stations mainly serve to observe animals and to protect natural reforestation in the lower reaches of the cloud forest.

The government of Costa Rica plans to eventually join the national parks of Guanacaste, Santa Rosa and Rincón de la Vieja into a gigantic megapark containing more than 100,000 hectares.

The Guanacaste National Park was created to protect native animal species, rather than to provide recreational areas for human visitors. For this reason very little has been done to develop a tourist infrastructure.

131

SANTA ROSA NATIONAL PARK

The 50,000 hectare Santa Rosa National Park consists primarily of dry tropical forest. It covers a large portion of the **Santa Elena Peninsula**. Established in 1971, it is one of the oldest and largest of Costa Rica's national parks. It got its name from the Hacienda Santa Rosa. The country's most famous battle took place in this area on March 20, 1856, when an army of hastily assembled volunteers defended Costa Rica against the invading rag-tag army of U.S. adventurer William Walker. The Costa Rican victory against the hardened soldiers of fortune was hailed as a miracle and is celebrated to this day.

The primary concern of environmentalists and scientists at Santa Rosa is the protection of the fragile environment of the tropical deciduous forest. The Santa

Above: The towns near the Nicaraguan border are quiet. Right: Even the animal world has its machos – the strutting frigate bird.

Rosa National Park contains the largest forest with this sort of vegetation in all of Central America. The park is also responsible for the long-term protection of beaches where various species of sea turtle come to lay their eggs. During the rainy season between August and December, especially during the months of September and October, the giant turtles can be observed laboriously crawling ashore to lay their eggs. Because of the crowds that gather to witness this sight, biologists have tried for several years to limit the number of tourists at Playa Nancite, the most famous of the turtle nesting beaches. For this reason only 25 people with special permits are allowed to witness this natural spectacle per night. It is not only the human visitors who threaten to overrun the park's shores, though: olive-green bastard turtles also drag themselves over the sand. More than 7,000 of them have already been observed on the beaches at the same time.

The park has 10 distinct habitats, including mangrove swamps, oak forests,

deciduous forests, evergreen forests, dry savannas and coastal and mixed forests. Small wonder that the fauna is also so varied. Scientists have recorded more than 4,000 various kinds of moths and butterflies in the park. This is the largest group, followed by 250 species of birds and more than 60 types of bats (*murciélagos*). There are also coatis, armadillos, coyotes, monkeys, raccoons, red deer, tree ocelots, pumas, jaguarundis and even the occasional jaguar among the animals that gather at watering holes or stalk the thick undergrowth. The forest floor of the national park crawls with snakes, iguanas, lizards and turtles.

The **Museo La Casona**, in the main building of the Hacienda Santa Rosa (built in 1895), is easily reachable via a paved road from the Panamericana. On the way you pass the park administration building, a monument to the heroes of Santa Rosa, and camping grounds. The museum exhibits photos, sketches, documents and maps, plus old weapons and uniforms from the battle of 1856. Santa Rosa was also the site of battles in 1919 (the Sapóa Revolution) and 1955. Other exhibits show agricultural implements and common objects in use at the turn of the century. There is also a small chapel and a typical country house kitchen from those "good ol' days."

Visitors to the museum are often accompanied by swarms of small bats which dash through the doors, for they nest inside the museum. The tree in front of La Casona is the national tree of Costa Rica, the Guanacaste (*Enterolobium cyclocarpum*), which gives the region its name.

A few meters north of La Casona a small hiking trail with the unusual name of **El Sendero Indio Desnudo** (Path of the Naked Indians) begins. The appellation recalls the popular name of the gumbo-limbo tree, which is commonly seen in this region. In the dry season, when it has dropped its leaves, its bright red bark takes over the process of photosynthesis and hangs in strips from its trunk. The Indians regret this misnomer

and wish it were called the "naked tourist tree," because its bark resembles the sun-burned skin of vacationing palefaces more than Indians.

Hundreds of Ticos visit the national park, especially during the dry season (from December to April). Entire families come, stopping first at the historic memorial, then observing the animals around the few remaining watering holes before settling down for a lively picnic under the shade of the gnarled oak trees. They round off their visit with a romp on the Pacific coast beaches, which also belong to the park. At the Playa Nancite, not far from the **Witches Cliff**, young Ticos bob up and down in the surf while surfers rides the waves.

La Cruz and Peñas Blancas

The village of **La Cruz** is near the northwest pinnacle of the Guanacaste

National Park. Light blue stone benches decorate the Parque Central, where shade trees provide a welcome respite from the midday heat. At the edge of the cliff, 100 meters away, the **Mirador Ehecatl** opens to the grandiose panoramic view of the pacific bay of Bahía Salinas. On a clear day you can see all the way to the Isla Bolaños Game Preserve from the Mirador.

From La Cruz it is 20 kilometers to the Nicaraguan border. Peñas Blancas is the name of the border station (open only from 8 a.m. to 6 p.m.) here. As it is not a town, it is not surprising that there are no overnight accommodations. Back in La Cruz, a six-kilometer-long gravel road leads to the small fishing village of **Puerto Soley** on the Pacific coast. Set in the narrow bay of Bahía Salinas, the tiny port town has little more to offer visitors than the sailors' bar and a simple restaurant. After stopping for a cool Costa Rican beer, you shouldn't miss the opportunity to rent a boat for a trip to the island of Bolaños.

Above: Jungle beauty – wings spread but well camouflaged. Right: Iguana.

134

Isla Bolaños

From Puerto Soley it is four kilometers by boat through the deep blue water of Bahía Salinas to the 25-hectare Isla Bolaños and its **Refugio National de Fauna Silvestre** (National Refuge for Forest Fauna). This park created to protect animals is especially rich in bird life. The American oystercatcher with its bright red bill and various types of gull dominate the coastal region.

A colony of 500 brown pelicans nests at the north of the island. In the south, 200 frigate birds return each year to raise their chicks. The highest point on Isla Bolaños is only 80 meters above sea level, but it's enough to act as a signal buoy for both birds and sailors. Landing on the island is only allowed for visitors holding a special permit.

Nicoya Peninsula

South of the Santa Rosa National Park (reachable from Liberia), the two-kilometer-long gray, but clean, sand beach of **Playa Hermosa** stretches along the Golfo de Papagayo. Many private vacation houses line the curved bay, and hotels of all categories offer overnight accommodations. These tend to be heavily booked on weekends and during peak vacation periods. Surfboards, kayaks, snorkeling equipment and mountain bikes are for rent at the entrance to the town, and fishing enthusiasts and divers can find boats for hire. At the northern end of the street, three kilometers from Playa Hermosa, is the less developed idyllic beach of **Playa Panamá**. At present there is only a small shop selling food and a beach bar, but all that could soon change. Plans for the development of Playa Panamá are just waiting in the filing cabinets of big investors, and the mighty brazilwood and mesquite trees will soon give way to their bulldozers.

The Playa Panamá joins the two-kilometer gray sand beach of **Bahía Culebra**. The bay is lined with low bush covered hills and small mangrove

swamps in which birds nest. The Pacific is so deep in this bay that it is said U.S. submarines anchored here undetected during World War II. The ruins of a pre-Columbian Indian settlement near **Na-cascolo** are an easy walk away at the western end of the bay.

The neighboring town of **Puerto Cule-bra** is reachable via a new street that now connects it to Bahía de Culebra. The gigantic and controversial *Papagayo* project, consisting of yacht harbors, hotels and apartment complexes, was to have been built here, but so far only a few smaller luxury hotels, such as the Malinche Real Beach Resort and the Costa Smeralda Hotel have been realized.

The beaches closest to Liberia, which lies 35 kilometers to the east, are the **Playas del Coco**, accessible by bus via

Above: A Coco Loco cocktail at the Playa del Coco. Right: Ernest Hemingway sends regards – sport fishermen fight the black marlin and other game fish off shore near the Playa Flamingo.

Comunidad and Sardinal, or easily reached by car. These beaches attract local young Ticos rather than foreign tourists, in part because, unlike many of the other beaches surrounding the village of Coco, these *playas* provide entertainment – day and night. Despite a strong undertow and sand that is not always clean and well maintained, the crowds seem to love the Playas del Coco and go there in ever increasing droves.

It sometimes seems that the number of beachgoers is well over any acceptable limit. Several simple cabins, hotels and campgrounds make a stay of a few days here possible.

Just three kilometers southwest of the Playas del Coco, almost vertical cliffs reach skyward. This is where the less frequented **Playa El Ocotal** lies almost hidden and reachable only by a rather poor road. In addition to good swimming conditions and few bathers, this beach provides a good area for snorkeling at its south end. The water is crystal clear and filled with soft coral, and is inhabited by colorful tropical fish and tiny sea horses. The best place to start underwater exploration along this 500-meter-long beach is to swim out in the direction of the rocky 14-kilometer-distant **Santa Catalina Island**. The island is easy to reach by boat. From March to September special kinds of sea swallows nest on the island.

Sport fishing enthusiasts regard the Playa El Ocotal as the gateway to the Golfo de Papagayo. They prefer to stay at the sport fishing resorts of Las Corridas and El Ocotal, and go to sea from the fishing village in boats especially equipped for deep-sea fishing in hopes of hooking a black marlin or hawkfish.

A modest road leads from the Playa El Ocotal via Zapotal, past Playa Pan de Azucar (Sugar Loaf Beach) and La Penca, which is generally known as Playa Blanca, both of which are good for snorkeling. A bit further is the two-kilometer-long white sand beach of **Playa Flamingo Potrero**. Both local and foreign visitors claim this to be one of Costa Rica's most beautiful beaches and call it the "Acapulco of Costa Rica." The name, Playa Flamingo (after the Flamingo Beach Hotel), is the clever marketing idea of the resort's local investors. Far and wide, there are no flamingos to be seen.

Playa Flamingo is more exclusive than other Pacific coast beaches in the northwest. Well-to-do Costa Ricans and Americans have built their elegant villas along the beach. International sports fishing enthusiasts followed on their heels and soon turned Playa Flamingo into the base for the largest sport fishing fleet in Costa Rica. Its harbor is busy throughout the year. Anyone arriving from international waters by yacht, however, has to complete customs formalities at Playas del Coco before entering the shallow water of Playa Flamingo. The accommodations along the beach fall, without exception, into the luxury category with prices to match.

The tiny **Playa Brasilito**, with its little fishing village of the same name, borders on the "Acapulco of Costa Rica." Small shops, restaurants, inexpensive accommodations and the possibility of horseback riding from the La Perla restaurant attract vacationers willing to brave the less than romantic road to Playa Brasilito. Its white sand beach is also fabulously beautiful but not developed for tourism.

Playa Brasilito runs south to the rocky spit of land called **Punta Conchal** (Shell Point). The Pacific surf sweeps lots of shells onto the sparking white sand, which always seems freshly washed. In addition to swimming and sunbathing, this beach is a good place to take long walks and gather some very exotic looking shells. A parasol provides a bit of shade, the shallow turquoise blue water laps at your feet and soon – who would have imagined anything else – the Playa Brasilito connects to another dream beach, **Playa Conchal**. Locals discovered Playa Conchal as a vacation destination only a few years ago, and plan to

137

expand its facilities. In 1996, Sol Meliá, the Spanish hotel chain, built a resort directly on the fine white sand beach. The sprawling Meliá Playa Conchal Beach and Golf Resort has 300 luxury suites, an 18-hole golf course, tennis courts, a fitness center and a diving school.

Playa Grande, popular with surfers for its long smooth waves, is on the road that goes through the villages of Puerto Viejo and Matapalo. Nature lovers also find many attractions nearby. A 400-hectare mangrove swamp at its southern end provides shelter for the crocodiles and sea birds that find an ideal habitat in its shade and brackish water.

Leatherback turtles come to Playa Grande to lay their eggs, and environmentalists have succeeded in obtaining protected status for the beach, despite a 10-year wrangle with developers who attempted to build resort facilities on it.

Above: Time clock, what's that? Right: You rarely have to go far even to buy the needed souvenirs to take home.

The beach has been administered by the National Park Service since 1990.

Las Baulas de Guanacaste National Ocean Park

After seeing so many beautiful beaches, and bodies covered in suntan oil roasting in the sun, many a traveler in Costa Rica longs for a change and the chance to slip away into areas where nature remains untouched except by the wild animals that live there. The 450-hectare **Las Baulas de Guanacaste National Park**, established in 1991 at the mouth of the Río Matapolo, fulfills such desires. Along with the **Tamarindo National Game Preserve**, Las Baulas is the most important area on the entire Pacific coast where leatherback turtles (*baula*) currently lay their eggs. During their laying season between October and April, as many as 100 female turtles have been seen on the beach. Most are leatherbacks, but some bastard turtles are among them. During the peak season, volunteer scouts

help biologists protect the turtles and their eggs from over-enthusiastic animal lovers, and poachers who try to steal the eggs and newly-hatched turtles. The large numbers of visitors have also raised the costs of running the park. Because of this growing demand, Las Baulas has recently started charging admission and assigning visitors specific places from which they can observe the turtles.

Las Baulas is more than just a beach where leatherback turtles lay their eggs. A mangrove biotope spreads out along the border to Playa Tamarindo and there are another 22,000 hectares of protected park under the sea for the preservation of underwater creatures.

From Las Baulas to Ostional

Globe trotters discovered **Playa Tamarindo** some time ago, and since then the beach and its fishing village have become increasingly popular and crowded, especially during the peak season. Accommodations are available in all price ranges, but it is best to reserve ahead if planning a trip during the dry season. Playa Tamarindo is known for its gray sand and gravel beach. It has deep water and magnificent tamarind trees that grow along the shore.

The pulpy fruit of the tamarind is found in its long pods and is somewhat of an acquired taste. Ticos call the fruit *pulpa* and love its sweet-sour taste. They eat the fruit's pulp sprinkled with a bit of sugar. They also make drinks, fruit syrup, candy and even spicy sauces (Worcestershire Sauce contains tamarind) from pulpa. The tamarind is also known for its laxative properties and is often eaten or avoided for this reason. Its young leaves and green pods can also be cooked and served as vegetables. Even the seeds are edible, and they are also used in the textile industry.

The Playa Tamarindo is also known, but less loved, for its stinging sandflies. In the evening, when the sun goes down, they can be especially nasty. Swimmers should be warned there are dangerous

currents, undertows and barely visible rocks just below the surface. Windsurfers and surfers find the Playa Tamarindo a paradise. There are three perfect "breaks," in surfers' language these are locations that guarantee the thrill that surfers travel half way around the world to experience. These are at Henry's Point, Pico Pequeño and at the mouth of the river. Other good spots for surfing are the beaches to the south, reachable by boat, Playa Negra, Playa Avella and Playa Langosta. But environmentalists ask surfers to be careful not to collide with the protected species of turtle found at these beaches.

Playa Junquillal, a broad beach near the villages of Pochote and Paraíso, is recommended for novice surfers. High waves attract surfers, but few swimmers use the beach because of strong undercurrents that make it dangerous. Numerous small channels, where anglers sometimes try their luck, slice through the three-kilometer-long Playa Junquillal. The excited chirping of birds at the mouth of the river is a sure sign that it is brooding place for many tropical species. Crocodiles have also been seen here on occasion

There is no village directly at Playa Junquillal, but a number of cabins and inns provide overnight accommodations for those who wish to spend more than a day at the beach. Camping is also allowed, but campers have to bring their own tents and equipment.

Such hardships are quickly forgotten when you pull something elegant and wrinkle-free out of your backpack and dress up for an evening at the open-air disco on the beach. There, under the stars of the vast sky above the Pacific, every dream of tropical paradise seems to come true. A large swimming pool offers an opportunity to cool down, and daytime entertainment includes a match at the tennis courts at the nearby hotel complex, along with the usual beachside activities.

Above: Rhythm that gets into your blood – open-air disco at Playa Junquillal.

Ostional National Game Preserve

Another game preserve is situated to the south, past Playa Lagarto and the mouth of the Río Tabac. The **Refugio Nacional de Fauna Silvestre de Ostional** (National Refuge for Forest Fauna of Ostional) also includes another 600 hectares of coastal water. It sprawls over 15 kilometers of coastline and includes the beaches of Playa Ostional, Playa Nosara and Playa Guiones. In the *Laboratorio de Investigación Tortuga Marinos* (Laboratory for the Investigation of Sea Turtles), young people from an international youth exchange program led by biologists volunteer their time to protect endangered species of turtles (*Proyecto de Tortugas*). In Ostional they concentrate on the bastard turtle, which lays its eggs between July and December, particularly on dark nights during the new moon in August and September. Only a small percentage of the millions of eggs yield baby turtles, and of these, few reach maturity.

At first glance it seems contradictory that the local inhabitants are allowed to plunder the nests during the first days of the egg-laying season in the Ostional Game Preserve. The biologists argue that, in the first place, subsequently arriving turtles crush many of the eggs that were laid earlier, and secondly, allowing people to harvest eggs also involves them indirectly in the conservation process and awakens their awareness of the importance of the regular return of turtles to their beaches. Once the Ticos have gathered and sold the first crop of turtle eggs to local restaurants, the nests are protected for the rest of the season.

The average seasonal rainfall of 2,000 mm during the rainy season, from May to December, along with the average temperature of 28°C during the day, promotes lush growth in the deciduous forests of Ostional. Jasmine and prickly pear cacti, with delicate, refreshing fruit, grow in the forest. Shade trees, however, do not grow along the beach and there is still no ranger station at Ostional.

Swimming is not recommended at the **Playa Ostional** because of the dangerous undercurrents. The entire coast of the game preserve offers visitors other diversions. Howler monkeys, coatis, kinkajous, iguanas and crabs are plentiful in the forest and scrub growth along the shore. The mangrove swamp, at the mouth of the Río Nosara, is the nesting place of more than 200 different kinds of birds including migratory plovers and magnificent royal terns.

Simple shops (*pulperías*) sell food and drinks to hikers so they can stock up for their next expedition along the paths leading through the park.

Playa Nosara, five kilometers from the village of the same name, also lies within the confines of the park. The village has several lively bars and restaurants and a number of family-run hotels. A large number of retired U.S. citizens live in small houses built along the wooded shore. Houses that can be rented by the week or month by vacationers are scattered among them. The limits placed on construction protects the forest and its monkeys, armadillos, toucans, colorful parrots and other protected species.

A path stretches the length of **Playa Guiones**, which is also part of the Ostional Game Preserve. Its perfectly straight white sand beach, small coral reef and warm water welcome visitors.

Bahía Garza, Sámara and Carillo

From Nosara there is a narrow unpaved road that bumps along for 26 kilometers to **Playa Sámara**. After about ten kilometers it reaches the soaring cliffs of a small bay called the **Bahía Garza** (Heron Bay). The white sand of the horseshoe-shaped beach is mixed with fine gravel and protected by a tiny island which is visible from the shore.

The **Hotel El Villagio** is worth a visit for its unusual architecture and pleasant atmosphere. The complex incorporates a unique blend of elegance and coziness, and features, for example, a large swimming pool with a small man-made waterfall. The hotel bar, *La Tortuga*, features dancing, and on warm Pacific nights it is the place where the hearts of young and old beat in unison. The bay also offers possibilities for horseback riding, fishing and snorkeling, leaving little time for boredom.

The inhabitants of the village of Sámara make their living fishing or farming. The village beach is made up of light colored sand and is one of the most visited vacation destinations on the entire Nicoya Peninsula, especially on weekends, when Costa Rican sun worshipers from the inland cities come out for a day or two of fun and sun.

Above: Red crabs are a common sight on the Pacific coast. Right: Kayak surfing provides good fun at Playa Sámara.

Playa Sámara is very well suited for swimming because there are no dangerous currents off its shore. It is also popular with backpackers from Europe and North America because of its inexpensive and plentiful overnight accommodations. Many well-heeled Ticos own summer homes at Playa Sámara. Among its most illustrious residents is former Costa Rican President and Nobel Prize winner Oscar Arias Sánchez.

A large ranch divides the village into two parts. The livelier south side has most of the restaurants, including the Italian restaurant Chora Inn, the discotheques Disco Tutti Frutti (in the Hotel Playa Sámara) and the disco in the Hotel Isla Chora.

Playa Sámara ends at the steep cliffs of **Punta Indio** (Indian Point). The horseshoe-shaped **Playa Carillo**, the southernmost beach of this region, begins at the point. Despite its lovely rows of coconut palms planted along the beach and less expensive quarters, Playa Carillo attracts few visitors because of its out-of-the-way

location. Even the interesting handicrafts shop under the giant fig tree on the beach is unable to attract visitors. Four kilometers east of Sámara is a luxury hotel complex managed by a Japanese company, the **Gunamar Beach Resort**. The resort's affluent guests prefer deep-sea sport fishing and water skiing. For fun they rent one-man kayaks and paddle out into the Pacific.

The east coast of the Nicoya Peninsula, with its parks and beaches, is described on pages 120-121.

Ciudad de Nicoya

The little town of Nicoya was once the Chorotega Indian capital. The Chorotegas were the largest Indian group in Costa Rica at the time of the Spanish conquest. It takes about an hour to reach Nicoya from Playa Casrillo along secondary highway 150; it is 80 kilometers from Liberia.

Nicoya, the oldest colonial city of Costa Rica, was founded in 1544 and named San Blas de Nicoya, in honor of Chorotega Chief Nicoya. The Indian chief was heartily greeted by Spanish conquistador Gil Gonzalez Davila as his tribal brother. Today the few surviving descendants of the Chorotegas live on the Matambú Reservation.

The heart of Nicoya is its **Plaza Central**, lined with mango trees. On one side of the Plaza, resembling a medieval fortress, rises the oversized Baroque façade of the massive **Iglesia de San Blas**. As was often the case in the history of Latin America, the conquistadors purposely built their church on the ruins of a Chorotega Indian ceremonial temple. The church symbolized the eradication of the old Indian religion and presented the natives with a new "true" symbol to take its place.

A fire completely destroyed the church in 1634. Ten years after the catastrophe, a new church had replaced it and has consoled many generations since, despite a number of small earthquakes. A museum inside the church exhibits pre-Columbian

143

silver, as well as bronze and copper icons, and contains a total of 160 religious items. The many pictures of saints, with locks of hair added by faithful worshipers, and the devotional items presented in gratitude for answered prayers from sick and suffering parishioners are also interesting. These often take the form of notes attached to the pictures, vivid testimony to the enduring strength of the Catholic faith in Costa Rica.

Every year on December 12, the faithful honor the dark-skinned **Virgin de Guadalupe**, the saint who first appeared in Mexico and is worshipped throughout Latin America. The worshipers carry the statue through the town, accompanied by the music of flutes and drums. This fiesta, as is often the case in Latin America, is not entirely free of elements of Indian religion. One of these is the Chorotega

Above: Old church tower and new church in Santa Cruz. Right: In Guaitil, Chorotega Indian women carry on the tradition of pre-Columbian pottery.

Indian legend of *La Yeguita*, which is celebrated at the same time as the feast of the Virgin of Guadalupe.

The legend tells of a small mare that ended the fight between twin brothers who were both in love with the same Indian princess. Only the intervention of the peace-making mare prevented the brothers from killing each other.

The religious procession ends in uninhibited celebration that includes bull fighting, concerts and nights filled with drinking, dancing and fireworks.

Early in the morning, before the first rooster has crowed, *bombas* (homemade fireworks), known for the ear-splitting racket they make, are shot from iron pipes. Many foreign tourists, unaware of the extent or the sound level of the celebrations, are frightened out of their beds by the noise. Even in front of the church – or perhaps *because* it is in front of the church – the bombas blast away without respite.

Beer, made of fermented corn, flows in streams during the fiesta. It is drunk out of hollowed-out gourds. All day long traditional Indian music can be heard on every corner, and ecstatic dancers crowd the streets.

Santa Cruz

Some 20 kilometers northwest of Nicoya is the city of Santa Cruz (Holy Cross), with its 10,000 inhabitants. Around 1,800 Spanish colonial rulers founded the city on the banks of the Río Diriá (named after the 16th-century Chorotega Chief Diriá).

The jewel of this colonial city is its **Parque Central**, filled, regardless of the season, with profusely blooming flowers and shady trees. A massive 19th-century **church tower** rises skyward on the southern side of the park. Its walls, which could easily have served as a fort, were badly damaged in a 1950 earthquake and still bear its visible scars. The new modern church built next door seems strangely out of place because of its design, apparently inspired by the architecture of the Sydney Opera House and the Cathedral of Brazilia.

Santa Cruz is primarily known as the folklore capital of Costa Rica. At the musical faculty of the University of Costa Rica, which was founded in the city, many of the students are occupied reviving the country's old musical traditions. Students perform dances, handed down by their forefathers, on stages throughout the Nicoya Peninsula, and earn a little extra pocket money with their performances in hotels.

On January 15 and July 25, Cruzeños celebrate their famous dance festival which attracts visitors from all over the country.

Guaitil

Folklore is to Santa Cruz what ethnic ceramics are to Guaitil. The pretty, quiet village is located 12 kilometers east of

Santa Cruz. Chorotega Indian women produce their red, black and ocher colored ceramics, just as they have done for many generations. Nowadays, though, the women are part of an art cooperative and support their families with the money they earn.

A stroll through Guaitil reveals many woman sitting in front of their houses making pottery. They form the graceful vases, bowls, pots, cups and mugs from clay, which they obtain close to the village. The style and shape of the pots is pre-Columbian, and the artists only use colors made from natural pigments found in the area, resulting in exquisite pieces that make wonderful souvenirs.

Most of the ceramics are sold in **San Vicente**, a town just two kilometers from Guaitil. The decorative pots also add a touch of local color to the region's hotel lobbies, inns and restaurants, where they are also often sold. Unlike the bazaars in some eastern countries where it is customary to bargain, haggling over price in Guaitil brings little reward.

BARRA HONDA
NATIONAL PARK

The attractive Barra Honda National Park is not far from Nicoya. Constant erosion during the last 70 million years has produced 42 karst caves over an area of 2,300 hectares. The caves were only discovered at the beginning of the 1970s, and to date only 20 of them have been explored. Very few of the caves are open to the public. Ancestors of Indians still living in Costa Rica inhabited the caves more than 2,300 years ago. The remains of skeletons and stone artifacts – particularly in the Nicoya Cave – confirm the human habitation.

In the 200-meter-deep **Cueva Santa Ana**, the deepest cave, is a chamber known as the "Pearled Hall," containing many stalactites and stalagmites. The limestone formations in some of the

Above: Little egret with her chicks. Right: One of the 200,000 exotic birds found in the Palo Verde National Park.

caves fire the visitor's imagination: lion's heads, fried eggs, popcorn and shark's teeth decorate the walls and ceilings. Certain pillars give off musical tones when tapped. In many places bats swarm in the dark areas only to swoop down, narrowly missing visitors' heads. In a cave called **Pozo Hediondo** (Stinkpot), bats have left their "souvenirs" – which has done nothing to prevent salamanders and fish from living there.

The descent into the caves is very strenuous and should be undertaken only with a guide and only in the dry season. On the path to the caves it is often possible to spot many of the wild animals that inhabit the national park: howler monkeys, red deer, agoutis, peccaries and anteaters.

Visitors who still have a surplus of energy after visiting the caves can climb the 442-meter-high **Barra Honda** for a lovely view of the Gulf of Nicoya. From its elevation it is also possible to see Las Cascadas, the limestone sediment along the bottom of the river that runs through the park.

PALO VERDE
NATIONAL PARK

Not far to the northeast, only separated from the Barra Honda by the Rio Tempisque, is the famous wild bird preserve of the Palo Verde (Green Stake) National Park. The 17,000-hectare park is renowned for the 300 bird species that make it their nesting ground. The park takes up a large part of the Tempisque Delta, the most arid region of Costa Rica. The water level of the river varies up to four meters and creates 15 distinct habitats in the park, including mangrove swamps, marshes, meadows, forests and limestone formations.

In the dry season (which is totally free of rainfall), from December to March, many forests suffer drought, drop their leaves and survive on the water reserves stored within their cells, until the rainy season brings the steady precipitation that floods the forest floor.

The river and swamps teem with waterfowl, especially from September to March: from spoon-billed herons (approximately 800 of them) to common herons, gray herons, ibises, geese and storks. Among the latter is the magnificent, majestic jabiru stork, also found in the tropical north of Australia. Palo Verde is the only place in Costa Rica where this, the largest of all storks, nests. Its long black legs and bright red beak make the jabiru instantly recognizable.

An estimated 200,000 birds live in Palo Verde. The park gives visitors to Costa Rica their best chance of discovering the country's incredible variety of bird life. Thousands of black-breasted ducks and green-winged teals with their striking coloring flutter into the air at the approach of a human being and land in the river a few meters away with a braking action, visible in the curl of spray they leave behind them.

Every now and then the visitor is rewarded with a glimpse of the large-beaked toucan or a flash of red indicating the presence of a member of the park's colony of red macaws – the only permanent colony in the tropical dry zone of the Americas.

In addition to the toucans and macaws (parrots), the forests are full of other birds. Palo Verde also provides an ideal habitat for iguanas, crocodiles, porcupines, peccaries and monkeys.

The bird island, **Isla de Pájaros,** lies in the middle of the broad Río Tempisque. The island shelters many rare birds, including roseat spoonbills, egrets, shy forest storks, white ibises and even the large jabiru stork. Ornithologists have also identified a large colony of Cayenne night herons on the island.

The best time to visit is during the months of December, January and February. In these months migratory birds as

well as those indigenous to the park are easiest to spot. During this dry period the birds are also easier to see in the bare trees. A further advantage of the dry season is that the paths remain dry and passable, and the mosquitoes are not as prevalent as at other times of the year.

Lomas Barbudal Nature Preserve

The Palo Verde National Park gives way in the north to several kilometers of farmland before the next park begins, the **Lomas Barbudal Nature Preserve** (*Reserva Biológica*). The park takes up a wide strip of land comprising 2,300 hectares. Almost 70 percent of the park is made up of deciduous forest, which its unusual name, Lomas Barbudal (Bearded Hills), aptly describes.

The months of November to March are especially dry, giving rise to types of trees adapted to the environment, among others, endangered species like mahogany, Panama redwood and rosewood. The corteza amarilla (*Tababuia och-*

racea) is especially spectacular. These trees all begin to bloom on the same day, usually a day at the end of the dry season. Within one short week they turn the park into a colorful carpet dotted with bright yellow.

The banks of the Río Cabuyo, which contains water all year round, are covered with lush forest sheltering more than 200 different types of birds, including the endangered king vulture. Howler and capuchin monkeys, as well as white-tailed deer and peccaries also come to the river to drink, giving visitors a chance to catch a glimpse of these exotic creatures.

Sitting on the shore, the observer is sure to note that this paradise on earth also contains many smaller creatures. There are 250 kinds of bees alone in the park. Their buzzing, as they go from flower to flower in search of nectar, fills the air. In addition, there are many types of butterflies and moths.

The African killer bee has also been spotted at Lomas Barbudal in the last several years. The bee has caused concern and fear throughout Central America since its escape from a Brazilian research laboratory in the mid 1980s.

Cañas

On the return trip to San José it is possible to reach the Panamericana by way of Cañas, a real cowboy city. The majority of the city's 26,000 inhabitants are *sabañeros*. The city got its name, however, from the wild sugar cane that still grows everywhere, even alongside the streets. Cañas is a good place to stop when traveling between Palo Verde, Lomas Barbudal and San José.

The town itself has little in the way of tourist attractions. For visitors interested in ecology, there is an interesting center five kilometers north of Cañas, the **Centro Ecológico La Pacífica**, which includes a park containing many interesting nature trails.

LIBERIA

Getting There: The bus from San José takes 4 hours. Departure (Av. 5, C 10-12) daily from 4 a.m., every 2 hours.
Accommodation: *LUXURY:* El Sitio, on the road to Nicoya, tel. 666-1211, fax. 666-2059, older luxury hotel with pool. **Las Espuelas**, 2 km south on the Panamericana, tel. 666-0144, fax. 225-3987. *MODERATE*: **El Bramadero**, (Panamericana, Av. Ctl.), tel. 666-0371, fax. 666-0203, restaurant, bar and pool. **La Siesta** (C.4, Av.4-6), tel. 666-0678, fax. 666-2532, good value, pool. *BUDGET:* **La Posada del Tope** (C. C., Av. 2-4), tel. 666-1313, rooms with shared baths. **Hotel Daysita** (Av. 5, C. 11-13), tel. 666-0197, out of the way but quiet, clean rooms. **Guanacaste** (C. 12, Av. 1), tel. 666-0085.
Restaurants: **Pizza Pronto** (C. 1, Av 2-4), nice place, wood-burning stove. **Pocopí Restaurant** (on the road to Nicoya), good but rather expensive. **Jardín de Azucar** (C. Ctl., Av. 3). Chinese restaurants are concentrated on Av. Central and Av. 1.

GUANACASTE NATIONAL PARK

Accommodation: *MODERATE:* **Los Innocentes Lodge**, at the north rim of the park, tel. 265-5484, guest farm with a view of Orosí volcano. *BUDGET:* **Santa Clara Lodge**, south of the park, arrive via García Flamenco, tel./fax. 666-0473, clean, shared bathrooms (cold water only). Accommodation also at the research station in the park.

RINCÓN DE LA VIEJA N. P.

Accommodation: *MODERATE:* **Rincón de la Vieja Mountain Lodge**, south of Las Pailas ranger station, tel./fax. 695-5553, nice atmosphere, rustic rooms, riding stables. **Buena Vista Lodge**, at the western edge of the park, arrival via Cañas Dulces, tel./fax. 695-5147, nice location on slope, good restaurant, riding stables. *BUDGET:* **Hacienda Guachipelín Lodge**, 4 km before Las Pailas, tel. 284-2049, rustic accommodations, all rooms with bath.

LA CRUZ

Accommodation: *MODERATE:* **Hostal de Julia**, (400 meters east of the park) tel./fax. 679-9084, new hostel. **Amalia Inn** (100 meters south of the park) tel./fax. 679-9181. Private home with great view and pool. *BUDGET*: **Cabinas Santa Rita**, near Parque Central, tel. 679-9062.
Restaurant: **Ehecatl / El Mirador**, at look-out point above Salinas Bay, good Costa Rican cuisine.

PUERTO SOLEY

Accommodation: *LUXURY:* **Ecoplaya Beach Resort**, tel. 289-8920, neat hotel complex on the sea, nice restaurant, pool, air-conditioning.

SANTA ROSA NATIONAL PARK
Accommodation: Camping only with own tent.

PLAYA HERMOSA
Accommodation: *LUXURY:* **Hotel Sol Beach Resort**, at north end of beach, tel. 221-2264, large complex with hotel and bungalows. *MODERATE:* **Hotel El Velero**, in center, tel. 670-0310, nice small seaside hotel, restaurant, pleasant rooms (no sea views). **Hotel Villa del Sueño**, south of road, tel./fax. 670-0027. New hotel with swimming pool, good restaurant, nice rooms, ca. 200 meters to beach. *BUDGET:* **Cabinas Playa Hermosa**, tel./fax. 670-0027. Older seaside complex. **Cabinas La Casona**, south of entrance, tel. 670-0205, clean rooms, ca. 300 meters from beach.

PLAYAS DEL COCO
Accommodation: *MODERATE:* **Hotel Coco Verde**, on access road, to the right, tel./fax. 670-0367, new hotel with pool, air-conditioned rooms, 400 meters to beach. **Hotel Villa Flores**, turn right in front of church, tel./fax. 670-0269, new private house in quiet location with garden, good rooms. *BUDGET:* **Hotel Anexo Luna Tica**, tel. 670-0279. Clean rooms near beach.
Restaurants: **Bar/Restaurant Beach Club Zebra**, nice place with sea view, expensive. **Hotel La Flor de Itabo**, right of town entrance, good Italian cuisine, expensive.

PLAYA EL OCOTAL
Accommodation: *LUXURY:* **Villas Los Almendros de Ocotal**, tel. 670-0401, luxurious apartments, close to beach. **Hotel El Ocotal**, tel. 670-0083, nice location overlooking sea, with swimming pool, tennis courts. *MODERATE:* **Hotel Villa Casa Blanca**, tel./fax. 670-0448, tastefully furnished rooms and apartments, ca. 600 m to beach.

PLAYA BRASILITO
Accommodation: *BUDGET:* **Hotel Brasilito**, tel. 654-4237, close to beach. **Cabinas Ojos Azules**, tel./fax. 654-4346, nice rooms with baths.

PLAYA TAMARINDO
Accommodation: *LUXURY:* **Hotel Jardin del Eden**, tel./fax. 653-0111. Nice location close to beach with pool and excellent restaurant. *MODERATE:* **Hotel Tropicana**, tel./fax. 653-0261, new hotel with pool, close to beach. *BUDGET:* **Cabinas Pozo Azul**, tel. 653-0280, no frills, rooms with baths, cheap.
Restaurants: **La Meridiana,** elegant Italian restaurant, air-conditioned dining room, expensive. **La Fiesta del Mar**, regional cuisine.

PLAYA JUNQUILLAL
Accommodation: *MODERATE:* **Hotel Villa Serena**, tel./fax. 680-0573, restaurant with sea view, pool, tennis courts. *BUDGET:* **Hotel Hibiscus**, tel. 680-0737, cabins with baths near beach.

PLAYAS DE NOSARA
Accommodation: *MODERATE:* **Hotel Casa Romantica**, tel. /fax. 682-0019, new hotel on Playa Guiones with good restaurant and pool. **Hotel Villa Taype**, tel./fax. 382-7717, close to beach, restaurant, pool, tennis court. *BUDGET:* Cheap lodgings in Nosara, **Cabinas Angel**, **Cabinas Chorotega**.

BAHIA GARZA
Accommodation: *MODERATE/LUXURY*: **Hotel Villagio**, tel. 680-0784, large vacation complex.

PLAYA SÁMARA
Accommodation / Restaurants: *MODERATE:* **Hotel Giada**, tel. 656-0132, pleasant rooms, reasonable prices. **Hotel Isla Chora**, tel. 656-0174, with pool, good Italian restaurant. *BUDGET:* **Belvedere B&B**, tel. 656-0213, nice location on slope.

NICOYA
Accommodation: *MODERATE:* **Curime Hotel**, at south end of town, tel. 685-5238, restaurant, pool. *BUDGET:* **Pensión Venecia**, next to church, tel. 685-5325, clean rooms in annex.

SANTA CRUZ
Accommodation: *BUDGET:* **Hotel La Pampa**, tel./fax. 680-0586, clean rooms, air-conditioning.

BARRA HONDA NATIONAL PARK
Getting There: From Liberia or Cañas via Puerto Moreno, from Nicoya by bus via Santa Ana and Nacaome (departs daily at noon). **Accommodation**: Camping, cottages at entrance, tel. 686-5680.

PALO VERDE NATIONAL PARK
Getting There: Via Bagaces (Panamericana), then by taxi. From Nicoya via Santa Cruz and Hacienda El Viejo. **Accommodation**: *MODERATE:* **Rancho Humo**, west bank of Río Tempisque, tel. 255-2463. **Albergue Las Sillas**, tel. 671-1030.

CAÑAS
Accommodation: *LUXURY:* **Hacienda La Pacifica**, 5 km north on the Panamericana, tel. 669-0266, fax. 669-0555, hacienda-style hotel, good restaurant, pool, hiking trails. *MODERATE:* **Cañas Hotel**, tel. 669-0039. *BUDGET:* **El Parque**, Parque Central, tel. 669-0915. **Guillén**, Parque Central, tel. 669-0070.

CENTRAL PACIFIC COAST

FROM TÁRCOLES TO QUEPOS
MANUEL ANTONIO N. P.
FROM PLAYA MATAPOLO TO
BALLENA N. P.
SAN ISIDRO DE EL GENERAL
CHIRRIPÓ N. P.

Without having to travel over long distances, it is possible to visit countless beaches along the Pacific Coast within just a few days. Their sand is fine and white, but is sometimes also gray. The **Parque Nacional Manuel Antonio**, Central America's most popular national park, attracts thousands of visitors from the central highlands like a magnet – especially on weekends. The rich and varied plant and animal life of the coastal game and nature preserves, plus the vast protected maritime area with its magnificent coral reefs, astound and delight even the most fastidious nature lovers.

The region also features the almost untouched **Chirripó National Park** in the Cordillera de Talamanca. It iss named for Mt. Cerro Chirripó (3,820 m), the country's highest mountain and greatest challenge for Costa Rica's mountain climbers.

FROM TÁRCOLES TO QUEPOS

In addition to the beaches south of Puntarenas, **Playa Tárcoles**, near the fishing village of the same name, is the first Pacific beach to be reached from the

Previous pages: Pure romance in the Manuel Antonio National Park. Left: Green iguana – a reminder of the dinosaurs.

capital. But the gray gravel beach is not the only reason for leaving the big city. The mangrove swamp that stretches 15 kilometers north to Punta Loros is worth closer inspection. It is especially exciting to watch various types of coastal birds at ebb tide.

From Costanera Sur, the coastal road, there is a gravel road just beyond the Río Caña Blanca that leads directly to **Playa Punta Leona**. Palm trees line the gray sand beach, which goes on for kilometers. Between July and December sea turtles crawl up onto the beach to lay their eggs.

In 1990, the beach saw a different kind of action when it served as the backdrop for a number of scenes in the film *1492*, in which Gerard Depardieu starred as Christopher Columbus and Sigourney Weaver appeared as Queen Isabella. Within 10 weeks the film's producers spent US $8 million, and they employed 150 *Indígenas* to play the roles of the Indians encountered by Columbus on his historic voyage. Another 350 mostly white inhabitants helped build the scenery, including a cathedral and an entire Indian village.

The **Playa de Jacó** is not occupied by Indians, but rather by Josefinos who come out on weekends, and by surfers, backpackers and Canadian travel groups

153

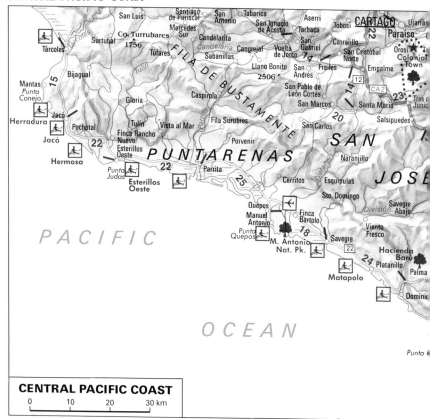

who come throughout the year. It is the nearest beach to San José and is one of the best developed beach and bathing facilities in the land. Jacó is especially attractive to young Costa Ricans, for whom this is *Party Beach*. Ticos also refer to this playa as *Boom Boom Beach*.

Not everyone would necessarily find the three-kilometer-long beach, with its palms, Indian almond trees and dark sand, attractive, since the dangerous offshore currents make the water unsafe for swimming. At high tide the beach is reduced to a narrow strip of sand, and the many hotels which have sprung up nearby have problems with their waste water disposal that can no longer be ignored. The private septic tanks built to serve the temporary needs of the hotels are now too small.

Avenida Pastor Díaz, the main street that runs parallel to the beach, is the town's only paved road. It contains banks, public telephones, a supermarket and bicycle and surfboard rental shops.

Surfers actually prefer the beaches south of Jacó, Tivives and Boca Barranca. Members of the international surfing elite, however, ride the waves of Jacó in the championships held here every year. In the evenings the action switches to the discotheques, La Central and Disco Club Los Tucanes. There is still no cinema. Jazz fans can enjoy their favorites during dinner in the restaurant of the El Jardín hotel. Other hotels also fea-

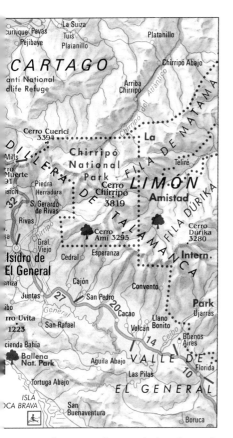

The seven-kilometer-long beaches of **Estilleros Oeste** and **Este** are well-suited for surfing. Although they are only a few minutes distant from Costanera Sur, the beaches seem remote. In the north, tidal pools form at ebb tide, yielding many small – and sometimes also hand-sized – rock fossils.

From this point the road heads inland and only returns to the Pacific coast at Quepos. **Parrita**, a small, dusty town surrounded by banana plantations, is built along the river of the same name. It is about a one-hour drive from Jacó. The origin of the town's name is curious: apparently there was a woman named Rita who was a postal worker there for many years. She was well known throughout the region, and when people from the neighboring villages wanted to send a letter or a package to the little village they would declare, *Es por Rita!* ("It's for Rita"). As a result, all female letter carriers in the town are now nicknamed Rita.

Today, Parrita is the commercial center for the huge 1,700-hectare ranch belonging to the United Fruit Company. Following its founding in 1895, the company planted thousands of African oil palms (*Elaeis guineensis*) along the road. The squat palms wave their feathery fronds in the sea breeze on either side of the narrow railroad bridge over the Río Parrita. They are planted in straight lines with almost mathematical precision.

The intensive odor (to put it very diplomatically) seeping through every window betrays the presence of the nearby factory that manufactures cosmetics and machine oil. The workers live in geometrically arranged settlements, some of which can be seen from the street. The wooden huts (some of which are on stilts) are painted turquoise blue or yellow and have wide country-style verandahs. This incongruous settlement, with its swaying palm trees, never fails to grab the attention of motorists driving past.

ture live entertainment during the peak season. There are accommodations in every category in Jacó, but they are more expensive than anywhere else on the Costa Rican Pacific coast.

Surfers can also find their mecca on the beaches to the south of Playas Hermosa, Estilleros Oeste and Este. **Playa Hermosa** (*Beautiful Beach*) stretches in a straight line for almost 10 kilometers and is best left to experienced surfers. A competition is also held at Hermosa every year in August. The pretty bay, with its turquoise-blue water, is not solely for the pleasure of those who shoot the curls; brown pelicans also bob on the waves. Delicious fresh fish is served in simple beach huts and bars.

Quepos

The next large town is **Quepos**, with 11,000 inhabitants. Its name is derived from the Quepoa Indians, a tribe of the Boruca people. They lived peacefully for centuries at the mouth of the Río Naranjo, where they farmed and fished. And, being excellent divers, they sought oysters bearing pink pearls 20 meters below the sea. The pearls were used in trade with other tribes. The Quepoas were decimated – as were many other tribes – through exposure to the diseases that the Europeans brought to the New World with them.

Today, the inhabitants live primarily from agriculture, for which they have at times cleared areas of virgin forest. In the 1970s, international tourism began to develop, helping to put a halt to the uncontrolled clearing. Lately, local people have

also begun to earn money from the growing stream of international sport fishing enthusiasts who have discovered the area.

MANUEL ANTONIO NATIONAL PARK

There are countless hotels (mostly large expensive complexes), but also some inexpensive hotels and restaurants, on the way from Quepos to Manuel Antonio National Park. Based on the number of visitors who come here, this is the most popular national park in the country; based on its size, it is Costa Rica's smallest. Otherwise, there is not much of interest in the area.

The 683-hectare park was established in 1972, just in time to rescue it from destruction through uncontrolled hotel and resort construction. The park features beautiful tropical beaches backed by thick forests, long narrow rocky points of land and – despite all the crowds that visit it – a wealth of animal life and a network

Above: The young man and the sea. Right: All of Costa Rica's beautiful Pacific beaches are worth a visit (Playa de Jaco).

of well-maintained paths. Visitors who want to enjoy the park have to acclimatize quickly to the high humidity. The average daily temperature throughout the year is 27°C. At the same time there is high humidity caused by the average annual rainfall of 8,000 mm, which is about 10 times the average in central Europe.

Drivers have to leave their cars at the southern end of the street and enter the park on foot, as do those who arrive by bus. It is important for hikers to bring enough drinking water along, as well as sun cream and insect repellent.

To enter the park visitors have to wade through the mouth of the Quebrada Camaronera, which, depending on the time of year, can be ankle to knee-deep. The path to the beaches and to Punta Catedral leads over an isthmus, a natural bridge (called *Tombolo*) made of alluvial sand.

To the northwest of the isthmus is a beach known as **Playa Espadilla Sur**, which is bordered by a patch of mangrove swamp. Southeast is **Playa Manuel Antonio** with its fine-grained white sand. This protected beach is the most popular one in the park and is also safe for swimming. Nearby, the remains of ancient semicircles formed of stone have been found. Archeologists think they may be the remnants of turtle traps once used by Indians.

The splendid view from **Punta Catedral** (Cathedral Point) stretches over the Pacific and takes in nearby rocky islands. It is worth the extra time and effort to hike further south to **Playa Puerto Escondido,** and to take the path through the forest to the 135-meter-high lookout point in the middle of the coastal jungle. This *mirador* (viewpoint) offers the best panoramic view of the park. It takes about one hour to walk here from Playa Espadilla Sur.

The Manuel Antonio National Park also provides first-time visitors a glimpse into Costa Rica's **animal world** and, with a bit of luck, a nodding acquaintance with capuchin and howler monkeys, as well as other animals. Whether you will catch a glimpse of any of the 350 yellow titi monkeys in the park is another matter; they are shy and – in the park at any rate – in danger of dying out. The masses of tourists who visit the park leave them far too little room and make far too much noise, which results in a disturbance of the titis' nesting habits.

Agoutis, on the other hand, are plentiful and may be easier to spot. The agouti is one of six types of American *Rodentia*, similar in their anatomy to rabbits. They are 40 to 60 centimeters long, but have small ears, paws that resembles hooves, and stiff bristled fur that ranges from reddish-brown to black. They eat roots, leaves and fruit and, much to the dismay of Costa Rica's plantation managers, also help themselves to bananas and sugar cane. Sloths and peccaries, armadillos and coatis also live in the park, along with the quick raccoons seen on the ground and in the trees. Lizards, snakes and iguanas creep along the forest floor.

One floor higher, in the tops of the trees, 350 different types of birds make their nests. There are still even a few colorful parrots in the jungle. Large numbers of these birds have been trapped and smuggled out of Costa Rica to be sold for huge sums of money to supposed animal lovers and laboratories abroad. Brown boobies and pelicans are found close to the water. Crabs, coral, sea snakes and sponges present a sampling of the colorful underwater world of Costa Rica. There is a small coral reef, but the water is usually not clear enough for snorkeling or other underwater sports. The fish most often found along this part of the coast has an unlikely military-sounding name – sergeant major. It has distinct verticle black stripes on its sides, and finds its way onto the menus of seaside restaurants, where it is generally served grilled.

The **flora** of the national park has much to offer. The manzanillo tree ("little apple tree" in Spanish) bears a small fruit similar to a crab apple. But the fruit, just as Adam and Eve discovered in the Garden of Eden, has its drawbacks. The manzanillo is poisonous! Its bark and leaves are toxic, and cause itching and burning when touched. Its wood can't be used, not even as firewood, because the smoke it releases contains etheric oils that can damage the lungs.

The wealth of animals and plants in the Manuel Antonio National Park, its protected beaches, and what is probably most important, its proximity to the capital have assured a heavy flow of visitors since its opening.

Every year approximately 100,000 people come to the park. That adds up to 1,000 per day outside of the rainy season. The park's administrators estimate that, ecologically, the park cannot sustain more than 300 visitors per day. In order to avoid the masses of tourists, it is best to arrive at the park very early in the morning, and, if possible, on weekdays rather than weekends. Better yet, visit the park during the rainy season. Special attention should be paid to personal belongings in the hotels and snack bars in the park, and on the beach.

FROM PLAYA MATAPOLO TO BALLENA NATIONAL PARK

Continuing along the coast you cross the Río Naranjo, which forms the eastern boundary of the Manuel Antonio National Park. Then we pass less heavily frequented beaches and bays. After the miles-long Playa Savegre the road crosses the river of the same name and reaches **Playa Matapolo**, a beautiful, long gray sand beach just two kilometers from the coastal road. Thousands of African oil palms grow here, and between them the smoking chimneys of the oil factories can be seen.

Just a few kilometers north of Dominical is a 320-hectare private nature

Right: Oil palm fruit awaiting transport to the oil factory.

preserve called **Hacienda Barú**. Meadow land, plantations and mangrove swamps surround the preserve, which contains 80 hectares of virgin rain forest at an altitude of 320 meters above sea level. The area also includes 75 hectares of rain forest that was cut in the 1970s, and which is now covered by secondary growth forest.

Jack and Diane Ewing (not to be confused with the fictional Ewings of the American television series *Dallas*) have been the owners of the hacienda since they moved to Costa Rica in the 1970s. Pre-Columbian settlements and cemeteries have been discovered in their park, along with a very rare Indian grave, one of the few in the country that has not been plundered by grave robbers.

Visitors to the park can also see no fewer than 10 very clear petroglyphs carved into the rock, and the remains of an old ceremonial site that was in all probability destroyed when the Spanish conquistadors swept through the area in the 16th century.

More than 300 different kinds of birds are found in the reserve, including spoon-billed herons, frigate birds, falcons, cormorants, darters and owls. There are also 23 different species of bat in the Hacienda Barú Nature Preserve. On the guided tours provided by the Hacienda Barú, visitors can see frogs, turtles and snakes, many of which have to this day not been classified. In addition, there are anteaters, ocelots, kinkajous, tayras, capuchin monkeys, jaguarundis and freshwater turtles.

The Ewings also offer special tours for bird watchers and riding adventures for horse lovers. There are no overnight accommodations at the hacienda. However, two kilometers away, a gas station owned by Hacienda Barú provides clean restrooms, a rarity in the area, usually found only in good hotels. It is also possible to buy food, drinks, supplies and hiking needs at the station.

Dominical, a pretty and quiet coastal village located 40 kilometers south of Quepos, features a four-kilometer-long

159

beach with warm water in which dolphins and whales are frequently seen. It has an abundance of inexpensive accommodations and restaurants. Swimming here can be a problem: not only are there occasional heavy underwater currents, but the water flowing from the Río Barú contains sewage that can be a health hazard. Young surfers and backpacking tourists let the powerful waves carry them to the south end of the beach where the water is presumed to be safer.

The beach offers other amusements. There are organized hikes and horseback-riding tours. Some years ago the *campesinos* (farmers) cultivated marijuana on their fields and tried to lure tourists by this means. But police have now become aware of the problem and are effectively eliminating this illegal crop.

Uvita ("Little Grape") is 15 minutes away from Dominical by car. It is the southernmost village worth mentioning on the Pacific coast. Farmers and cowboys still live and work in individual *fincas*, here called by their Mexican name *ranchitas*, much as they did 100 years ago. Uvita is also the northern gateway to the mangroves and gray sand beaches of Costa Rica's fascinating Ballena National Park. From its main street it is only three kilometers to the Río Uvita. The beach spreads out to the southeast, fringed with palm trees and backed by steep hills.

Ballena Ocean National Park

The **Ballena Ocean National Park** was first established in 1990, but has not had many visitors. The 13-kilometer-long park directly south of Uvita consists of 4,500 hectares, primarily made up of mangrove swamps, river estuaries and nesting areas for birds. The park is best known for its coral reef; the longest along the entire Central American Pacific coast. The Spanish word *ballena* means

Above: Uvita – oncoming traffic on the main street. Right: Divers discover Costa Rica's underwater paradise.

"whale." This refers, on the one hand, to a whale-shaped island off the coast, and on the other hand, to the humpbacked whales that migrate from Alaska via Baja California to Costa Rica. They are frequently sighted between December and April when they swim in the warm waters of the Pacific with their young.

The mighty sea mammals are not the only creatures that represent the richly varied **fauna** of the park. Frolicking dolphins can be seen throughout the year. Birds, including frigate birds and blue-footed boobies, nest on Whale Island. Bastard and loggerhead turtles crawl onto its beaches in September and October to lay their eggs.

Iguanas, basilisk lizards and – especially noticeable – the green iguanas that feed on algae in the salt-water pools and sun themselves on the beaches or rocks also live here. Once their body temperature has reached 37°C following a sunbath on the beach, they are warm enough to take another dip and eat another portion of green algae.

In terms of **flora**, it is worth noting that all five kinds of mangrove found in Costa Rica are present in this park: red, tea-colored, black, white and buttonwood mangrove. At ebb tide you can swim out from the beach and snorkel among the corals, sponges and sea anemones that create a colorful underwater landscape.

The construction of the new coastal road is an obvious threat to the delicate ecology of the reef. Oysters, mussels and tropical fish – the entire eco-system of the underwater world – could be effected. The first attempt to widen the coastal highway in the 1980s was disastrous, and resulted in 60 percent of the reef being destroyed, but the planners and politicians did not seem to have learned anything from the experience.

The Ballena National Park has no hotels, but camping is still allowed on the beaches. The ranger station in the village of Bahía has information about the park, especially about good places to snorkel. From here, too, boats for island tours can be chartered.

SAN ISIDRO DE
EL GENERAL

Several kilometers beyond the Hacienda Barú, a paved road leads up to the Valle de El General and the small city of San Isidro. The 40-kilometer-stretch of road, with its sharp curves, runs through the Cordillera de Talamanca and requires a good two hours to complete. It is beautiful, but it is without doubt also a very dangerous road. It is no accident that the Ticos have aptly named it the "Death Stretch." Road building and deforestation over a period of decades have led to serious problems caused by erosion. It is not unusual that landslides suddenly wipe out the entire road, forcing cars to make a long and arduous detour.

The small town of **San Isidro de El General** is situated at an altitude of 709 meters above sea level. The town serves as a center for the coffee plantations, cattle ranches and nurseries that employ most of its 40,000 inhabitants. El General refers to the river delta nearby, and San Isidro is the patron saint of the local farmers. For years the *campesinos* have brought their animals into the town every year on May 15, the feast day of San Isidro. There, amid a festive celebration, the priest blesses the animals assuring them health, and guaranteeing another year of prosperity for the farmers.

San Isidro is fortunate to have a number of interesting attractions. The small **Museo Regional del Sur** (Calle 1, Avenida 2) has a number of interesting exhibits which vividly represent the social life, history and archeology of the San Isidro area. The **Museo Perez Zeldon** specializes in historic photographs, and the **Centro Cultural**, in the same complex of buildings, contains a theater, lecture hall and an art gallery featuring the works of local artists.

Right: The Río Chirripó snakes through thick tropical vegetation.

The well-groomed **Parque Central** forms the heart of the city. The banks along its perimeter provide a place to change currency. One block further south, there is a post and telegraph office. The architecture of the modern **church** is purely functional. It is worth seeing for the bareness of its concrete walls, but it may not be to everyone's taste. During the day the sunny terrace of the **Hotel Chirripó** is the meeting place for globetrotters and San Isidrans of all ages. Given San Isidro's average daytime temperature of 22°C throughout the year, the terrace is the ideal place to exchange stories and share travel tips while enjoying a cool drink.

The slow drive on the road from San Isidro de El General, via Rivas and Canaán to San Gerardo de Rivas, is characterized by hairpin curves and spectacular views into deep green valleys and up to the high mountains. Quetzals, an endangered bird species, still inhabit the slopes. In the valley, the **Río Chirripó Pacífico** tumbles over boulders and rushes down to the Valle de El General.

San Gerardo de Rivas, at 1,350 meters above sea level, enjoys a comfortable climate throughout the year. It is the gateway to the Chirripó National Park. The ranger station is one kilometer beyond the sleepy village on the road to San Isidro. From the ranger station it is only possible to continue on foot.

Before visiting the national park, a small excursion to the village of **Herradura**, three kilometers north of San Gerardo, is recommended. The tiny village features relaxing hot springs. From there it is possible to stop off at the pond of the Río Blanco or head directly to Cerro Chirripó.

CHIRRIPÓ NATIONAL PARK

Many nature lovers and hikers find a visit of several days to the 50,000 hectare Chirripó National Park the high point of

their trip to Costa Rica. The name of the country's largest national park comes from its main attraction, the 3,819-meter Cerro Chirripó, Costa Rica's highest mountain.

The entire Chirripó massif is part of the Cordillera de Talamanca, the mountain chain that runs the length of Costa Rica in a northwest to southeast direction. In the east, the national park borders on the 193,000-hectare La Amistad International Park.

Contrasting zones of vegetation are characteristic of Chirripó National Park. Low-lying meadow land gives way to forests with lush ferns and thick groves of bamboo. Other regions of the forest feature hanging moss and epiphytes.

Further up the mountain the slopes are marked by impassable virgin cloud forest, which covers more than half of the park's total area. Still further up, above the tree line at the sub-alpine *páramo* level, created millions of years ago, is a unique landscape composed of various alpine grasses, herbs, mosses and low

bushes. In this region the rugged scenery is mirrored in the crystal clear, ice-cold water of mountain lakes created by glaciers that formed the land millions of years ago. The landscape reminds some visitors of northern Scotland or the Andes.

Most people visit the Chirripó National Park, with its three more than 3,800-meter-high peaks, during the dry season between December and April. It can get crowded during *Semana Santa*, the week preceding Easter. Last year a total of 2,000 people visited the park. The best weather is in February and March. On weekends the mountain cabins are usually completely full, occupied by local hiking groups.

Huge forest fires spread by strong sea winds caused great damage in 1976 and again in 1985. In April 1992, another 2,000 hectares of forest went up in flames. Fortunately, the animal world of Cerro Chirripó was largely spared. Several hundred different kinds of birds, including a kind of warbler with a fire red

throat, live in the park. In addition, there are tapirs, even jaguars and pumas (especially in the region known as the "Savannah of the Lions." Small animals like squirrels, blue and green frogs, and white caterpillars also live here.

Cerro de la Muerte

The road from the Chirripó National Park to the capital passes through bamboo and oak forests and sisal plantations. A very dangerous stretch of road, known and somewhat feared for its sudden fog and icy cold winds, awaits the traveler at **Cerro de la Muerte**, the "Summit of Death."

This poetic name for the 3,491-meter-high mountain, the highest point on the Panamericana, dates back to the turn of the century. Prior to that it was known as the Cerro Buenavista for its beautiful panoramic view.

Above: Moss, vines and epiphytes at Cerro de la Muerte.

One year, cowboys and ranchers, who had been traveling for several weeks in order to bring their cattle from the Valle de El General to the markets of San José, spent the night on the icy pass (3,300 meters). Many of them got ill with pneumonia, which was, at that time, a deadly disease.

The "Summit of Death" is the northernmost peak of the Páramo, a landscape that is characterized by wind-swept highland bushes, moss, heather and tussock grass During the day, with a little bit of luck, you can spot a native sooty robin or a silken flycatcher. A bumpy trail (a four-wheel-drive vehicle is necessary) leads from the pass to the summit (takes about 45 minutes on foot.

The hinterland has a number of lodges catering to bird lovers – for this is one of the best places to spot the almost legendary quetzal, "the bird of the gods." One such lodge is the privately-owned **Cloud Forest Preserve Genesis II** (on the access road of the Panamericana at km 58, tel. 381-0739, 225-6055; also camping).

PLAYA TARCOLES
Accommodations
MODERATE: **Hotel Villa Lapas**, tel . 288-1611. *BUDGET:* **Hotel Las Palmas**, tel. 661-0455. **Cabinas Villa del Mar,** tel. 661-2478.

PLAYA HERRADURA
Accommodation: *BUDGET:* **Cabañas del Río**, left of town entrance, tel./fax. 643-3275, 200 meters to the beach.

PLAYA DE JACÓ
Accommodation
There are many, mostly expensive, hotels in Jacó, but it is best to reserve early for holidays and weekends, especially Easter week.
LUXURY: **Jacó Beach and Villas**, tel. 643-3065, largest and most crowded. **Hotel Jacó Fiesta**, tel. 643-3147. **Hotel Club del Mar,** tel. 643-3194. **Hotel Cocal**, tel. 643-3067. *MODERATE:* **Hotel y Restaurante El Jardín**, tel. 643-3050. **Club Marparaíso**, tel. 643-3025. **Restaurante y Chalet Tangerí**, tel. 643-3001, rooms with ocean view. **Hotel Poseidon**, tel. 643-1642, nice hotel in town center. **Hotel Colibri**, tel. 643-3419, nice seafront property with pool. Italian management. *BUDGET:* **Hotel Lido**, tel. 643-3171. **Cabinas Alice**, tel. 643-3061. **Cabinas Chalets Santa Ana**, tel. 643-3233. **Cabinas Gaby**, tel. 643-3080. **Cabinas Zabamar**, 643-3174.
Restaurants
Marisquería Los Manudos, on the beach, excellent fish dishes. **El Jardín**, tel. 643-3050. **El Gran Palenque**, fine menu, Flamenco music, large choice of wines. **Pancho Villa**, Mexican specialities served under a thatched roof. **Café Chatty Cathy**, cake, fruit juice and globetrotter information.

PARRITA
Accommodation
MODERATE: **Ruta del Sol Hotel**, 441-0008.

QUEPOS
Accommodation
LUXURY: **El Byblos**, on the road to the Manuel Antonio National Park, tel. 777-0411.
MODERATE: **Kamuk Hotel**, tel. 777-0379, with casino and good international restaurant. **Hotel Sirena**, tel./fax. 777-0528, new hotel with restaurant and pool. **Villas Mar y Sol Inn**, tel. 777-0307, quiet location, clean air-conditioned rooms.
BUDGET: **Cabinas Villas Cruz**, tel. 777-0271, new air-conditioned rooms. **Malinche Hotel**, tel. 777-0394, clean rooms with baths. **Hotel Ceciliano**, tel. 777-0394, some rooms with shared baths, inexpensive.

Restaurants
Marisquería Juiberth, right of town entrance, nice fish restaurant. **Viña del Mar Restaurant**, in front of the bridge on the right, nice oceanside location. **El Gran Escape**, in town center, very popular and lively.

Excursions
Ríos Tropicales, tel. 777-0574, arranges sea tours in kayaks and tours of the mangrove swamps. **Paraíso Aquatico**, tel. 777-0514, organized by Hotel Paraíso, deep-sea fishing, surfing, waterskiing, sailing trips and boat rentals. **Unicorn Adventures**, tel. 777-0489, specializing in horseback-riding tours of nature parks.

MANUEL ANTONIO NATIONAL PARK
Getting There
Buses leave several times daily from the Coca Cola bus station in San José. The information center for Playa Manuel Antonio is open from 7 a.m. to 4 p.m.
Accommodation
LUXURY: **Hotel Mariposa**, tel. 777-0355, one of the most beautiful and expensive hotels in the country.
MODERATE: **El Mirador del Pacifico**, tel./fax. 777-0119, on slope, pool, all rooms with sea view. **Hotel California**, tel. 777-1062, beautiful location on slope, pool, private nature preserve. **Hotel La Colina**, 2.2 km beyond Quepos (to the right), tel. 777-0231, small hotel, good rooms.
BUDGET: **Cabinas Ramirez**, Playa Espadilla, tel. 777-0003, near ocean, often fully booked. **Cabinas Los Almendros**, tel./fax. 777-0225, clean rooms with bath, some air-conditioned.
Restaurants
La Mariposa, in hotel of the same name, international cuisine. **Mar y Sombra**, beach restaurant of Hotel Ramirez, for those who enjoy eating. **Barba Roja**, tel. 777-0331, on the beach, good fish dishes, small art gallery.

SAN ISIDRO DE EL GENERAL
Accommodation
MODERATE: **Hotel del Sur**, 6 km south, tel. 771-0527, with swimming pool and tennis courts. *BUDGET:* **Hotel Chirripó**, at the Parque Central, tel. 771-0529, with restaurant. **Hotel Iguazú**, near Panamericana, tel. 771-2571. **Hotel Astoria**, at the Parque Central, tel. 771-0914.

CHIRRIPÓ NATIONAL PARK
Reservations (from San Isidro) for the cabins at the summit are necessary; also possible from San Gerardo, since all hikers who reserve cabins do not show up. Camping in tents on the summit is forbidden as the vegetation of the paramo is very fragile.

THE SOUTH

DÚRIKA

LA AMISTAD

BORUCA / SAN VITO

GOLFITO

PENINSULA DE OSA

ISLA DEL CAÑO

ISLA DEL COCO

What is your spontaneous reaction to the word "south"? Sun, palm trees, clear blue sea water, sand beaches, vacation with warm or hot days and cool nights, relaxing evenings spent swinging in a hammock? Perhaps also impassable jungle with gigantic green trees and exotic animals? The south of Costa Rica has all this to offer. The Panamerican Highway, the dreamiest road in the world (here often called the *Carretera Interamericana*), brings travelers headed for the Equator closer to their dreams.

DURIKA NATURE PRESERVE

The Panamerican Highway leads south from San José via San Isidro de El General, sometimes downhill, sometimes uphill, at times over long stretches of straight road, sometimes in hairpin curves. Most of the villages are not directly on the road, but are rather a few kilometers away. This is also the case of a tiny town, located 65 kilometers southeast of San Isidro, **Buenos Aires**.

The town with the same name as the capital of Argentina is reachable from the north via Volcán and Cañas. The route is

Previous Pages: Even adults are dwarfed by the giants of the jungle. Left: Children on the Boruca Indian Reservation.

full of reminders of the terrifying catastrophic consequences of the massive clearing of the forests that once covered the area. Deep erosion fissures and landslides are the result. Unscrupulous business people ordered hundreds of hectares of forest to be cleared for their pineapple plantations. Even today, Ticos know Buenos Aires first and foremost as a center for pineapple cultivation. A tour of the **pineapple plantation** and the adjacent factory are possible.

Just 20 kilometers north of Buenos Aires on the slopes of Mt. Dúrika in the Cordillera de Talamanca, there is an unusual **private nature preserve** called **Dúrika**. It is where some 50 people have started a project that makes it possible for them to live independently. They give courses in meditation, yoga and healthy nutrition (whole grain products and vegetarian dishes), and dedicate their leisure time to the protection of plants and animals. Visitors are welcomed heartily and can hike the paths of Dúrika and observe the birds.

Buenos Aires is also the starting point for visits to the Boruca Indian Reservation and the gateway to the seldom visited and hardly developed La Amistad International Park. A 10-kilometer dirt road leads from the town to Ujarrás, which lies directly to the north.

169

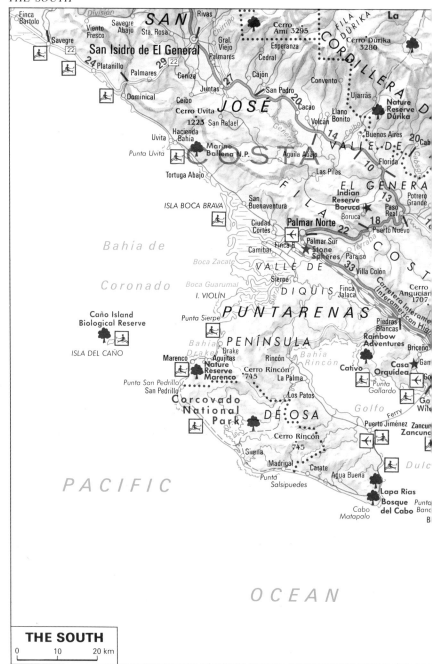

THE SOUTH

0   10   20 km

LA AMISTAD

La Amistad, meaning "friendship," with its 193,000 hectares, is Costa Rica's largest nature preserve and, at the same time, is an international park. Another 440,000 hectares lie on Panamanian soil on the other side of the border. When the Costa Rican protected areas of Chirripó, Hitoy Cerere, Tapantí, Wilson Botanical Garden, Las Tablas and Barbilla are added, there are another 340,000 hectares, making this entire area one gigantic biosphere preserve.

In 1982, UNESCO granted La Amistad the status of World Heritage Site. The park has really earned both the title and the added protection that it accords. Seven Indian reservations are found within its borders. Eight different zones of plant and animal life (following Holdridge's classic definitions) are represented. The park contains 60 percent of all species known to exist in Costa Rica, including 10,000 tropical plant species, 1,000 orchid families, cloud forest and the sub-alpine landscape known as paramo. The park covers an area that ranges in altitude from 150 to 3,549 meters above sea level. The highest mountain in the preserve is **Cerro Kámuk** near the Panamanian border.

The animals native to the park are also varied. Half of Costa Rica's wild animals live in La Amistad, one third of which are endemic to the area. Hikers who love isolation and untouched wilderness (no one should attempt this without an experienced guide) can set off in search of the tapirs, giant anteaters, jaguars, jaguarundis, tiger cats, pumas and ocelots, all of which live in La Amistad.

If you look upwards from the thick underbrush to the treetops, you can see up to 500 different kinds of birds, of which 50 are native species. Whoever has not had the opportunity to see the fabulous quetzal bird in other national parks or game preserves, has a good chance of

171

seeing the bird in La Amistad, because the park has the largest number in the country. Quetzals have been coveted since Aztec and Mayan times for their long, brightly-colored tail feathers. The harpy eagle, another endangered species, is also found in the park.

The infrastructure of the park is still largely undeveloped. Most of the visitors are scientists who hope to find new species of animals or plants. Until now they have discovered 120 kinds of fish, and 220 species of reptiles and amphibians. Zoologists also conduct research into the behavioral practices of animals in La Amistad.

Visitors to La Amistad have the choice of four entrances, marked by ranger stations: the main administration center in Progreso, 30 kilometers northeast of San Vito; La Escuadra, 14 kilometers northeast of Agua Caliente; Estación Tres Colinas, 12 kilometers northeast of Portrero Grande; and, finally, Station La Amistad, 27 kilometers northeast of Guácimo. Before entering the park, hikers should ask the rangers about conditions of the hiking trails and a weather forecast – although the weather here is usually hard to predict.

BORUCA INDIAN RESERVATION

From Buenos Aires, the Boruca Indian Reservation is best reached via Brujo and Térraba, or by the Paso Real along a dirt road. The center of the settlement is in a lush green valley 20 kilometers south of Buenos Aires, but only eight kilometers from the Panamericana. It serves various small settlements and scattered farms. Here, unlike many other Indian villages in Costa Rica, visitors are welcome.

This hospitality, however, is not without its motives; the Indians also want to

Right: Mangrove swamp on the Río Térraba near Palmar Norte.

172

sell souvenirs and handicrafts to the few visitors who make the trip to La Amistad. It is a way to earn a bit of extra income needed to supplement the meager living they make from their subsistence farms.

Both young and old women in Boruca sit in front of their huts, working at traditional looms that have changed little since pre-Columbian times. They weave tablecloths, fabric for dresses and belts. Some also produce decorated wallets made of leather.

The men carve balsa wood masks and engrave intricate landscapes (some quite artistic) on gourds (*jícaras*). In comparison to the way they lived before the arrival of Columbus, it doesn't seem that the highly touted white civilization has had much to offer the Boruca Indians. They live their lives in a quiet and unspectacular way. Their work rewards them little and feeds them more poorly than well.

Paso Real and Palmar

From the Boruca Indian Reservation, get back onto the Panamericana and drive southeast to the next larger settlement and traffic junction, **Paso Real**. Here the Carretera Interamericana meets the Río General and the Río Térraba. The signs are modest considering this is one of the main roads in Central America. To travel straight ahead in the direction of San Vito, take the ferry crossing the Río Térraba. It operates all day and night.

Before continuing on to San Vito, it is possible, staying on the Panamericana, to make a short excursion from Paso Real to **Palmar Norte** and Palmar Sur. These two towns, separated by the Río Térraba, are also more of a traffic junction than a tourist attraction.

There are several hotels, one gas station, a bus stop and a bank. This modest collection of buildings comprises the center of the banana planting agro industry in the Valle de Diquis. In the nearby

delta of the **Río Térraba**, mangrove swamps harbor a large population of crocodiles and many kinds of water birds. From Palmar, notable for the large number of Chinese who live there, roads lead to Cortes and Sierpe. From there it is possible to take a boat on the Río Sierpe and travel by river to Bahía Drake on the Osa Peninsula (see page 185).

Palmar Sur has a small airport. The main square holds the town's chief attraction, a rusting **steam locomotive** – a souvenir of banana transport from the good old days. More interesting for most travelers in the region are its **archeological finds**. Archeologists dug up stone balls with a diameter of up to one meter. The local inhabitants call these mysterious balls *esferas de piedra* or *bolas grandes*. They were made by Indians before the arrival of Europeans on the American continent. Similar objects have been found on the Isla del Caño. At present it is still not clear who made the balls or what purpose they served. Perhaps they have some meaning related to the

advanced astronomical knowledge of the Mayan civilization. Today the stone balls lay under the open sky, scattered around the banana plantations and fields.

SAN VITO

Back in Paso Real, take the ferry across the Río Terraba and follow the route southward along the steep winding road that offers excellent viewpoints along the way. You can't go very fast on this road, but you are rewarded with a splendid view of the Valle Coto Brus and the mountains of the Cordillera de Talamanca. After 50 kilometers the road reaches **San Vito de la Jaba**. The small town, situated at 990 meters above sea level, refreshes the traveler with cool mountain air – a welcome relief after the tropical heat and humidity of the lowlands. The city of 13,000 inhabitants has a short but unusual history. It was founded at the beginning of the 1950s by Italian immigrants. An Italian organization for agricultural colonization pur-

chased 10,000 hectares of land from the government of Costa Rica. In 1952, the first Italian immigrants arrived armed with tractors and other farm machinery, and began to farm the land intensively and to raise cattle.

By the 1960s and 1970s, they were very successful and many Ticos moved to the flourishing city. Today it is difficult to find any particularly Italian charm in the town and there is little to distinguish San Vito from other Costa Rican cities. The town does have an Italian cultural center, but the visitor will search in vain for typical Italian houses or Old World churches.

One thing does become immediately apparent, though; unlike other Costa Rican cities, San Vito is not laid out in a grid pattern. The Italian atmosphere is more evident in the Italian restaurants, for example the Mamma Mia Restaurant

Above: Archeologists found mysterious stone balls like this one near Palmar Sur.
Right: Red passion flowers in full bloom.

that serves delicious pasta and pizza, homemade spaghetti and glasses of real Chianti. Italian is still occasionally heard over an espresso in the cafés, but it is usually spoken only by the older citizens of San Vito. Not far from Costa Rica's version of Little Italy (here called *Italia Chica*) in a location halfway up the slopes of Mt. Fila Zapote, is another attraction of southern Costa Rica.

The **Wilson Botanical Garden** was founded in 1963 on 10 hectares of land by Robert and Catherine Wilson, a couple from Miami. They are also buried here. The property is more than simply a botanical garden, and allows visitors to experience the tropical rain forest firsthand in a comfortable and pleasant way. The garden contains an amazing 1,000 plants from 200 families, which visitors can examine without overexerting themselves as they stroll through the garden and explore its wooded paths.

The grounds are surrounded by 145 hectares of virgin forest, which, like the garden itself, have been part of the bio-

sphere preserve of La Amistad since 1983.

Hobby botanists can have a field day exploring this tropical paradise along 10 kilometers of paths with self explanatory names like Fern Way, Orchid Path, Bromeliad Way, Bamboo Path and Heliconia Circle Path. The garden possesses the world's most extensive collection of palms, and epiphytes as tall as a man. There are bromeliads, agavas and various kinds of lillies.

Picnic benches provide a welcome break and a chance to rest your feet before starting off again. Most of the paths require half an hour from start to finish. The path along the river, however, takes about three hours.

Many animals can be spotted from the paths: butterflies and hummingbirds, pacas, anteaters, opossums, kinkajous, porcupines, armadillos, sloths, tayras, monkeys and bats. There are around 315 types of birds in the garden, as well. Since its founding, the Wilson Garden has served as an intensive zoological and botanical research facility and a training center where scientists can continue their education.

The best time to visit is during the dry season from January to April. The area where the garden is located gets an average of 4,000 mm of rain during the wet season. There is little danger of freezing here; the temperature throughout the year remains an average 26°C.

Anyone wishing to remain for longer periods can do so. The garden has about 50 beds for visitors.

Continuing to Golfito

From the Wilson Botanical Garden the road continues straight south via Aguas Buenas until it rejoins the Panamerican Highway. **Ciudad Neily**, a pretty and friendly little town, is at the intersection. It is in the valley of the Coto Colorado, just 50 meters above sea level, which guarantees it a hot moist climate, ideal for cultivating bananas and African oil palms. From here it is 17 kilometers to

175

Panama. **Paso Canoas** is the most important border crossing between Costa Rica and Panama. The town is hardly what you could call attractive, but the stands and shops along its main street attract thousands of bargain-hunters every day into this free-trade zone. The duty-free goods – clothing, shoes, perfume, food and luxury items – are especially interesting to the Costa Ricans and Panamanians who live near the border. On weekends, however, people come from as far as San José to shop at Paso Canoas, though the merchandise does little to tempt international tourists.

Services include a gas station and numerous street money changers. Travelers continuing to Panama should change their remaining colones or spend them, because they are not worth very much in Panama.

Above: Zebu oxen work on the palm oil plantation near Golfito as draft animals. Right: Golfito on the Golfo Dulce – the "Sweet Gulf."

GOLFITO

Those who choose to remain in Costa Rica can continue their journey from Paso Canoas along the border via the towns of La Cuesta and Laurel, traveling in a large arc via Pueblo Nuevo (New Village) to Golfito on the Golfo Dulce, the "Sweet Gulf." Many destinations in southern Costa Rica can be reached from here: the Golfito Game Reserve, beautiful bays, and the Osa Peninsula, with its dreamy beaches, national parks and idyllic small fishing villages.

The United Fruit Company (UFC) founded Golfito in 1938, when it moved its central administrative center from the Caribbean coast. During the Second World War, many sailors aboard battle ships stopping there were attracted to the town's ladies of pleasure. Golfito's reputation as a city of sin soon traveled across the sea. It wasn't until 1945 that bananas regained their importance in the city's economy. By the 1950s, multinational concerns were shipping 90 percent of

their banana crop from the harbor of Golfito. The jobs and the major source of its income disappeared suddenly 30 years later when the UFC, following a series of strikes, closed its facilities and left Golfito. They left behind a quiet, typical one-street village built along the six-kilometer main axis at the mouth of the Río Golfito. It is surrounded by heavily wooded mountain slopes, lies protected within a large ocean bay, and is connected to the outside world by an airport.

The United Fruit Company also left behind its division of Golfito into two parts. In the north is the *Zona Americana*, a quiet residential neighborhood with pretty bungalows, generously furnished schools, a hospital and playing fields. UFC's managers occupied the Zona Americana. Today it is full of U.S. and Canadian retirees who come here to spend their golden years in a climate without cold and snow.

In the south is the second part of the city, known as *Pueblo Civico*. Until 1985 it was a typical blue-collar neighborhood.

Today all that remains are simple houses, a few cheap bars, hotels and a handful of bordellos. The differences between the two parts of town have diminished since UFC's departure, and are less and less noticeable every year.

Hundreds of jobs disappeared when the United Fruit Company left Golfito. The inhabitants were threatened with poverty, and the city was on its way to becoming a ghost town. In order to slow down its decline, the Costa Rican government established a free trade zone in the city (*depósito libre*). In practice, however, the move meant that a shopping center containing 50 stores was built north of the American Zone.

Golfito, fortunatley, also has something more to offer, the **Golfito Game Preserve**. The park's Visitor Center now occupies the old administration building vacated by the United Fruit Company. The 1,300-hectare Golfito Game Preserve was established, first and foremost, to protect the area's rivers and bay, which are so vital to the lives and welfare of

177

Golfito's inhabitants. The plants and animals have also benefitted from the establishment of this protected zone.

The rain forest and its fern trees, kapok and butternut trees is spreading rapidly. More than 150 bird species, including hummingbirds, toucans and trogons, nest in the park. Anteaters, coatis, monkeys, peccaries, agoutis, tree ocelots, raccoons and jaguarundis have found protection in the preserve.

Punta Encanto

Just half an hour away by water taxi, or 10 kilometers as the crow flies, from Golfito is the Punta Encanto "Charming Point" Lodge, established in 1992. The lodge is surrounded by a 7.5-hectare private nature preserve with hiking trails, waterfalls and clear water for swimming,

Above and right: At night can you listen to the romantic sounds of nature; during the day, the noise of howler monkeys is impossible to ignore.

snorkeling, canoeing and fishing. It is truly an enchanted place where vacation days fly by only too quickly. The lodge has pleasant rooms, good local cuisine and a very relaxing atmosphere.

Casa Orquídea

The area surrounding Golfito features other attractions. Halfway between Golfito and Playa Cativo, 10 kilometers northwest of the town and reachable only by boat, is a private botanical garden called Casa Orquídea.

Planted several years ago by a family named MacAllister, it soon grew beyond their first modest plans. They started out by planting fruit trees intended originally to supply the family's own needs, but the orchard soon developed into a real park. It now contains more than 100 different kinds of orchids and other decorative exotic flowers, tropical fruit trees, bromeliads, palms and ferns that attract many tropical birds. Paths through the jungle and guided tours permit visitors to

smell the heady tropical fragrances and touch some of the exotic plants, the Casa Orquídea is certainly a worthwhile day trip for anyone staying nearby.

The small evergreen orchid trees stemming from a family of legumes (*leguminosae*) immediately attract attention at the Casa Orquídea. Orchid trees are found throughout the world and come in more than 300 varieties. A few examples found here include the *Bauhinia blakeana* (the purple blossoms of which are the national flower of Hong Kong), the *Bauhinia monandra*, whose red flowers striped with yellow suddenly turn pink after one day, and the *Bauhinia purpurea*, whose large purple flowers have light-colored veins.

The Costa Ricans use these orchid trees not only as decorative plants, but as a source of wood and food as well. Even its bark is used to extract fiber. The Indians had long ago discovered that the leaves of one kind of orchid tree had medicinal properties and could be used for healing.

Rainbow Adventures

Another three-quarters of an hour from Golfito is a private game preserve called Rainbow Adventures at Playa Cativo. The adventures include hiking, swimming, snorkeling, or simply lying in the sun on the one-kilometer-long Playa Cativo. Occasionally, a howler monkey or lemur works up the courage to come closer and makes sure that no one gets bored. The Playa Cativo has an unusual three-story wooden lodge furnished with antiques. The fine carpets and elegant paintings, and the fresh flowers that fill the dining rooms, are certainly worth the trip from Golfito. Those who want to stay longer can book a room with a large balcony overlooking the sea and the rain forest.

Playa Zancudo

Another excursion from Golfito to the beaches of the Golfo Dulce ("Sweet Gulf") could end at Playa Zancudo. The

beach stretches along the mouth of the Río Coto Colorado, about 15 kilometers south of town. The black sand beach is the most popular and among the most beautiful in the area. During the dry season it is the favorite beach of locals. The estuary of the Río Coto Colorado is characterized by mangroves whose branches attract a wealth of birds. Many exotic plants grow along the moist banks of the river that delivers enough fresh water to give the gulf its name, "sweet." The tropical sun and the gentle waves lapping the black sand make time go by only too quickly.

Zancudo means "mosquito" in the language of the Indians. These unpopular insects, though not really a plague, are certainly well-represented. The village of Zancudo, located on a short spit of land, has a number of hotels and restaurants. Many U.S. retirees make their dreams of paradise come true at Zancudo.

Above: Playa Pavones is ideal for surfers.
Right: Toucan in the Punta Banco Preserve.

Pavones

A bumpy road ends a few kilometers to the south at the village of Pavones. Its beach is known to surfers all over the world for its grandiose waves – some days up to 1,000 meters long. The best waves, called "tubes" by the experts, develop during the rainy season between April and October. An ideal "long left" offers experienced surfers three minutes of surfing heaven at one stretch. The village of Pavones consists only of a few simple houses, a soccer field, a restaurant, and a few budget hotels.

Punta Banco

Near the border to Panama, 28 kilometers south of Golfito on the southeastern bridgehead of the Golfo Dulce, is a 100-hectare area of virgin rain forest rich with rivers and waterfalls. It is the private **Punta Banco Biological Preserve**, which began as a test farm for tropical fruit. The preserve contains the greatest

variety of tropical fruit in Costa Rica. The always-colorful and exotic-smelling fruit gardens attract not only tourists, but parrots and toucans as well, which are easier to observe in the garden than in their native jungle.

In addition, there are tidal pools full of salt-water animals. The **Tiskita Lodge** is in the heart of the Punta Banco. It has 20 beds, a rustic dining room and a small library. A solar energy and hydroelectric power plant which belongs to the lodge ensures that it is always well supplied with energy.

OSA PENINSULA

Puerto Jiménez

After exploring all the possibilities for excursions from Golfito, some travelers may feel the urge to explore new shores. No problem: all you have to do is take the ferry to Puerto Jiménez on the Osa Peninsula. Leave the Panamericana at Piedras Blancas ("White Stones"), or more pre-

cisely at Chacarita, a village with at restaurant and a gas station. Take Highway No. 245 via Mogos and Rincón where the paved portion ends; continue southward until you come to Puerto Jiménez, the only major town (4,000 inhabitants) on the Osa Peninsula.

Until 1964, Puerto Jiménez was a sleepy hamlet. Then the Costa Rican lumber industry discovered it and began cutting down the rain forest in the area. Later a few lucky prospectors found gold. The village boomed and the land suffered great damage through clearing and pit mining.

Today, Puerto Jiménez is a relaxed, easy-going place where young backpackers make up the bulk of the tourists. Several white sand beaches south of the town provide ideal sunning and bathing conditions. Surfers try their luck at the beaches of Platanares, Tamales, Pan Dulce ("Sweet Bread") and Carbonera. On weekends many Ticos from the north come here to shop in the free-trade zone and combine a few days shopping with a short vacation on the beautiful neighboring white beaches. Puerto Jiménez has survived its boom and bust years, and now first and foremost serves Costa Rican travelers and globetrotters as the gateway to the nearby Corcovado National Park.

Corcovado National Park

The **Corcovado National Park** was established in 1975 to protect the landscape from rapid and uncontrolled deforestation and from destruction caused by sporadic digging by gold prospectors. For centuries the region had provided Costa Rican Indians with gold for their ornaments. In 1980, the national park again experienced a sort of gold rush when 3,000 illegal gold prospectors pushed their way into the protected area, stirring up the rivers, cutting down the trees, building campfires and digging up the earth. In short, they systematically damaged the environment. Six years after the beginning of the gold rush they were finally forced to leave the environmentally protected area. It is still occasionally possible to find an illegal gold prospector in the park, furtively sloshing water in a tin pan in search of gold nuggets.

The 42,000 hectares of tropical coastal rain forest receive abundant rainfall year after year. The average annual precipitation in the area is 5,500 mm, fostering low forest growth along the coast and mountainous forest in the up to 750-meter-high hills of Cerro Rincón.

Stone cliffs, waterfalls and 50-meter-high trees with trunks up to one meter in diameter characterize the landscape of the park. Many unique forms of vegetation have found their ecological niche in the humid region, and live with the help of host plants to which they attach themselves. Lianas, bromeliads, hanging figs,

Right: A red macaw in the Corcovado National Park.

orchids, staghorn ferns and other examples are found in the park.

In the course of millions of years, Nature's cycle has reached absolute perfection in the park. The moldy, damp humus soil sends off a strong odor in the tropical heat, which transforms all waste into fertile soil and provides nourishment for new generations of plants.

The plants in turn feed a great many animals. There are 400 different kinds of birds, including brilliant red macaws that lend a touch of welcome color to the dark green background of the jungle's thick vegetation. Harpy eagles (which have virtually disappeared elsewhere in Costa Rica) and hummingbirds are an integral part of the region's ecosystem.

The Corcovado National Park also provides an ideal habitat for the peccary, a mammal resembling the wild boar. Banded peccaries with bands of darker fur at their necks and white-bearded peccaries can reach a length of one meter and weigh up to a hundred pounds. They eat grass, leaves, roots, seeds, fruit and small animals such as frogs and reptiles. In the warmer season they feed only in the mornings and evenings and spend the remainder of the day sleeping in the shade, their own variation of the popular Latin American siesta.

In Corcovado, peccaries live in groups of eight to 10 animals and move about constantly in search of the large amounts of food they need to survive. This characteristic prompted Brazilian Tupi Indians to name the peccary, "Animal that Makes Many Paths through the Forest."

In addition to peccaries there are many other animals, including about 150 different mammals, such as ocelots, jaguars, long-tailed cats and coatis.

Near the lagoons of Corcovado and Buena Vista is a tidal zone characterized by palms and mangroves. Crocodiles are also around wherever it is warm and humid. Glass frogs, with their transparent skin, adapt very well to this damp envi-

ronment. The rivers are filled with various kinds of reptiles and sea turtles. Even sharks have been seen near the coast, their dorsal fins high out of the water as they inspect the delicacies which the rivers have swept into the sea.

Five forest stations provide information about Corcovado National Park. The park administration is in Sirena, south of Lake Corcovado near the small airport. The main entrance to the park is at San Pedrillo at the northwestern corner of the protected area.

Lapa Ríos and Bosque del Cabo

South of Puerto Jiménez on the southeastern point of the peninsula, another private nature preserve was established in 1993. The entrance to the 400-hectare park is near **Lapa Ríos**. Following the investment of millions of dollars to reforest the preserve and create hiking paths, the only thing it lacks is visitors willing to spend their dollars and colones on swimming, surfing, snorkeling and hiking. The

Mexican-style hotel is said to be the most exciting accommodation on the entire Pacific coast.

Somewhat smaller (140 hectares), but equally attractive, is the **Bosque del Cabo Forest Preserve** on Cabo Matapalo, the southernmost cape of the Osa Peninsula. Bungalows with a view of the Pacific, and whales, which can often be spotted between December and March as they swim past the hotel, attract visitors from all over the world.

Marenco

Just a few kilometers north of San Pedrillo – or four kilometers southwest of Bahía Drake – is another private rain forest preserve called Marenco. The 500-hectare area offers the nearest available overnight accommodations to the Corcovado National Park.

Marenco is a good example of ecologically positive "gentle" tourism. The protection of nature and information targeted at environmentally concerned tourists are

the primary concern of this resort. Marenco is managed by Sergio, a Costa Rican who runs a biological research station with a staff of scientists who also work at the resort. The scientists at Morenco entertain guests with informative lectures and slide shows focusing on the geology, geography and biology of this unique privately-owned protected nature area.

Morenco has four kilometers of excellent, well-maintained hiking trails, which guests can explore on foot or on horseback, with or without a guide. Eight distinct types of jungle are recognizable along the trails. One path runs parallel to the rocky beach to Río Claro, a river that in several places tumbles in waterfalls and cascades into small fresh-water pools, providing hikers with refreshing showers or baths in the cool pools. The waters of the Pacific hereabouts are often

Above: Bathing fun at Corcovado National Park. Right: An adventure on horseback on the Peninsula de Osa.

warmer than vacationers seeking refreshment might prefer.

All four species of monkey native to Costa Rica are found in Morenco. In addition, there are some 400 different species of bird: flocks of pelicans can be seen from the shore scooping up fish; bright red macaws fly through the thick forests while giant parrots break the silence with their cries; hummingbirds flutter around the brimming cups of tropical flowers, sipping nectar; and brilliant tanagers and flycatchers flit among the trees, clearly audible and visible from the hiking trails. The Morenco Lodge occupies an idyllic location, crowning a rocky hilltop in the center of a vast tropical area of untamed nature. It offers a superb panoramic view of the park and its spectacular surroundings.

Transportation to the lodge and room reservations should be made well ahead of time, preferably before leaving San José. Other arrangements and reservations for excursions to the Isla del Caño can be made from Marenco.

Bahía Drake

Bahía Drake – an unusual name for a place in a country where Spanish and Indian names are the rule – got its name from the legendary English pirate Sir Francis Drake. According to research by historians, Sir Francis Drake sailed into the bay that now bears his name in March 1579, during his circumnavigation of the globe in his ship the *Golden Hind*. He dropped anchor in the two-kilometer-long bay on the Osa Peninsula, north of Marenco (reachable by boat from Sierpe). The village of **Agujitas** is Bahía Drake's center. A small food store supplies basic needs and a public telephone provides communication with the rest of the world.

The residents of Agujitas manufacture exquisite appliquéd cloths (*molas*), only found here and on Panama's San Blas Islands. Their intricate decoration, showing fruit and birds of the jungle, make them unmistakable. Agujitas has a number of lodges for visitors who have lots of time on their hands. It is possible to snorkel in the Pacific or watch for the whales that often swim quite close to shore. These ocean giants appear to be greeting the humans on shore with fountains they blast from their blow holes – a tribute not unlike the cannon shot fired by Sir Francis Drake and his pirates. A word to the wise – sharks have also been sighted in the clear blue water of Bahía Drake.

The inhabitants earn their living working on coffee and cocao plantations surrounding the bay. Guavas are another popular crop grown in the area. The tennis-ball-sized fruit belongs to the myrtle family. Although now found all over the world, guavas are native to Central America. The gnarled, unremarkable trees reach a height of 10 meters. The delicious round fruit with yellow-green skin is sweet and rich in vitamin C. Ticos make jam, juice, liqueur and wine from guavas. The local people even use the leaves, from which they extract medicine which is said to be effective in treating digestive disorders.

Visitors with a romantic bent or love of adventure can rent a canoe and paddle along the shore to the mouth of the Río Agujitas. There is an anchorage for sailing ships and other attractions.

ISLA DEL CAÑO

Anyone who still hasn't had enough of rapturous descriptions of southern Costa Rica's natural beauty has no choice but to turn to the "open sea." Two islands, neither of which is easy or inexpensive to reach, merit closer inspection. They are the Isla del Caño and the "Treasure Island," Isla del Coco.

The 300-hectare Isla del Caño, 20 kilometers west of Bahía Drake, is a protected biological preserve surrounded by another 5,800 hectares of protected ocean area. Steep cliffs with small beaches at their bases and a massive rock plateau covered with lush tropical vegetation soars out of the ocean.

Snorkeling or diving at Isla del Caño in 30°C water and exploring the coral banks, far from civilization, can become an unforgettable experience. Unfortunately, parts of the reef have been damaged because there is not enough personnel to guard the island. During the egg-laying season, bastard turtles swim up onto the beaches and drag themselves across the sand to lay their eggs. In the ocean, dolphins and whales on their way south from Alaska cavort in the waves.

There are no overnight tourist accommodations on the island. Scientists studying the island's fauna and flora, which is not as varied as that of the mainland, can stay at the ranger station. Isla del Caño is a destination for people who want to explore the final summit of Costa Rica. They can climb the old lighthouse, which now serves as an observation tower, or hike up the cliffs to the 110-meter summit of the island. Near its highest point archeologists have discovered stone balls made by Indians in pre-Columbian times. It remains a mystery how the giant orbs were made. Graves and burial caves have also been discovered on the Isla del Caño, leading scientists to believe it may have served as a cemetery for high ranking members of the tribe. Researches have also found corn mortars and prehistoric stone tools. Recent excavations indicate that the island may have been used in earlier times only for ceremonial purposes.

In 1973, the island's peace and quiet was threatened when a Spanish real estate company leased the island and announced they were going to build a vacation complex on it. The project was cancelled only after massive protests by students of the university in San José and Costa Rican biologists. Lately, deep-sea fishing enthusiasts have also discovered the island. The rangers are not happy with this development because such sports can disturb the delicate balance of nature in the sea.

ISLA DEL COCO
NATIONAL PARK

Still further away and still more mysterious than the Isla del Caño is the Pacific Isla del Coco, 500 kilometers southwest of Costa Rica. Also called "Treasure Island," Isla del Coco ("Coconut Island") has an area of 52 square kilometers (circa 12 x 5 kilometers) and is the world's second-largest uninhabited island and a Costa Rican national park. The island is the northernmost link of a chain of volcanoes, most of which are under the surface of the sea. They stretch across the Equator all the way to the Galapagos Islands. The Isla del Coco is long and narrow and has a hilly surface. The Cerro Iglesias (634 meters) is its highest point. Steep cliffs up to 100-meters-high rise from the sea and make access to the

Right: The trip to Isla del Caño lasts an hour and a half.

island difficult. Waterfalls, which pour off the cliffs directly onto the shore or into the sea, lend the island its particular charm.

Spanish seafarer Juan Cabezas discovered the Isla del Coco in 1526. By 1542 it had already appeared for the first time on a sea chart. Since this time, seafarers from all the world's seagoing nations have at one time or another landed on the island for fresh water (the island gets 6,000 to 7,000 mm of rain a year) or coconuts. No one has until now lived on the small Pacific island permanently. A group of exiled prisoners spent a number of years on the island in the 18th century. For them, the sentence to "paradise" may not have been all that attractive. The judge who pronounced sentence is rumored to have said, "They were ripe for the island."

A number of famous people have visited Isla del Coco of their own free will. President Franklin D. Roosevelt landed on the island several times, and French oceanographer Jacques Cousteau also visited the island and carved his name on one of the cliffs.

For centuries Coconut Island has also attracted people with more sinister motives. According to legend the island's hills contain chests full of gold bullion. More than 500 expeditions have searched for sunken Spanish ships that are believed to have sailed for Spain loaded with Inca gold. The "Treasure of Lima" aboard the *Mary Deer* was especially valuable. It was supposed to have been shipped secretly home to Spain in the 18th century by order of the Colonial Governor. Its present-day value is believed to be about three billion dollars.

German adventurer August Gissler was the most persistent of all the treasure hunters. He spent 18 years on the island, built himself cabins, planted fruit trees and fields, and obtained permission to prospect for ore. The government of Costa Rica was to have shared in any discoveries he made. Whether Gissler ever actually found anything, and whether he really returned to New York to die a rich

man are questions that have never been clearly answered.

A few years ago two German journalists published findings that once more created excitement and raised speculation about buried treasure on the Coconut Island: P.D. Lauxmann and C. Pfannenschmidt claimed in their article, *The Authentic History of Stevenson's Treasure Island*, that Isla del Coco was indeed the Treasure Island that Scottish author Robert Louis Stevenson had in mind when he wrote his great classic.

Because of its isolation, Coconut Island has developed a unique natural environment which attracts naturalists who visit it to study its animal and plant life. There are no land animals native to the island with the exception of two types of lizard, while there are 80 species of birds found here. Three of them are endemic, a cuckoo, a finch and a variety of flycatcher. At the same time, more than 70

Above: Hammerhead sharks near the Isla del Coco provide excitement for divers.

different types of plants are endemic to the island, making it even more fascinating to botanists. The majestic frigate bird nests on the island. Boobies, shearwaters and gulls feed on the plentiful supply of fish in the sea around it.

The more than 5,000 wild pigs, descendants of domesticated animals set free on the island by sailors in the 18th century, are less attractive to naturalists. Everywhere there are signs of mud-wallowing orgies and uprooted plants, which the pigs leave behind along with a depressing trail of destruction. When multiplied by the number of grunting wild pigs on the island, the damage is considerable and produces erosion which subsequently also harms the coral reef. The pigs, which were probably regarded as a delicacy by stranded pirates and treasure seekers, have other imported animals to keep them company. Goats, rats and cats also live on Isla del Coco.

Divers regard the sea around Isla del Coco as the world's best diving ground. Sharks, however, cast a shadow on this underwater paradise. Galapagos sharks, white spotted sharks and hammerhead sharks have been sighted feeding on the plentiful supply of fish that fills the sea around the island. Divers claim that the sharks prefer juicy fresh fish to tough humans packed in neoprene suits, but they keep a respectful eye on the toothy giants nonetheless. Rays, pilot whales, flying fish and dolphins also populate the colorful underwater world.

But even on Coconut Island paradise is not perfect. The fish population is being thinned by illegal catches of lobster and tuna (within a five-kilometer protected perimeter). The Costa Rican national park police who are responsible for patrolling the island and sea around it are too few and far between to effectively stop such poaching.

Visits to the Isla del Coco are only possible by taking a cruise ship journey lasting several days.

BUENOS AIRES
Getting There
By bus from San José to San Isidro. Buses from there leave every two hours.
Accommodation
BUDGET: **Cabinas El Buen Amigo**, tel. 730-0188, quiet location, clean rooms.

PALMAR NORTE / SUR
Getting There
By plane with SANSA, daily from San José or daily with TRAVELAIR. By bus from San José (C. 14, Av. 3-5), six times daily.
Accommodation
BUDGET: **Cabinas Casa Amarilla**, three blocks east of the Tracopa bus stop, tel. 786-6251. **Cabinas Tico-Alemán**, on the Panamericana , north of town. tel. 786-6232.

SAN VITO
Accommodation
BUDGET: **El Ceibo Hotel**, tel./fax. 773-3025, clean rooms with baths. **Cabinas Las Huacas**, tel. 773-3115, acceptable.
Restaurants
El Ceibo Hotel restaurant is excellent. *ITALIAN:* **Lilliana**, pasta and pizza. **Pizzería Mamma Mia**, nicely furnished, elegant, good food.

WILSON BOTANICAL GARDEN
Getting There
6 km south of San Vito. Open daily 8 a.m. to 4 p.m.
Accommodation
In the research station, must be reserved by calling OET in San José, tel. 240-6696.

GOLFITO
Getting There
By plane: SANSA flies twice daily. TRAVELAIR flies daily. By bus: Tracopa from San José (C. 14, Av. 3-5), daily at 7 a.m. and 3 p.m.
Accommodation
MODERATE: **Hotel Sierra**, tel. 775-0666, wooden house with verandah and nice atmosphere. **Hotel Las Gaviotas**, tel. 775-0062, good seaside location. **Hotel El Gran Ceibo**, tel. 775-0403, clean.
BUDGET: **Hotel Golfito**, tel. 7750047. **La Purruja Lodge**, on the right at entrance to town, tel./fax. 775-1054, quiet location, nice rooms, restaurant. **Cabinas Miramar**, tel. 755-0169, inexpensive.

CASA DE ORQUIDEA
Private botanical garden, open Sun.-Thur. 8 a.m. to 11 a.m. It is 10 km northwest of Golfito.

PLAYA ZANCUDO
Accommodation / Restaurants
BUDGET: **Cabinas Los Almendros**, tel. 775-0515, clean rooms, nice restaurant with sea view. **Cabinas/Restaurant Sol y Mar**, tel. 775-0014, local cuisine. **La Luna Linda**, two cabinas with palm-thatched roofs. **Pensión Fin del Mundo**, at entrance to town, right side, clean rooms, shared baths, good food.

PAVONES
Accommodation
BUDGET: **Bahía Pafromes Lodge**, 2 km south of town. **Pavón Tico**. **Cabinas Mira Olas**.

PUERTO JIMÉNEZ
Accommodation
MODERATE: **Manglares Hotel**, on the bridge, tel. 735-5002, nice garden, restaurant. **Playa Preciosa Lodge**, 4 km from Puerto Jiménez, alone on unspoiled beach, tel. 735-5062. **Cabinas Agua Luna**, at ferry port, tel. 735-5034, beautiful rooms.
BUDGET: **Cabinas Marcelina**, 2 blocks south of soccer field, riding, gold prospecting and fishing. **Cabinas Puerto Jiménez**, tel. 735-5090, entrance to town on left, seaside, clean rooms.
Restaurants
El Rancho Bar y Restaurant, tel. 735-5120, the hot spot of Puerto Jimenez, with bocas, music and lots of young people. **Agua Luna**, good fish dishes. **La China**, good Chinese food, inexpensive.

CORCOVADO NATIONAL PARK
Getting There
By boat from hotels on Bahía Drake or by group taxi from Puerto Jiménez (Mon.-Sat. 6 a.m.).
Accommodation
Camp of Costa Rica Expeditions 1.5 km west of Carate, 500 meters to southern border of the national park. Either for self-sufficient campers, or in the park station, tel. 735-5036.

BAHIA DRAKE / MARENCO
Accommodation
LUXURY: **Marenco Lodge**, tel. 221-1594, good location, private preserve, expensive. **Aguila de Osa Inn**, tel. 296-2190.
MODERATE: **Bahía Drake Wilderness Camp**, tel./fax. 771-2436. **La Paloma Lodge**, tel./fax. 239-0954. **Río Sierpe Lodge**, simple and inexpensive, tel. 284-5595.
BUDGET: **Casa Mirador**, tel. 227-6914.

ISLA DEL CAÑO
Getting There: Boats from Bahia Drake, Sierpe and Uvita. No hotels, camping forbidden.

SOUTHERN
CARIBBEAN COAST

FROM SAN JOSÉ TO
PUERTO LIMÓN
TOWNS AND BEACHES
AROUND PUERTO LIMÓN
PUERTO VIEJO DE TALAMANCA
GANDOCA-MANZANILLO

FROM SAN JOSÉ TO
PUERTO LIMÓN

Aerial Tram

Whoever travels from San José overland to the Caribbean coast, driving on
the new road to Puerto Limón (Carretera
32), arrives at an attraction of a special
kind after just 50 kilometers. At the edge
of the Braulio Carrillo National Park is
the **Aerial Tram**, a 1.3 kilometer cable
car that travels just above the forest floor
in one direction, and at tree-top level in
the other. The Aerial Tram permits park
visitors to see the rain forest from a new
and exciting perspective. With luck they
are able to catch a glimpse of birds and
other tree dwellers at close range. A tractor brings visitors from the parking lot to
the cable car station. The tram is open
Tuesday to Sunday, from 6 a.m. to 3:30
p.m., and from 9 a.m. to 3:30 p.m. on
Monday (tel. 257-5961).

The first larger city along the way is
Guápiles, the business center of Río
Frío, Costa Rica's tradition-rich banana
growing region. The completion of the
new paved road has turned Guápiles into

*Previous Pages: In the black sand of Playa
Negra, Puerto Viejo. Left: Siesta time in
Puerto Limón.*

a traffic junction for travelers on their
way to Puerto Viejo de Sarapiquí, Rara
Avis and the Caribbean coast.

Guápiles was established in 1910 on
the property of the vast Hacienda Guápiles cattle ranch. The railroad had been
planned to go through the town, and
Guápiles was meant to get a station. The
mountains of the Cordillera Central,
however, proved to be more than a match
for the railway pioneers. After several fu-
tile attempts the road was laid to Turrialba and Siquirres instead. Ticos still
call the stretch from Guápiles to Siquirres, *Linea Vieja*, the "Old Line." During construction the railway workers
discovered a great many pre-Columbian
artifacts in the jungle. Guápiles takes
handicrafts seriously. Good looking baskets and bamboo rocking chairs are made
here and sold along the main street.

Guácimo

Guácimo, 12 kilometers in the direction of the Caribbean coast, is where the
Escuela de Agricultura de la Región
Húmeda (EARTH), the school for tropical agriculture is located. Future farmers
spend four years at the school learning
environmentally sound and effective
ways of farming and animal husbandry,
suited to the fragile tropical ecosystem.

Siquirres

The name Siquirres comes from the language of the Indian tribe who lives in this area and means "colored reddish." The town is 110 kilometers east of San José, two kilometers beyond the bridge over the Río Reventazón. Until 1992, it was an important railroad terminus for passenger trains as well as banana transport to the coast. Very few historic buildings of any note remain in Siquirres, but the town has three monuments. Two are in honor of local large land holders (*patrones*), and one commemorates those who died in the civil war, the *Mártires del Codo del Diablo*, the martyrs of the 1948 revolution.

The lively market, Mercado Central, right next to the former railway station, is worth a visit. All the town's streets are limited to one way traffic.

Above: Not cheap but original – a trip through the rain forest on the aerial tram. Right: White-water trip on the Río Pacuare.

The town lost its importance in 1987 with the completion of the highway. It received another serious blow in 1992, when the Atlantic Railway was taken out of service following earthquake damage. Most individual travelers choose Siquirres as a midway stop on their way to Tortuguero and the southern Caribbean coast. They usually have lunch in one of the town's many restaurants.

Río Pacuare

Río Pacuare, which flows nearby, is Costa Rica's second most important river after the Río Reventazón. Its quieter stretches are good for rafting in inflatable boats, but the river also has exciting passages through narrow gorges and rapids for thrilling white water trips.

The river flows through virgin rain forest. From the raft it is possible to enjoy scenic views and to get a close-up view of the heavily wooded mountain slopes that rise almost perpendicular on both sides of the river.

Puerto Limón

The overland road ends on the Caribbean coast at Puerto Limón. Today the city has 55,000, mostly black, inhabitants, but it is honored as the birthplace of Costa Rica's "white" history. In 1502, Christopher Columbus landed on the small offshore island of Uvita, dropped anchor and went ashore in the belief he had arrived at the Kingdom of Siam. Columbus named the island *La Huerta*, "The Orchard," after the lush green land on the opposite shore. Isla Uvita is now a protected historic area, reachable from Puerto Limón by boat. It has trails that take the visitor around its rugged stone cliffs and caves.

The Costa Rican government made Porto Limón the capital of the 9,000-square-kilometer Limón Province in 1872, just two years after the beginning of construction on the Atlantic Railway. The move was in anticipation of its future role as a port for shipping coffee to Europe. Contrary to their expectations, the city developed into a center for industry, oil refineries and banana transport. Soon the harbor proved to be too shallow for modern freighters.

Around the turn of the century the government began construction of a new harbor, seven kilometers further north at Bahía Moín. At that time the city began its slow decline into poverty. It was accelerated in the 1950s when banana exports drastically declined.

The colorful mansions in the former center, with their fanciful wrought-iron balconies, are falling to ruin. The one-time docks are deserted and covered with piles of rubbish. Vultures, lazy from the midday heat, pick at garbage in the streets. The city has still not recovered from its most recent blow, delivered by the earthquake of 1991. Broad cracks in the buildings, broken sidewalks and streets, as well as the tectonically raised coral reef, now used as a garbage dump by the residents, give the city a dismal and forlorn appearance nearly a decade after the catastrophe.

The lemon tree that gave the city its name in the last century is long dead. It once stood in front of the **Alcaldia**, the bright, stucco-decorated city hall, which remains a beautiful example of Caribbean tropical architecture, featuring wide balconies, open arcades and bay windows. The city, which was originally founded in a swampy area plagued by yellow fever and then moved to higher ground, still wakes up early in the morning. Most residents try to accomplish their tasks before noon in order to escape the merciless heat of the afternoon. They allow themselves a long relaxing siesta after lunch. The shops and bars remain open until late into the night. Some local residents pass seamlessly from siesta to fiesta. The two top meeting places in town are the lively **Caribbean Market** (Avenida 2, Calle 3-4) and the **Parque**

Above: On the road along the southern Caribbean coast to the next watering hole. Right: Puerto-Limeños celebrate their carnival on October 12.

Vargas, a miniature jungle complete with vines, waving palm and banyan trees and bushy bromeliads. The park displays a bust of Christopher Columbus and his son Fernando erected in 1990, commemorating their landing on the nearby island of Uvita in 1502. Another bust shows Balvanera Vargas Molina, the governor at the turn of the century.

Even though Puerto Limón has few tourist attractions to speak of, it is still interesting and worth visiting because of its people. The inhabitants of the city are primarily black, the descendants of Jamaican slaves imported to work on Costa Rica's banana plantations. Their Creole culture gives the city a unique character. It is especially apparent in their cuisine with its exotic dishes and drinks, in their reggae and calypso music, and in their popular medicine which uses ancient herbs for healing a variety of ailments.

Pidgin English is spoken on the Costa Rican Caribbean coast rather than Spanish. When you greet one of the many Rastafarians with their shoulder-length

dreadlocks on the streets of Puerto Limón, a greeting is more often "all right," than "hello," and instead of "good bye" they are more likely to say "okay." But this is only scratching the surface of the Creole culture in Puerto Limón.

Increasing tourism in the past few years has raised the living standard of the inhabitants, and at the same time, accelerated their assimilation into the Spanish dominated Costa Rican culture.

The contrast between the different worlds of the poor and unemployed native inhabitants and the casual, strolling, and comparatively well-to-do vacationers is hard to ignore.

Once a year, however, the residents of Puerto Limón forget their problems for the week leading up to October 12, the anniversary of the discovery of America. For an entire week they celebrate the **Limón Carnival**. The pulsating rhythms of reggae, salsa and calypso music reverberate through the streets and alleys. The Indians join in with tribal dances that have been all but forgotten. Even the Chinese living in Puerto Limón join in the lively festivities.

The people paint themselves from head to toe, and this could just as well be New Orleans or Trinidad. For visitors it is important to realize that Puerto Limón and its people have to be accepted totally, the good along with the darker side of their make up. It is all or nothing, and those who cannot accept this vibrant culture are better off leaving for other parts of the country.

TOWNS AND BEACHES AROUND PUERTO LIMÓN

Four kilometers north of Puerto Limón (toward Moín) are two small beaches. **Playa Bonita** has a fine yellow sand beach with palm trees, passable hotels, but not ideal water conditions. **Playa Portete** has a dock for local fishermen who land here with their catches. Further north is the tiny village of **Moín**, where the government built an industrial harbor for freight ships in the 1980s. Here crude

197

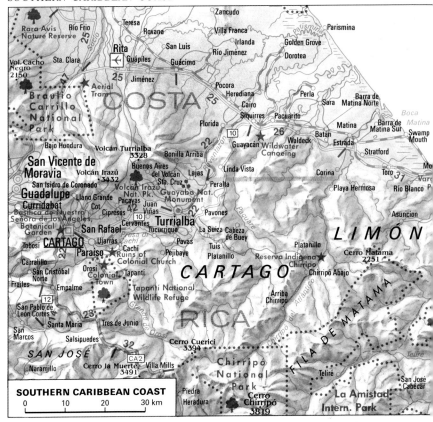

oil arrives in huge tankers for the refineries further inland, and bananas are packed into containers for transport to Europe and the United States.

Traveling north along the canals (*Los Canales*, see page 211), that were so popular with tourists before the 1991 earthquake, you arrive after about 50 kilometers at a small town at the mouth of the Río Parismina. The village, also named **Parismina**, is well known among sport fishermen for its two excellent fishing lodges. Deep-sea fishing enthusiasts from all over the world come here to catch tarpon and snook in the turquoise waters of the Caribbean. The lodges rent out fishing rods, and sell fishing accessories and bait.

Selva Bananito

On the way south from Puerto Limón there is a turnoff at the village of Bananito. From there a bumpy road leads to the new **Selva Bananito Lodge**, at the edge of an 850-hectare private nature preserve. The lodge is an ingenious combination of comfort, nature and ecology. There are seven well-designed wooden bungalows, each with its own tiled bath with hot water (heated by solar energy), and a beautiful verandah hung with hammocks. The restaurant serves delicious typical Costa Rican dishes and commands a splendid view of the mountains. The owner of the hotel accompanies her visitors on hikes into the rain forest on

198

The private game preserve that belongs to the property contains a great many sloths. Biologists are conducting a scientific research project to determine the habits of these slow moving tree dwellers. In the 1991 earthquake the coast in this region rose almost one meter out of the water. Since then the island has been connected to the mainland.

Valle del Río Estrella

Large flocks of white cattle egrets (*Garcilla bueyera*) often circle the sky over the valley of the Río Estrella, which flows out of the west to Penshurst. Citrus fruit, such as lemons and oranges, as well as cacao, are planted in the valley.

The low cacao trees bear red fruit, up to 20 centimeters long. The seeds are embedded in sweet, creamy white fruit pulp which Ticos call *pulpa*. At harvest they separate it from the seeds and use it for making desserts and sweet, aromatic drinks.

Hitoy Cerere Biological Preserve

The **Reserva Biologica Hitoy Cerere** is 30 kilometers, as the crow flies, inland from the Caribbean Coast. The preserve is located at the foot of the Cordillera de Talamanca at an altitude of 150 to 1,000 meters. The preserve contains more than 9,000 hectares, and is difficult to reach. It is virtually undeveloped: not surprisingly, it is also one of the least-visited parks in Costa Rica; no more than 500 people visit the preserve each year. It is surrounded by three Indian reservations: Estrella, Telire and Talamanca. Hitoy Cerere is most important as a watershed for drinking water needed by the people who live on the coast, and as protection for the tropical evergreen rain forest from inevitable lumber operations. Many large and small rivers flow through the park. Water is not a problem; the park receives an annual rainfall of 4,000 to 7,000 mm.

foot, horseback or mountain bike, as well as providing guests an opportunity to prove their tree climbing skills.

Aviarios del Caribe

Further south on the road to Cahuita is a lodge opened in 1992, **Aviarios del Caribe**, the "Caribbean Aviary." Visitors can explore the estuary of the Río Estella in row boats and take advantage of the isolation and unspoiled nature to catch a glimpse of one of the more than 300 different kinds of birds that nest in the area. In addition to birds, the guides also point out poison arrow frogs, river vipers, alligators and monkeys living in the park.

The Indians who originally lived in the area give the park its name. Hitoy and Cerere are Indian names for two of the rivers in the park. Cerere means "River of the Clear Waters." The park, with its challenging terrain, is best suited for well-trained, energetic adventurers. Anyone who wants to conquer this jungle should begin by following the river. Hikers may encounter beautifully spotted margays and other wildcats. The jungle is also full of peccaries, agoutis, deer, tapirs and monkeys. Ever rarer harpy eagles circle the sky above the forest. Cuckoos, blue-headed parrots, toucans and Montezuma oropendolas inhabit the treetops.

Cahuita

The next destination is Cahuita, back on the Caribbean Coast. The village, with its 4,000 inhabitants, is especially loved by young backpackers and low-budget travelers. It is usually fully booked during the holidays and during Costa Rican school vacations because Ticos, too, come here in search of sun and relaxation. Sun and sea are the true attractions of this village, which consists of little more than a long main street with several intersections and houses that look as if they might collapse at any minute. The ancestors of the current village residents stem from Jamaica (as in Puerto Limón) and came to Costa Rica in the middle of the 19th century.

White sand beaches fringed with coconut palms, a relaxing atmosphere, and a total absence of hectic activities or stress attract young people. Backpackers mingle with Rastafarians who wear their hair in meter-long dreadlocks. The lively beat of reggae music, Rastas and *ganja* (marijuana) characterize this resort. What could be better than spending a lazy day

Right: The right tool for the job? In any case, the sweet cool coconut milk is a most refreshing drink.

on the beach, swimming and sunning? Nights are dedicated to never-ending parties and an seemingly endless supply of tropical pleasures.

The best months to go are March and April or September and October, because there is very little rain during those months. Sudden tropical showers can occur throughout the year, however, generally ending as quickly as they began and leaving brilliantly clear blue skies behind them.

There are three beaches near the village. One is on the other side of the Punta Cahuita cliffs and is protected by a coral reef. Another one, which is less frequented, is several kilometers long and lies north of Cahuita. The third beach stretches toward Cahuita National Park.

A note of warning regarding personal security and belongings in Cahuita and in nearby Puerto Viejo de Talamanca: Pickpocketing and thefts from hotel rooms and beaches are common. Nowadays, a domestic police force recruited from the village patrols the beaches, and the number of such incidents has reportedly gone down.

Cocaine and marijuana are openly sold on the streets and beaches. Often the sellers are undercover police agents. Never pay in advance for boat charters, hiking guides or horseback-riding tours. Single women traveling alone have been approached by native men – sometimes very aggressively – with offers of short-term affairs, frequently followed by demands for payment.

Cahuita National Park

The Cahuita National Park begins east of the village. It is made up of 1,000 hectares of land including 14 kilometers of beaches, countless palm trees, dense forests and mangrove swamps. The park was established in 1970 to protect the 240-hectare coral reef which was threatened by pollution. Today this park is

heavily visited because it is easy to reach, has beautiful beaches, acceptable hotels, rich fauna and good diving and snorkeling at its coral reef.

The best way to discover the beauty of the park is to hike. From Kelly Creek Ranger Station at the eastern end of Cahuita village, a seven-kilometer-long trail runs along the beach to Punta Vargas at the southern end of the park. On the way to the nearby rocky spit of land called Punta Cahuita hikers wade through the Río Perezoso, a stream named after the sloth. Tannic acid from the trees and leaves of plants have dyed the water blackish-brown. The trail provides a pleasant hike that proceeds along the beach and dips further inland; it takes a total of two hours.

Those who pay close attention to nature are rewarded by glimpses of the park's many animals. Pacas, raccoons, sloths, anteaters, agoutis, howler and capuchin monkeys, toucans, green-winged macaws, hummingbirds, ibises, large Central American great currasows (*Crax rubra*) and macaws fill the forests and fly among the tree tops. The shores of the rivers are also alive with many fascinating creatures, including caimans, coatis and poisonous snakes. The beaches are full of sand crabs and frequently provide sun-warmed nests for turtles who lay their eggs in the sand.

Snorkeling is best at Punta Cahuita and Punta Vargas, for which the dry season provides the best conditions. During the rainy season the rivers of the Talamanca Mountains swell with the torrents of rain, washing mud and pesticides from the plantations into the sea, thereby polluting the water.

Snorkelers can discover some 40 different types of coral, including the easily identified brain and elkhorn coral. There are well over a hundred different sorts of fish, marked with an almost unbelievable variety of color and design, such as the iridescent, startlingly beautiful blue parrot fish. The pure, uninhibited fantasy of nature seems limitless. Snorkelers are delighted, but paddle away with great re-

201

spect when they come face to face with a full-grown moray eel.

Bribrí

Bribrí lies south of Cahuita, approximately 10 kilometers inland from the Caribbean Coast. It is the administrative center for all the Indian reservations in the neighboring area. The Indian influence is first apparent in the town itself. Bribrí has little by way of tourist attractions, but does provide a bank for changing currency, a post office, a public telephone, and a hospital, set up by the Department of Health for the inhabitants of Puerto Viejo de Talamanca and the Indian reservations.

The reservation, with the unusual name of Kéköldi, covers an area of 3,500 hectares, but not all of the land is fully owned by the Indians. Kéköldi merges into the Gandoca Manzanillo Park and, along with the reservations of Bribrí and Cabécar and the protected natural area of La Amistad-Talamanca, forms an enormous park.

Some 200 people live on the reservation and participate in the park's comprehensive projects of reforestation and the protection of endangered species. No commercial exploitation of nature is allowed within the reservation. Only Indians have the right to hunt and use plants growing in the park for their own needs.

PUERTO VIEJO DE TALAMANCA

When you return to the coast from the Indian reservation, you feel as if you are entering another world. Puerto Viejo de Talamanca, similarly to Puerto Limón, was also founded as a Caribbean harbor. Since the completion of the road, Carre-

tera 36 (the town is now six kilometers off the beaten track), fewer visitors stop at the village. Tourists have just recently started returning to this idyllic old harbor, surrounded by rain forest and influenced by a fascinating mixture of black and Indian cultures.

Today the residents earn their living largely through agriculture, planting cacao, citrus fruit and coconut palms, or by seasonal fishing for lobsters. But ever more families are discovering that extra money is to be made from renting rooms to tourists.

The clock seems to tick slower in Puerto Viejo. Every activity appears to take place in slow motion. The popular greeting on the streets is a casual, "What's happening?" In its shortened pidgin English form it sounds like, "Wa'apin, man?"

The nearly white, palm fringed sand beach of **Pirikikí** is used by visitors as well as residents for swimming and relaxing. Apparently inexhaustible surfers ride the waves between December and March. They come in large numbers during these months in search of "killer waves," such as the legendary six-meter-high wave referred to as *La Salsa Brava* by the locals.

At night everyone – surfers, Rastafarians, Indians and package tourists – meet in discos with exciting names like Old Harbor's, Standard's and Johnny's Place. Music video clips show another world, and cold beer flows down dry throats. For many young local men the evening has only one logical end – *amor, amor!*

Playa Cocles, Playa Chiquita and Punta Uva

Playa Cocles, two kilometers east of Puerto Viejo, is perfect for surfing. Two hotels cater especially to surfers, and a lively bar with the name of Kapalapa supplies them with all their basic needs. At night the daring wave-riders move to the

Right: Many fishing families at Puerto Viejo have discovered that tourism can provide a good second source of income.

beat of a different drummer on the Kapalapa dance floor, and watch short videos in lieu of seeing movies.

Playa Chiquita adjoins Puerto Viejo four kilometers to the east. The beach is just as beautiful and exciting as Playa Cocles. The Villas del Caribe hotel complex, which primarily attracts young travelers, is built along the beach. The owner is Maurice Strong, a well-known Canadian environmental activist who organized the International Environmental Summit in Rio de Janeiro in 1992.

Punta Uva, three kilometers further to the east, is not really a village, but rather a collection of wooden huts along a dirt road. From here you can start guided hikes through the forest, for example, along the Quebrada Ernesto trail. Horseback riding is also possible.

Naturales, a restaurant located on a hill with an excellent view of the turquoise blue water, serves typical Costa Rican dishes and sells traditional handicrafts in its little shop. From Punta Uva, a magnificent black sand beach stretches for five

kilometers to the village of Manzanillo, and to the Gandoca-Manzanillo Game Preserve.

GANDOCA-MANZANILLO GAME PRESERVE

The village of **Manzanillo**, named after the ancient towering manzanillo tree that stood on the village plaza until it died in the 1940s, lies 12 kilometers east of Puerto Viejo and forms the gateway to the Gandoca Manzanillo Game Preserve. A trail leads from the village up to Punta Mona (Monkey Point, which is said to have been named by Columbus himself after the many howler monkeys he found there) and Gandoca Lagoon, a 50-meter-deep lagoon with two outlets to the sea. South of the small settlement of Gandoca is an area where rare red mangroves are still to be found. Especially good hikers can continue to the Sixaola River, which forms the border with Panama.

The tiny villages of Manzanillo and Gandoca are within the borders of the

huge game reserve, which covers just under 10,000 hectares. Almost half of the park's 4,500 hectares are made up of coastal water, with nine kilometers of beach and a living coral reef that is 200 meters offshore. The reef is a paradise for snorkelers. The land portion of the preserve covers more than 5,000 hectares of meadow land and forest. By hiking and riding through the park you can get acquainted with its tropical plants and animals. The forest, with its impassable undergrowth, contains mahogany trees, which are still felled and sold for a pittance to illegal dealers.

In a swampy area covering 400 hectares near Punta Mona is a grove of holillo palms, loved by tapirs. Red mangroves grow in the Gandoca River estuary and the natural oyster bank attracts Caribbean lobsters. Tarpon, beloved by sports fishermen, lay their eggs in the river. Crocodiles, caimans, margays,

Above: Family picnic on the inviting sand beach of Playa Chiquita.

sloths, manatees and ocelots represent the fauna. Between January and April sea turtles swim to the beaches of Gandoca-Manzanillo to lay their eggs.

Sixaola

Sixaola, located in the midst of banana plantations, marks the southernmost end of the Caribbean coastal road and functions as a seldom-used border station to Panama. The actual border is formed by the Sixaola River, which is named after one of the Indian tribes of this area. Indian families who lived scattered throughout this region experience the unrelenting pressure of Western civilization. The profit-oriented banana and cacao industries, with their massive use of pesticides and constant expansion, have forced the Indians to give up their traditional way of life. The acculturation process, which is accelerated through constant contact with modern life, is far more rapid than it was in the time of the Spanish conquistadors.

GUÁPILES
Accommodation
LUXURY: **Hotel Suerre**, at the eastern edge of town, tel. 710-7551. *BUDGET:* **Casa Río Blanco B&B**, quiet location, family atmosphere, managed by a couple from the U.S., tel. 382-0957.

SIQUIRRES
Accommodation
BUDGET: **Centro Turistio Pacuaré**, on the road to Puerto Limón, renovated rooms, pool, tel. 768-6482. **Hotel Don Quito**, 3 km east of town on the Río Pacuare, tel. 768-8533.

PUERTO LIMÓN AND SURROUNDING AREA
Accommodation
LUXURY: **Hotel Maribú Caribe**, 3.5 km toward Moín, tel. 758-4010, beautiful sea view.
MODERATE: **Hotel Matama**, tel. 758-1123, 4 km toward Moín, near beach. **Hotel Acón** (Av. 3, C. 2-3), tel. 758-1010. **Hotel Miami** (Av. 2, C. 4-5), tel. 758-0490. **Hotel Tete**, tel. 758-1122, at the central square, clean rooms.
BUDGET: **Cabinas Cocorí**, tel. 7582930. **Hotel Paraíso** (Av. 4-5, C. 2-3), tel. 758-1506. **Hotel Río**, tel. 758-4511. **Hotel Linda Vista**, tel. 758-3359.

Restaurants
Arrecife, 500 meters northwest of town on the road to Portete, tel. 758-4030, fish dishes. **Springfield**, tel. 758-1203, Jamaican cuisine.

MOÍN
Accommodation
BUDGET: **Hotel Moín Caribe**, tel. 758-2436. **Cabinas Chita, Cabinas Colón**.

PARISMINA
Accommodation
LUXURY: **Parismina Tarpón Lodge**, tel. 771-2583. **Río Parismina Lodge**, tel. 236-0348.
MODERATE: **Happy Monkey Jungle Resort**, tel. 222-6055.
BUDGET: **Soda Iguana Verde**, tel. 798-1494.

SELVA BANANITO
Accommodation
Selva Bananito Lodge, tel./fax. 253-8118 (San José number).

AVIARIOS DEL CARIBE
Getting There
Any bus going toward Cahuita. The bus stops at the entrance.

Accommodation
Aviarios del Caribe, tel./fax. 382-1335, organized canoe trips on the Río Estrella.

HITOY CERERE
Accommodation
BUDGET: In the **Ranger Station**, tel. 758-3996; to make advance reservations, call 233-5473; also through the National Park Service in San José, tel. 323-5055.

CAHUITA
Accommodation
MODERATE: **Selvamar Hotel**, between Limón and Cahuita near the sea, tel. 758-2861. **Atlantida Lodge**, Playa Negra, tel. 755-0213, beautiful property with garden. **Magellan Inn**, tel. 758-0035, very quiet, best accommodations in town. **Cabinas Hibiscus**, directly on the sea, tel. 755-0021, pleasant rooms. **Hotel Jaguar**, tel. 755-0238 (ext. 238), near beach, 2 km from center. **Casa Kelly Creek**, at entrance to national park, tel. 755-0007, large rooms in a wooden house with a verandah.
BUDGET: **Cabinas Sol y Mar**, near park entrance. tel. 755-0237. **Alby Lodge**, nice cabins, quiet, tel. 755-0031. **Cabinas Sol y Mar**, tel. 755-0237. **Cabinas Jenny**, tel. 755-0256, sea view. **Cabinas Arrecife**, tel. 755-0081, near the sea.

Restaurants
Miss Edith, Caribbean specialities, simple and inexpensive. **Kelly Creek**, great Spanish cuisine. **Ristorante Cha Cha Cha**, Italian cuisine, fish. **Casa Creole**, excellent Caribbean cuisine, high priced.

PUERTO VIEJO DE TALAMANCA
Accommodation
LUXURY: **El Pizote Lodge**, tel. 229-1428, before Puerto Viejo, to the right. **Las Palmas Hotel**, tel. 255-3939, unique location. **Hotel Best Western Punta Cocles**, near Punta Uva beach, tel. 234-8055 (San José number). **Hotel Villas del Caribe**, tel. 233-2200 (San José number).
MODERATE: **Cabinas Picasso**, 20 meters from the sea. **Chimuri Lodge**, 1.5 km north, earthy location in rain forest, tel. 758-3844. **Escape Caribeño**, 400 meters south. **Kashá Lodge**, tel. 284-6906, 5 km south. **Playa Chiquita Lodge**, Playa Chiquita (6 km south), tel. 233-6613 (San José).
BUDGET: **Cabinas Selvins, Cabinas Surf Point, Cabinas Salsa Brava, Hotel Puerto Viejo**, in center. **Cabinas Playa Negra**, tel. 556-1132. **Cabinas Maritza**, in center, tel. 758-1844, bungalows. **Cabinas Grant**, tel. 758-2845. **Cabinas Yucca**, on the sea. **Cabinas Casa Verde**, in town center, tel. 750-0015. **Casablanca**, tel. 750-0001, natural setting.

Restaurants
Jacaranda, Caribbean, vegetarian, excellent. **Amimodo**, good Italian food. **Vista Verde Restaurant**, 200 meters south, Spanish, expensive.

GANDOCO-MANZANILLO GAME PRESERVE
Accommodation
There are no hotels, but camping is allowed (no sanitary facilities, however).

NORTHERN
LOWLANDS

RARA AVIS
LA SELVA
LOS CANALES
BARRA DEL COLORADO
TORTUGUERO NATIONAL PARK

Following a couple of days fighting the traffic in the bustling Costa Rican capital of San José, where time is spent going to museums and theaters, and where Costa Rican fiestas go on night after night, many visitors long to return to nature and the quiet of the rain forest. An excursion to the Barra del Colorado Nature Preserve in the northern lowlands and to Tortuguero National Park are just the right thing in this case.

An early start is recommended, but you can leave your warm sweaters at the hotel. You can look forward to an excursion providing a varied and scenic landscape, fresh air, warm days and mild nights, an unforgettable encounter with nature – and with any luck, a glimpse of a green sea turtle (still called soup turtle in some parts of the world) in the national park – not in the soup tureen!

The road passes Heredia and La Virgen, and continues via Chilimate La Selva to Puerto Viejo de Sarapiquí. An alternative route goes through the Braulio Carrillo National Park, stopping first at **Las Horquetas**. This small town on the dusty road harbors the Rara Avis office.

Previous pages: On a bird-watching expedition in Tortuguero National Park. Left: American darter, one of the many exotic birds found in Costa Rica.

The bird sanctuary and nature preserve is still 15 kilometers away.

RARA AVIS

Amos Bien, former director of the research station La Selva, has created the **Rara Avis Nature Preserve** in a 5,000-year-old stretch of virgin rain forest on the eastern edge of the Braulio Carrillo National Park. The 1,335-hectare park has become world famous in the meantime. Visitors are only admitted if they call ahead for reservations at the Rara Avis (the name means "rare bird") office in San José. The visit requires a minimum of two days but provides an unforgettable adventure involving a gentle form of environmentally safe tourism.

It is possible to explore the park with or without a guide on permitted paths. Rara Avis has 330 different types of birds, including macaws, hummingbirds, toucans and quetzals. This is where American biologist Donald Perry did his research on the jungle canopy, which he later described and illustrated in his book *Life on the Roof of the Jungle – A Researcher in the Canopy of the Rain Forest*. The park is also where he first tried out his cable car system, which would later be the model used for the Aerial Tram (see page 193), located further

south on Carretera 32. Secured by ropes, It is possible to learn to "climb" trees and visit Perry's tree house in the park.

Puerto Viejo de Sarapiquí

It is only 17 kilometers from Horquetas to the larger town of Puerto Viejo de Sarapiquí. Before the road and railroad were built, the town served as an important stop on the arduous trade route from the Caribbean, via the San Juan and Sarapiquí rivers, into the Meseta Central. Today Puerto Viejo de Sarapiquí, with its 5,000 inhabitants, is the starting point for tours into the Barra del Colorado Nature Preserve and the Tortuguero National Park. It also serves as the northern entrance to the Braulio Carrillo National Park (see page 83).

In January 1996, when two European women were kidnaped at Boca Tapada,

Above: Biologist Amos Bien founded Rara Avis. Right: Animal watching on the Río Sarapiquí.

30 kilometers to the northwest near the Nicaraguan border, this area made headlines around the world.

LA SELVA

A nature lodge and the La Selva biological station are very close to Puerto Viejo de Sarapiquí. La Selva, "The Jungle" in English, was founded in 1963. Nearly 50 universities and museums from all over the world participate in this institution, which is dedicated to researching new ways in which the rain forest and other natural resources in the tropics can be used sensibly without destroying their fragile ecology. The Organization for Tropical Studies supports La Selva's lecture rooms and research laboratories, and finances the experimental stations.

A day trip to this prestigious biological research station, one of the oldest in the country, is very worthwhile, but must be arranged beforehand. La Selva is first and foremost a research facility and an obser-

vation post for the ecological system in the wilderness area surrounding it. Visitors definitely take secondary priority at La Selva. The research facility is located on the road between Puerto Viejo and the Braulio Carillo National Park.

Unlike other regions of Costa Rica, the area around Puerto Viejo does not have a real dry season. It is true that there is less precipitation in the first five months of the year than during the rest of it, but even February, the driest month of the year, gets some 200 mm of rain, which is still about a third of the annual average precipitation for central Europe. December, the wettest month, receives 500 mm of rainfall.

In an area covering 3,500 hectares, biologists have so far identified more that 450 different kinds of trees, 49 sorts of amphibians, 113 different mammals and 400 species of birds.

La Selva has 50 kilometers of well-kept trails available to scientists and visitors alike. It is also possible to spend the night at the research station, but reserva-tions have to be made weeks in advance, because there is a limited capacity of only 60 beds.

Returning to Puerto Viejo de Sarapi-quí, it is possible to continue by boat to Barra del Colorado (see page 216). A dirt track leads from Puerto Viejo to the small settlement of Pavas, where the Río Toro and Río Sarapiquí flow together. From there it is possible to charter a private boat and sail down the San Juan River to Barra del Colorado. The Río Colorado Lodge also offers this service.

TORTUGUERO NATIONAL PARK

Tortuguero was founded in 1975 to protect endangered sea turtles (see page 213). Even getting to this park is an adventure, requiring several hours by boat through the 150-kilometer-long system of natural canals known as **Los Canales de Tortuguero**. The network is composed of lagoons and natural canals that have for centuries provided the only

possibility for transportation in this swampy area. The canals were used for the transportation of travelers and were the only means available to planters of getting bananas from their plantations to the markets. Most of the way the boats slide silently through thick carpets of blue flowering water hyacinths, while swarms of yellow and orange colored butterflies flutter above the water.

At the end of the 1960s, the Costa Rican government had four new canals built in order to connect the existing system of natural canals and lagoons into a navigable network of water highways for the northeastern lowland region.

The powerful earthquake that hit Costa Rica in April 1991 brutally rearranged this fine system of waterways and destroyed parts of it. It is still possible, however, to travel back and forth on canals between Siquirres, the Río Pacuare and Moín, Tortuguero and the Río Colo-

Above: The ancient art of making a dugout canoe can be seen in Barra del Colorado.

rado, the Río San Juan, Pavas and Puerto Viejo de Sarapiquí. The canals between Moín and Tortuguero are the most heavily used. Countless small and large motorboats ply this stretch in both directions. The leisurely boat trip on the Tortuguero-Moín canal lasts about three hours. The rotting piles of tumble-down huts appear again and again on the shores. The people who live in them scrape a meager existence out of their corn fields, and fish for tarpon and gar in the waterways. Their 10-meter-long canoes or dugouts are no match for the larger and faster motorboats that ply the waterway. Often the canoes are sent wildly rocking in the wake of a motorboat, and far too often the pile of coconuts on their way to market are sent tumbling into the water.

Travelers enjoy the refreshing wind and try to find a bit of shade from the merciless sun. After a trip of several hours they arrive at the village of Tortuguero.

Tortuguero

The village of Tortuguero lies directly on the long beach where turtles lay their eggs. It is appropriately called Playa de las Tortugas ("Turtle Beach"). Most of the 2,000 inhabitants are descendants of slaves brought to Tortuguero in the 19th century by North American lumber companies that came to cut ebony in the forest. The rusting machines and vehicles that lie around everywhere are also reminders of that bygone era. They lend the village a special kind of charm that lies somewhere between open-air industrial museum and tropical junkyard. The machines also symbolize how little human life was worth a century ago. The U.S. lumber concerns that shipped these machines and men to Costa Rica simply left them behind when they had outlived their usefulness. The black lumber workers turned to fishing and farming to survive.

Much later the tourists arrived, giving the villagers a chance to earn a little extra money.

Today the village is significant only as the gateway to the Tortuguero National Park. The 10,000 visitors who come to the park every year have little economic impact on the daily life of the villagers. Most of the tourists come in organized tours that arrive in the morning and leave again the same evening. Others spend the day in the park and travel on to the Barra del Colorado Nature Preserve. Very few tourists actually spend the night in the inexpensive and very basic lodges available in the village. Individual travelers who plan a longer stay and who have had their fill of fish should bring other supplies with them, because the menu in the village restaurant consists solely of fish, served seven days a week.

Very close to the village, reachable in just a few minutes on foot and built on one of the canals, is the most important of the park's three forest stations: the administration office of Tortuguero. Visi-

tors can pay their entrance fee at the station, obtain information material and ask the rangers about the turtles, and where they happen to be coming ashore to lay their eggs at that particular time.

The Turtle Experience

The Tortuguero National Park is unique in the world. Only eight kinds of sea turtles are known to exist on our planet, and six of these species lay their eggs on Costa Rican beaches; four of them come to Tortuguero. Since the 1950s, the egg-laying process of these endangered species of turtles has been observed and protected in this park.

The turtle population has slightly increased since then. Most visitors come to witness a turtle laying eggs, which, along with the boat trip along the canals, is reason enough to come to this 19,000-hectare park with its 5,000 to 6,000 mm of average annual rainfall.

The rangers and researchers in the park allow visitors to watch the turtles lay

their eggs, and later to observe the new hatchlings as they see the first light of day – in any case always from a distance calculated not to disturb the great sea creatures. Visitors who want to take photographs should not use their flash. The newly-hatched turtles orient themselves to the light of the sun or moon, and the flash from a camera or flashlight can seriously confuse them. Those who want to test this should only do so by shining the light over the water, but even so, bright flashlights can irritate the baby turtles.

In order to observe all the different kinds of turtles that come to Tortuguero, you would have to spend virtually the entire year in the park. **Leatherback turtles** crawl up on the beaches between February and July. The 3,000 green sea turtles that visit the park each year arrive

Above: Sport fishing in the Barra del Colorado Nature Preserve – a tarpon puts up a good fight. Right: Fisherman's hut near Barra del Colorado.

between July and October. During the same months the rarer **loggerhead turtle** also appears. Single turtles may show up throughout the year.

The easiest to observe is the green sea turtle. Costa Rica has three beaches where **sea turtles** still regularly come to lay their eggs. Two of them are on the Pacific coast (one of which is in Santa Rosa) and one is on the Caribbean in Tortuguero National Park.

Five species of sea turtle are known in Costa Rica: the leatherback, the bastard, the green sea turtle, the hawksbill and the loggerhead turtle. These living fossils (their family tree goes back 200 million years) show up on Costa Rican beaches twice a year: in April and between October and December. They come ashore when the tide is exactly right, on nights when the moon is full. The dig themselves a pit in the sand and lay up to 100 eggs in a single night before swimming back out to sea.

The heat of the sun beating down on the eggs under the sand incubates them, and two months later the young turtles hatch and try, as quickly as possible, to reach the safety of the sea before being picked off by hungry vultures circling above the beach. Those that survive remain at sea, swimming thousands of miles, and only see land again when they reach maturity.

The females return after seven years to their birthplace to lay their first eggs. Females ready to lay eggs wait in a protected spot near the shore until the moon is full and the tide is high, so that they only have a few meters to crawl onto the shore, where they make their nest above the tide line.

In the morning they have to return to the sea, despite their weakened state. Those that remain will dry out in the merciless heat of the sun or succumb, despite their hard shells, to the insistent attacks of vultures. Fully grown the turtles weigh hundreds of pounds and reach up to 1.5

meters in length, and 70 to 80 centimeters in breadth. The animals leave a very specific trail in the sand. It differs from species to species, and even laymen can easily learn to identify them in this way.

Green sea turtles can lay eggs up to seven times in one season, but usually limit themselves to two or three times. They only lay their eggs every three years, and always on the same beach.

Green sea turtles do not enjoy a particularly carefree existence. One of their worst enemies is the vulture, which seems intent on pecking away at the giant animals. Vultures especially like to attack female turtles on their way back to the protection of the sea in a weakened state from the strenuous process of scooping out their nest in the sand and laying eggs.

Nor do the freshly-hatched baby turtles come off much better. The vultures first snap off their heads and only return to their stored up booty when they find no more living turtles. Most of those that survive the harrowing race to the sea will fall victim to sharks and other sea crea-

tures. Only a very small number – perhaps a mere one percent of the hatchlings – survive the first months of their lives and live to maturity. Sometimes the male turtles come ashore to defend the females against the attacks of the vultures.

The worst enemy of the sea turtle, however, is man – worse than the vultures and the sharks together. Even today, despite conservation efforts, turtle poachers are as active as they ever were. Shells of bastard turtles and the tender meat of green sea turtles bring high prices on the black market. Huge sums of money are paid even for the eggs, which are eaten raw and are believed to improve sexual potency (for which there is still no scientific proof). The only thing that interests black-market operators, however, is making a quick profit.

Turtles are the most fascinating animals in Tortuguero National Park, and have justly lent their name to this great place. But many other animals fly and crawl in the park, as well. The long beaches are not all that merit attention.

Excursions along the rivers and into the forests reveal an amazing array of mammals, birds, amphibians and reptiles, which alone would merit a visit to Tortuguero. Howler, capuchin and spider monkeys, along with sloths, anteaters, raccoons and kinkajous, enliven the upper canopy of the rain forest with their presence. Down below, peccaries and tapirs snort along the forest floor, and jaguars and ocelots stalk the thickest parts of the forest. From a boat you can explore the rivers and observe freshwater turtles warming themselves in the sun, basilisk lizards with their high comb, caimans, crocodiles and dozens of snakes (among them, for example, the poisonous fer-de-lance viper) and red-black poison arrow frogs.

The sky is full of birds. More than 300 different types, including many migrating birds from the United States and Canada, are to be found here. The easiest to

spot are the different kinds of herons, plovers, sandpipers, egrets, royal terns, kingfishers and jacanas. Hummingbirds flit through the forest, along with rarely seen manakins, such as the golden manakin. Visitors who want to return the quickest way possible to San José also have to take to the air.

BARRA DEL COLORADO

Near the estuary of the Río Colorado, about an hour's boat ride north of the village of Tortuguero, is the tiny village of Barra del Colorado. The name means "sandbank of the colored river," and refers to an arm of the larger Río San Juan that flows through the delta. The 1,500 inhabitants of Río Colorado live in a village that is divided in half by the river and is reachable only by boat or airplane.

In terms of tourist attractions, Río Colorado has little to offer except for a few bars and simple cabins, as well as lodges that have specialized in order to meet the

Above: A network of natural waterways flows through the Tortuguero National Park.

needs of North American sport fishing enthusiasts.

Sport Fishing in Barra del Colorado

Its isolation and the deadening heat that doesn't let up throughout the year seems to have effected all phases of life in Barra del Colorado. Even the Ticos who live here seem to move more slowly than elsewhere. The crocodiles also seem to be slowed down by the relentless heat and while away their time looking bored on the banks of the rivers and streams in the delta. Perhaps the town will prosper again and expand to its former size when trade with Nicaragua is restored following the ending of the fighting there.

The town still does not have paved roads. An irregular footpath leads visitors from the river through the center of the village. Run-down wooden huts, built on rotting piles, line the path. The village may seem romantic to tourists from industrial countries, but in reality it testifies to the bitter poverty of the native inhabitants. The discrepancy between rich and poor is also evident in their boats. The tiny fishing boats of Barra del Colorado's residents are patched and oft-repaired, held together by oddly assorted planks and kept afloat only with great effort. They present a striking contrast to the luxury yachts of the sportsmen from Texas, Toronto or Tokyo – the three areas that supply most of the tourists who come to this isolated region to fish.

Barra del Colorado is one of several sport-fishing centers on the Costa Rican Caribbean coast. The native residents make their living from lobster fishing, and by working as guides on the sport-fishing yachts which come mainly from the United States. Exclusive sport fishing in the area surrounding Barra del Colorado has a long tradition. Isla de Pesca, Río Colorado Lodge, Casa Mar and Silver King Lodge are among the oldest sport fishing camps in the country. Pas-

sionate anglers meet here and spend hours at the end of a long strenuous day telling each other detailed accounts of the duels they won against meter-long fish. From hour to hour, or rather from cocktail to cocktail, the fish become longer and heavier. You know what they say about fishermen's tales...

In actual fact, tarpon, up to two meters long, are often hooked in these warm Caribbean waters. It is even said that once a monster of a fish sprang into a yacht and made it capsize. In addition to the tarpon, which is highly prized as a game fish, the waters contain shark, sea bass, sawfish, wreckfish and rays.

Barra del Colorado Nature Preserve

The Barra del Colorado Nature Preserve is not exclusively for sport fishing. Hikers and animal lovers find it fascinating. It is in the northeast corner of the country, and with an area of 92,000 hectares Barra del Colorado is the second largest protected area in Costa Rica. In the north it borders on Nicaragua, in the east it ends at the Caribbean coast, and in the south it is a buffer zone for the Tortuguero National Park.

Barra del Colorado is a paradise made up of many square kilometers of virgin rain forest. The very humid evergreen jungle receives more than ample rain. The nature preserve is among the wettest regions of the country. Between 4,500 and 6,000 mm of rain fall here annually either in the form of steady rain that goes on for hours or days, or as sudden tropical showers.

Along with humidity, the constant temperatures create an ideal environment for the park's lush vegetation. The forests give way to a mangrove zone that stretches as far as the eye can see. Old raffia palms mark the banks of countless rivers. The forests contain massive ficus trees, and gigantic trees are covered with bromeliads. A canopy of leaves obscures

the light, and vines are so heavy that the host tree often breaks under their weight.

A trip to the park at the end of the year is an especially exciting experience because the yellow alemandas are in bloom and brighten the dark green shadows of the jungle with their brilliant golden blossoms.

A rich and varied supply of fauna completes the picture of this attractive nature preserve. Ornithologists have identified 240 different kinds of birds in the treetops and skies over Barra del Colorado. Giant green macaws seem to own the skies. Other parrots and parakeets are seen among them. Black and yellow toucans, with their enormous colorful bills, are seen as well as heard. The tiny flycatcher lives high up in the canopy of the jungle. Majestic jabiru storks sail high above and stalk a huge hunting territory that often stretches beyond the confines of the park. Large colonies of white

Above: A turtle in the Tortuguero National Park on its way to lay eggs.

ibises have been spotted in the clearings and near farms or in swamps. Sometimes it is possible to get near enough to observe them without field glasses or a telephoto lens.

The river is alive with darters, beautiful wading birds with long graceful necks. With luck observers can see them as they gulp a fish, and watch it wriggle down the bird's long neck. Birds must have a sharp eye and a good hunting instinct to feed in the cloudy water of the rivers and lagoons.

Not only the air space is crowded in the Barra del Colorado Nature Preserve. Many creatures also inhabit the river banks and deep forests: caimans, manatees (sea cows), peccaries (long-haired wild boar), pacas, sloths, jaguars, tapirs and monkeys. Turtles also tempt nest robbers at Barra del Colorado, but the park is not as famous for turtles as the Tortuguero National Park, which is further to the south.

A curious sort of ant, called the army or legionary ant, lives in and on the earth of the nature preserve. Army ants seem to be paramilitary in their organization. They march rank and file in long colonies through the jungle. The front lines of this ant army carry off the first supply of food, but take care to leave something behind for the troops that follow, and they never break their persistent march.

Should the first ranks or scouts make a mistake or lose their orientation, it can happen that they rejoin the ranks at the end of the marching colony. This phenomenon has been observed by researchers. And then something really strange happens. The brave, duty conscious scouts of the first rank continue running in circles until they run themselves to death.

Farmers plant corn and raise animals on scattered farms and tiny villages within the park, most of them are reachable only by boat. The sparse population in this area, however, has not effected the main problem that the park's management faces. In various places rangers have found proof of illegal lumbering activities. The cutting is graphically visible in satellite photos. The few environmentalists active in the park are powerless to stop the damage or prevent the theft of the valuable exotic wood.

Occasionally the destruction is officially tolerated or approved at a higher level. So that, for example, the British banana company Geest received permission from the Ministry of Agriculture to help itself to the forests of the Barra Colorado Nature Reserve.

Environmentalists hope that the long-planned merger of the Tortuguero National Park to the south with the Barra Colorado Nature Preserve will soon be possible, and that this will help to prevent illegal felling in their forests. The merger would make more efficient deployment of personnel possible, and give park officials enough additional rangers to patrol the vast stretches of jungle and prevent illegal activities.

RARA AVIS
Accommodation
El Plástico Lodge, **Waterfall Lodge** (somewhat expensive), **River Edge Cabin** (romantic). Transportation to the sanctuary, guided tours and food included in price. If you call ahead (tel. 253-0844) you will be picked up by tractor at Las Horquetas.

PUERTO VIEJO
Getting There
The Río Frío bus leaves San José (Av. 7-9,Ca. 12) at 6:30 a.m. and at noon, direction Puerto Viejo de Sarapiquí.
Accommodation
MODERATE: **El Bambú**, tel. 253-2608. **El Gavilán Lodge**, at boat dock, tel. 234-9507. *BUDGET:* **Mi Lindo Sarapiquí** (Av. Principal), tel. 766-6281. **Cabinas Monteverde**, tel. 766-6236.

LA SELVA
The *Organización para Estudios Tropicales* (OET), tel. 240-6696, organized day trips (US $34) telephone reservations are obligatory.

BARRA DEL COLORADO
Getting There
With TRAVELAIR airlines daily, with SANSA 3 times a week; by boat from Puerto Viejo via Río Sarapiquí and Río San Juan to Barra del Colorado or from Tortuguero.
Accommodation
LUXURY: **Samay Laguna Lodge**, 4 km south of town, tel. 284-7047, canoe tours, horseback riding. **Río Colorado Lodge**, tel. 232-4063. **Casamar**, tel. 443-8834. *MODERATE:* **Isla de Pesca**, tel. 239-2405. **Tarponland Lodge**, at the airport, tel. 710-6917. **Tropical Tarpon Lodge**, tel. 225-3336, also organizes fishing trips.

TORTUGUERO NATIONAL PARK
Getting There
TRAVELAIR has connections to San José and Puerto Limón; the airport is 2 km north of village on the beach. It is reachable by boat from Moín and along the Río Reventazón (via Siquirres).
Accommodation
LUXURY: **Tortuga Lodge**, tel. 710-6861 (res. at Costa Rica Expeditions, tel. 257-0766). *MODERATE:* **Ilan Ilan Lodge**, tel. 255-2031. **Jungle Lodge**, tel. 233-0133. **Mawamba Lodge**, tel. 222-5463. **Pachira Lodge**, tel. 256-7080. *BUDGET:* **Cabinas Sabina**, romantic, directly on sea. **Cabinas Brisas del Mar**, **Cabinas Bananero**.
Restaurants
All hotels and cabinas have their own restaurants. **Miss Junie's** has a large selection of dishes.

VOLCANOES AND EARTHQUAKES

What would Costa Rica be without its majestic volcanoes, its deep gorges, its roaring white-water streams and its thundering waterfalls? The climb to the summit of Cerro Chirripó, a hike through the gorge of the Río Pacuare with its tropical flora, a kayak trip on the Río Reventazón or a cool shower under the cascades of the Río La Paz are among the high points of a vacation in Costa Rica. Were it not for the intensively active geological zone on which Costa Rica lies, these mountainous natural wonders would not have been possible.

Geology is the explanation for many of the country's scenic wonders. The earth's crust is not one solid layer, rather, it consists of six large and many smaller

Previous pages: A hummingbird sips nectar from a hibiscus flower. Banana plantation. Above: Volcán Poas. Right: The eruption of Volcán Irazú in 1964.

movable continental plates. They float on a mobile layer called the *asthenosphere* and are in constant motion.

The molten mass of magma surrounding the earth's core pushes through weak spots in the earth's crust and forces its way to the surface. It also forces the plates further apart, which causes them to collide with other continental plates. Where two plates collide, one overrides the other forming subduction zones.

This process, which has been going on for millions of years, is very active in Costa Rica. The Caribbean Plate and the Cocos Plate collide forming a deep trough. The Cocos Plate pushes under the Caribbean plate which floats west, its sunken part becomes liquid, and under the enormous heat that is formed creates new magma. In addition, this subduction zone sucks part of the sea floor into the molten mass. The water turns to steam, the gases mix with the magma, and tremendous pressure builds up and pushes toward the surface.

This is where volcanoes appear. The magma rises, at first slowly, through the inner funnel of the mountain until it comes up against the upper blockage that acts like a cork. When it can no longer withstand the building pressure from below, it is forced out in a violent eruption or explosion that releases the molten magma. Examples of this kind of stratovolcano are the Volcán Poás and the merely 4,000-year-old Volcán Arenal, which erupt periodically spouting lava or loose earth onto the surface.

This type of volcanic activity also produces geothermal phenomena such as geysers (hot springs that shoot high into the air with regularity). An example is to be found at the foot of Volcán Rincón de la Vieja, north of Liberia. When (as at Volcán Poás) interrupted emissions of steam and gas occur, the volcano has a fumarole. Fumaroles are often filled with or surrounded by mud so that they are constantly bubbling and simmering.

The exciting scenic landscape that visitors experience in Costa Rica is primarily the result of the large number of its high volcanoes. Of a total of 100 volcanoes that are known to have once existed in the country, few now remain recognizable. Centuries of change and erosion have sometimes intervened since their last eruptions. Only 10 volcanoes are clearly visible today. These volcanoes are responsible for the varied vegetation and the many climatic zones that exist in this small country.

An excursion early in the morning to a "lookout" volcano, e.g., Irazú or Poás, is an absolute must for every Costa Rican holiday. The effort is rewarded by deep crater lakes that crown the volcanic giants, incredible panoramic views and a unique unforgettable volcanic landscape. Geologists classify volcanoes according to how often they erupt into active (in Costa Rica, at present, definitely Volcán Arenal), resting or dormant (Turrialba, Irazú and Poás) and extinct volcanoes (Cerro Congo and Barva).

Costa Rica's subduction zone, resulting from the depression of the Cocos Plate, creates more than volcanoes and volcanic activity. It is the source of the many earthquakes that have plagued the country during the five centuries of its "white" history. The massive waves of destruction account for the nearly total absence of large colonial churches and other historic buildings.

The earthquakes of 1841, 1910 and 1991 were especially destructive, and have turned many elegant colonial structures into rubble. On April 22, 1991, Costa Rica experienced the most powerful earthquake in its history. Exactly four months previously there had been a warning quake, two days before Christmas Eve. The 1991 earthquake was recorded at 7.4 on the Richter scale. Its epicenter lay directly south of the Caribbean port city of Puerto Limón, but was felt in the highlands and throughout the country. The few minutes during which the earth shook left 60 people dead, hundreds wounded and thousands homeless.

COSTA RICA'S
WORLD OF PLANTS

Tropical Paradise in Danger

Costa Rica's world of plants can also only be described in superlatives – both positive and negative. More than 12,000 kinds of plants, including 1,500 different types of trees and 1,200 species of orchids grow within its small territory. New plants are discovered every day; others are forever lost as rain forests and tropical deciduous forests are cleared. In 1950, forests still covered 40,000 square kilometers of the country. In 1996, the forests had shrunk to less than 9,000 square kilometers. Every year 40 to 60 hectares of forest are cut down, most often to clear more land for cattle ranches that produce meat for large hamburger chains. In 1993, the government was

Above: Typical landscape in dry paramo.
Right: The magnificent heliconia loves a warm, humid climate.

forced for the first time in its history to import lumber. This is paradoxical in view of the fact that forests covered 99 percent of the country when the first white settlers arrived. But Costa Rica still has an immensely rich selection of plants.

According to L. H. Holdridge's classification of the world's vegetation, there are 116 different life-supporting zones; 12 of these are found in Costa Rica. The zones are determined by temperature, average annual and seasonal rainfall, altitude and the quality of the soil. The result is a varied and delicate ecosystem which ranges from mangrove swamps influenced by tides on the Pacific coast, to the austere sub-alpine paramo landscape found on Cerro Chirripó.

Taking simpler statistics into account, you can divide Costa Rica's vegetation into three types: rain forest, cloud forest (high altitude rain forest) and dry or deciduous forest.

The tropical **rain forest** which covered most of the earth's land surface at the time of the dinosaurs still contains the world's densest and richest collection of flora. It is now confined to a narrow belt in which the unique climatic conditions for its vegetation are present: a minimum temperature of 20°C, less than a 15°C difference between day and night temperatures, and an atmospheric humidity of at least 60 percent. The trees grow to a height of up to 70 meters (the tallest trees in Costa Rica). The canopy of the rain forest is where 90 percent of its photosynthesis takes place. But even far below, on the forest floor, plants are struggling toward the sunlight. Even the most humus-poor forest soil is thickly covered with mosses, vines and mushrooms.

The **cloud forest** has fewer kinds of plants, but a fascinating variety of large and small epiphytes (bromeliads and orchids, for example) and vines, which find it an ideal habitat. A huge variety of giant ferns (800 different kinds) and large-leaved plants (e.g., *sombrilla de los pobres*, or "the poor man's parasol") grows in great profusion on the shady slopes of hilly cloud forests. Under the canopy of the cloud forest there is a layer of middle-sized trees, and under them, a further layer of thick undergrowth filled with thorns.

Hiking in the private cloud forests, Monteverde and Braulio Carrillo National Park, for example, can be a mystical experience, especially in the cloudy morning hours when the forest is still half dark and sunk in mystery.

The plant world of the dry or **deciduous forest** is still less varied but is no less fascinating. First, the trees are decidedly lower (seldom more than 15 meters high). The deciduous forest is much lighter than the rain forest or cloud forest. Most of the trees lose their leaves in the dry season (December to April).

In the middle of the seasonal drought many trees burst, as if on command, into bloom, like the amazing yellow *cortezas amarillas*, orange-colored flame trees, violet jacarandas and white-pink oaks.

Only two percent of Costa Rica's deciduous forest (300 square kilometers) has survived into the present. It is found, for example, in long stretches along the banks of the Río Tempisque in Guanacaste. In general, there are far fewer deciduous tropical forests than rain forests because the dry deciduous forest is more susceptible to forest fire.

Further deforestation in Costa Rica would be a catastrophe for many reasons. For one thing, after its people, scenic nature is Costa Rica's greatest treasure. The rain forest could, in the near future, develop into a constant source of income, in addition to tourism. For the last several years the U.S. pharmaceutical concern Merck (the largest in the world) has been sharing income from sales of pharmaceuticals made from healing plants with the InBio Institute of Costa Rica. InBio workers discovered the plants while cataloguing vegetation in the rain forests. Perhaps this could be the beginning of a wonderful new economic relationship, which will also benefit mankind.

227

FASCINATING FAUNA

Costa Rica's location as a corridor between two giant subcontinents accounts for the marvelous variety of its animal life. The Jardín Zoológico in San José, the country's butterfly farms, the game preserve near Cartago and the Rara Avis bird sanctuary on the eastern edge of the Braulio Carrillo National Park afford the visitor his first glimpse of Costa Rica's fauna – but even that is a limited picture. The variety of its animals is truly extraordinary. If you love to watch animals, you should really go to Costa Rica's national parks and game preserves with an experienced ranger or guide.

Our nearest relatives in the animal world are the primates. **Monkeys** are among the first residents of Costa Rica's forests that most visitors are likely to see. In the case of the howler monkey, per-

Above: Squirrel monkeys are good tree climbers. Right: The basilisk lizard can walk on water.

haps the first that they hear. Monkeys were the first mammals from North America to reach Central America and then migrate further south. In the course of evolution, four distinct monkey varieties developed: capuchin, howler, red-faced spider and squirrel monkeys. Today they are found in the treetops of nearly all of Costa Rica's rain forests, and in the thick growth of the country's deciduous forests.

Sloths are much quieter creatures. They spend most of their time rolled up sleeping in treetops. They need up to 18 hours of sleep each day and spend little or no time on bodily hygiene. When action becomes inevitable, their movements resemble something taken with a slow-motion camera. When absolutely necessary they can push themselves to cover one kilometer within three hours. Even their digestion is slow. It takes one week for nutrients that they have eaten to be processed and expelled.

The **wildcats** that inhabit the Costa Rican jungles are among the country's most fascinating and endangered animals. With a great deal of luck, hikers may spot one of them in the national parks of Santa Rosa, Corcovado or Tortuguero, where ocelots, jaguarundis and jaguars stalk the thick undergrowth. They were already admired in pre-Columbian times for their elegance. To the Maya and Aztecs they symbolized strength and power. Costa Rica's wildcats are excellent climbers and swimmers, weight up to two hundred pounds and can reach lengths of up to two meters. When they are not napping, they hunt for smaller animals that live in the trees, in the water and on the forest floor. But wildcats will also not hesitate to devour a full-grown cow, which they can kill in seconds.

Similar in its unusual appearance to the sloth is the **tapir**, which does not live in a family unit, but spends its time entirely alone feeding on plants that grow on the forest floor. With its long snout the tapir,

Central America's largest and heaviest mammal, roots among the plants seeking out the most succulent leaves and tender branches. When chased it can easily keep up with a human being. Jaguars and human beings have hunted the tapir to near extinction. A small number, approximately 300, are still known to exist in the Corcovado National Park.

Anteaters live in the middle and lower levels of trees and are generally no larger than a house cat. Only the giant anteater, which lives on the forest floor, is considerably larger. With their long sticky tongues, anteaters lap up ants and termites from their nests in trees or on the ground, and often devour bits of wood and sand along with the insects. In Costa Rica the giant anteater is only found on the Osa Peninsula. **Raccoons**, **kinkajous** and their long-nosed relatives **coatis**, on the other hand, are found throughout the country. They prefer moving from tree to tree at night or – to the concern of animal protectionists – on the beaches where they feed on turtle eggs.

The water is also full of countless exotic animals. **Sea turtles** come to lay their eggs on the beaches of Costa Rica and are among the world's endangered species. Five kinds are known in Costa Rica: leatherback, hawksbill, loggerhead, bastard and green sea turtles. Despite their dwindling numbers, poachers still steal the eggs, which are sold for their alleged potency-restoring qualities. At the right time of year, visitors to Tortuguero and Barra del Colorado national parks and on the Pacific coast of the Nicoya Peninsula (*Playa Grande*) can observe the giant armored creatures as they crawl onto the beaches to lay their eggs.

Costa Rica is fortunate to have three types of very unusual **frogs**: the tree-climbing frog, the golden toad and the poison-arrow frog. The latter have developed a poisonous substance that discourages its enemies from turning them into their dinner. Indians discovered this unique poison, dipped their arrows into it, and used it as a deadly weapon against larger animals.

The extremely rare golden toad, perhaps extinct in other parts of the world, was discovered in 1964 in the cloud forest of Monteverde. It is characterized by its gold-orange, neon-bright skin. Tree-climbing frogs also come in bright colors (green, blue or red) and are inedible. It is important for hikers to keep their eyes open while walking through Costa Rica's natural parks in order to spot the glass frog (*Centro lenella euknemous*), the leaf-green red-eyed frog, the fat gray Mexican burrowing toad, the Surinam toad (with its pointed ears) and the various kinds of harlequin frogs.

Frogs are easy to overlook, but **manatees**, or sea cows, are hard to miss. The animals, which resemble toothless walruses, have long been hunted by man for their delicious flesh. At one time they were decimated by hunters but now are beginning to recover, at least along the Caribbean coast where they are often seen in the Tortugero National Park. Visitors are advised to give them (and agoutis) a wide berth because they suffer all their lives from flatulence. Manatees eat up to 100 pounds of algae and water hyacinths ever day, gulping considerable air along with the vegetables, which causes their malodorous problem.

Crocodiles, such as the pointed crocodile (up to seven meters long) and caiman (up to four meters long), are perfectly camouflaged in the mud of jungle river banks. With a bit of luck visitors can spot them from boats as they sun themselves along rivers in Palo Verde, Corcovado and Tortuguero national parks. The giant lizards, descended from dinosaurs, are still hunted for their valuable skin, while dogs, iguanas and foxes eat their eggs.

Lizards are the crocodile's smaller relatives. They live in the forests and feed mainly on insects. The magnificent black iguana is wonderful to photograph. The green iguana is endangered, and the tiny,

Above: Red-eyed frogs are tree frogs that are active at night. Right: River turtles are often seen on the Caribbean coast.

six-centimeter-long anole lizard, like most of its relatives, is harmless. The gecko, which every visitor sees sooner or later on the wall of his hotel room, climbs walls with the help of tiny suction cups on its feet, and feeds on cockroaches, mosquitoes and flies.

Only a few of the many **snakes** in Costa Rica are venomous. Among the poisonous varieties are the coral snake, a number of sea snakes and the feared fer-de-lance (a member of the viper family), which grows up to three meters long and is considered very aggressive. Visitors have a good chance of seeing a boa constrictor. They often live in fields and are not poisonous, although the grip of a full grown boa can be deadly. Costa Rica's venomous snakes proved a few years ago that they not only take lives, but that they can also save them: the venom of the fer-de-lance helped pharmaceutical giant Hoechst develop a life-saving medication for heart patients.

For most visitors to Costa Rica's national parks the kings of the air are the country's most interesting animals. There are more than 850 kinds of **birds** in Costa Rica. The variety is so extensive that even ornithologists have problems distinguishing all the different types. It is a good idea to buy a basic reference book in San José before setting out. A number of works with the names of birds in Spanish and English are available in the capital's book shops, and make intelligent bird watching even more fun.

Hummingbirds, quetzals, pelicans, frigate birds, crimson macaws, sooty robins (Costa Rica's national bird), bellbirds, toucans, herons, cormorants, kingfishers, flamingos, curassows and brown pelicans are just a few of the more spectacular birds that soar through Costa Rica's skies.

Butterflies are just as extraordinary in their almost endless variety. Costa Rica has more kinds of butterflies than the entire African continent. In the Corcovado National Park alone more than 200 varieties have been identified. Around 1,400 different types live in the country.

231

BANANAS AND COFFEE

**Chiquita, Del Monte and
Uncle Tuca**

The victory of the banana in Costa Rica began with a freight train that chugged into Puerto Limón on the newly built Atlantic railway. Minor Kooper Keith, from the U.S., had made an agreement with the Costa Rican government that when he completed the Atlantic Railroad, he would get a 99-year lease to use 3,000 hectares of fertile land. In 1894, he imported a type of banana known as *Big Michael*, and he began to plant and export the golden fruit. In 1899, he joined his many small individual companies and founded the United Fruit Company (UFC). Afterwards, Keith negotiated tax-free status for his company and obtained a transportation monopoly. The UFC

Above: Costa Rica's climate provides ideal conditions for planting bananas. Right: Bananas are washed in chlorinated water.

controlled harbors and had its own private fleet of seagoing freighters. Minor Kooper Keith was further allowed to determine the working conditions of his employees at his own discretion. Thanks to his unscrupulous business methods, the UFC developed very quickly into a state within a state and turned Costa Rica into a banana republic. In the 1920s and 1930s, when the Panama Sickness and the Sigatoka banana blight swept through most of the Atlantic plantations, the UFC moved its operations to the still undeveloped Pacific region.

Banana plantations in Costa Rica meanwhile account for 45,000 hectares of land out of its total area of 51,000 square kilometers. That is five times as much land as was used for bananas in 1967. Since 1985, production has grown 50 percent. In 1985, the United Fruit Company withdrew from Golfito, its Pacific administration center and port, following a 72-day strike. Since then, most of the banana crop has been grown in the Atlantic lowlands. In 1994, 60 million cartons of bananas (at 18 kilos per carton) earned Costa Rica an income of US $500 million, including a one dollar export tax per case. The banana monocul ture is concentrated between Puerto Limón and Sixaola on plantations ranging in size from 200 to 400 hectares.

Costa Rica has become, after Ecuador, the second-largest exporter of bananas in the world. Bananas create jobs, but otherwise benefit the country very little. On the contrary, the soil is irreversibly damaged through the massive use of pesticides. Most of the business is in the hands of three multinational companies: United Brands (formerly UFC), Standard Fruit and Del Monte. The three companies also control the planting of bananas in Panama, Guatemala and other Latin American companies.

The labor done by the 20,000 *bananeros* is difficult. *Cortador* (cutter) *cargador* (carrier) and *carrero* (trans-

porter) are terms used to describe the generally strong men who work in banana fields where pesticides are sprayed. The *desfloradores* (literally, "flower removers") are usually women who wash the bananas in a chlorine bath, sort and pack them into cartons. The tropical fruit leaves the land labeled *Del Monte*, *Chiquita*, *Uncle Tuca*, *Bonita* and *Turbana*. Captains of the freight ships that transport the expensive cargo across the world's oceans have to make sure that the bananas are stored at a constant temperature of 14°C during the transport which can last for weeks. Payment at the final destination is only for fruit that arrives in perfect condition.

Since 1985, free unions have been systematically forced out of the banana fincas and plantations. They have been replaced by employer-friendly obligatory workers' associations which every worker must join. No one is employed unless they possess a valid membership identification. Many workers are only employed for a three-month trial period, and are

then fired in order to save the employer the costs of social benefits. Workers are forced to change plantations, and the process begins all over again.

Many of the workers are illegal immigrants from Nicaragua who are satisfied with the meager wages, and who are in no position to organize against their employers. A typical family working on a banana plantation earns about US $420 a month for working 50 to 60 hours a week. They have to work on weekends and holidays as well. Every two weeks an armored car for money transport rolls up to the plantation. The workers then have to line up, sometimes waiting up to three hours, to get their salary of US $125 in payment for two weeks of back-breaking work. The average age of the men and women who work on the plantations is 30. Those who noticeably exceed the age limit are regularly weeded out.

The time-coordinated labor done in teams, at temperatures of 35°C and 90 percent humidity, is physically very strenuous and can hardly continue beyond the age of 30. The strongest men are selected to work as *cargadores*, heaving the 35 to 50-kilogram green banana stalks onto conveyer belts. They lift up to 200 stalks per day. If any of the bananas are damaged, the cost is subtracted from their wages.

Since the beginning of the 1980s, large banana producers in Costa Rica have cleared another 30,000 hectares of rain forest to create new plantations and to expand existing ones. The cleared stretches are no longer ruled by nature, with its rich variety of species, but are subjugated to chemistry. In Costa Rica it is customary to use six kilos of poison, consisting of herbicides and fungicides, per hectare each year. This is about 10 times the international average for land in agricultural use. Even the plastic bags which are placed over the nearly ripe fruit to protect it from insects and birds are treated with insecticide. For this reason, banana orchards generally have a very unpleasant smell. Agro-chemicals are the highest cost factor on a banana plantation. Each year a mid-sized plantation produces 3,500 tons of highly poisonous waste. The deep, once fertile soil is rapidly used up and drowned in pesticides and chemical fertilizers. Today's export bananas are mostly *Giant Cavendish* and *Robusta* varieties. These are hybrid varieties that are far thicker and longer than wild bananas. The banana plants are also much higher and thicker, and have to be staked to keep them from falling over under the weight of their fruit. These "fruit" bananas are rarely eaten in Costa Rica. Ticos prefer the starchy, smaller, more aromatic "cooking" banana which they boil or fry and serve with meals.

The European market regulations initiated on July 1, 1993 (and since modi-

Above: The painting "Alegoría," in the Teatro Nacional in San José, is Costa Rica's most famous work of art and shows coffee and banana harvests in 1897.

fied), have had their effect on Costa Rica. In order to protect the banana production of Portugal, France and Spain, only two million tons of the so-called Dollar Bananas (primarily from Central America), can be imported into European Union countries each year. Customs duty of 20 percent is levied on all the bananas, and 170 percent is charged for those that exceed the import limit.

Costa Rica's Coffee

What could be finer on a trip through Costa Rica than spending the afternoon on a shady restaurant terrace overlooking the spectacular landscape that spreads out before you like a panorama of paradise, and relaxing with a cup of hearty, aromatic native coffee from the Costa Rican highlands? It is the perfect way to end a sweaty jungle tour or a strenuous long climb to the summit of a volcano through the merciless tropical sun.

The first coffee beans were imported to Costa Rica from Jamaica in 1808. Costa

ENTRAL DE COSTA RICA

CINCO COLONES

THOMAS DE LA RUE & COMPANY, LIMITED

Rica provided ideal conditions for the planting of coffee, a crop then still little known in the Americas. The division of the year into a rainy and dry season made it possible for farmers to harvest their crop during the dry season and to ship the coffee a short time later along dry roads. Costa Rica also had land at an ideal altitude (800-1,700 meters) for highland coffee; the best quality variety. The absence of any frost, in contrast to the south of Brazil, and fertile soil combined to make Costa Rica the perfect choice for growing the new crop.

The new state could also invest in coffee plantations because coffee had no competition among other cash crops of the day. Bananas would have to wait another hundred years before becoming an economic factor in Costa Rica. In addition, there were few financial problems: for decades the government freed coffee of taxes, making the crop a very interesting option for many farmers. The government financed the introduction of coffee, in large part, through money that

flowed from gold mines discovered in 1821 near Alajuela.

By 1829, the *Grano d'oro* or "golden bean" was Costa Rica's most important export product, amounting to 20,000 kilos per year. German coffee baron Georg Stiepel was meanwhile able to establish important contacts abroad, and coffee exports to European countries soon followed. In 1885, the *finqueros* were loading their ox carts for the overland journey to the 100-kilometer-distant Pacific harbors with more than 50 million kilos of coffee beans. Coffee by that time occupied 10,000 hectares of land.

Most of the coffee shipped at this time made the long and dangerous trip around Cape Horn. The journey took three months to Great Britain, where the beans became known as *Café Chileno*. Following Minor Kooper Keith's completion of the Atlantic Railroad to Puerto Limón, the journey was shortened by several weeks. Profits soared and hard currency poured into the country. The new wealth was spent on impressive mansions,

theaters and opera houses. Much of it flowed into improvements of the country's infrastructure. In San José, electric lighting was installed and streets were paved.

Small farmers dominated the coffee economy of Costa Rica until the turn of the century. Then the ruling clans managed to "buy out" most of the small farmers within just a few years. All means were used to this end, including unscrupulous business deals. From that time on, the *Aristocracía cafetalera*, or coffee aristocracy, dictated government policies and led the country into an ecologically and financially risky monocultural economy.

Today coffee only plays a subordinate role but remains the most important agricultural product of the Costa Rican highlands. Coffee beans, despite sinking prices on the world's markets, still bring

Above: Coffee pickers will never get rich from their work in the fields. Right: Coffee tester at an auction.

Costa Rica almost 300 million dollars annually, which comprise 11 percent of the country's total exports.

Coffee guarantees employment to around 200,000 workers, who harvest more than 150,000 tons of the "black gold" each year. Growers keep about one quarter of the money paid for the crop. Most of the profits go to middlemen.

What botanists know as *Coffea Arabica* is cultivated as the coffee plant, stemming from the madder family. It grows in the form of a bush, which reaches up to 1.5 meters in height. The main stem or trunk in the center of the plant has many straight branches. Thanks to the mild climate, the plant bears fruit twice a year. Its white blossoms open following the rainy season. Coffee berries are covered with a number of layers. Underneath the tough outer shell is a hard parchment-like skin that covers the two halves of the bean (actually a seed). The seeds are enclosed in a thin silvery skin.

Costa Rican coffee is harvested by poorly-paid day laborers or seasonal

pickers (*peones*, most of whom come from Nicaragua, the poorer country to the north of Costa Rica). The beans have to be picked by hand because they ripen individually at different times. The harvest can stretch over a period of six weeks. Often entire families, including women and children, pick beans. They have to live for months from the money they earn during the harvest.

High-quality coffee comes only from fully ripened berries. These are reserved for export. The coffee drunk in the country is usually brewed from beans of inferior quality.

Following the harvest, the red beans are spread out on the ground and dried in the sun for days. The beans have to be turned over many times. The shelling and removal of the silver skin is done by machine. Once shelled, the beans can be stored almost indefinitely.

After processing, only about 20 percent of the harvested weight remains. The shells can be used either as fuel for drying coffee beans, or they can be spread between the coffee plants to discourage weed growth and help retain moisture in the soil. The average life of a coffee plant is around 25 years, after which the amount of fruit it bears rapidly declines. The farmers then have to pull up the plants and replace them with new ones that need another two to three years before they begin to bear fruit.

Coffee tours at highland coffee plantations, such as the Café Britt (near Heredia) or the Orosí Coffee Adventure in the Orosí Valley, show visitors various phases of coffee processing and give them the opportunity of tasting various kinds of coffee that have been roasted in different ways.

Roasted coffee beans, packed in small sacks, are sold in many souvenir shops and at the *mercados*, or markets, in larger towns. Freshly-roasted coffee loses its aroma within a few weeks. For this reason most beans are exported green, and are roasted in the countries where they are sold to the final consumers. Coffee beans are roasted at 200 to 250°C.

GALLO PINTO AND PATACONES

Costa Rican Cuisine

In Costa Rica, a pleasant dinner in a restaurant means more than just going out to eat. Mariachi music belongs to the experience as well as people watching, making new acquaintances, and trying new exotic dishes and drinks. Even the simplest and cheapest *soda* (meaning not the fizzy drink, but rather a snack bar) and the *mercado central*, which is found in every town, serve delicious typical Costa Rican dishes.

A hearty breakfast consists of *gallo pinto*, a dish of fried rice and beans with eggs, onions and *salsa picante* (chili sauce). *Casado*, or the main dish, typically consists of pan-fried beef (*carne de res*), chicken (*pollo*) or fish (*pescado*).

Above: In Costa Rican cuisine vegetables from various climatic zones all go into the pot. Right: Mamones (Rambutan).

Side dishes include rice with beans (*arroz con frijoles*), *tostones* or *patacones* (fried cooking bananas) and *ensalada* (salad). It goes without saying that *tortillas*, flat unleavened fried bread made of corn, are included.

Caribbean regional cuisine is also based on the principle of "rice and beans." Grated coconut is often sprinkled on top and the dish is served with a cakelike bread called *pan bom*. Fresh palm hearts, *palmitos*, are served everywhere as a popular side dish. They are so tender they almost melt in your mouth.

Those who prefer fish or seafood can order *tilapia* (a type of perch), *camarones* (shrimp) or whatever happens to be the catch of the day. The coastal waters and fresh-water lakes of Costa Rica teem with fish.

Small snacks called *bocas* are especially interesting and varied. They are served as appetizers in the finer restaurants but also as simple snacks at the rolling kitchens along the streets, at stands in the *Mercado Central* and in *sodas*. *Empa-*

nadas, pastry baked with a spicy meat or cheese filling, can be a meal in themselves. *Tamales*, made of cornmeal mush wrapped in banana leaves, come from a long tradition of Indian dishes. So do *elotes* (corn-on-the-cob), which is delicious either roasted (*asados*) or boiled (*cocinados*), spread with butter and seasoned with salt and pepper or paprika. They are popular between-meal snacks that can keep you busy picking the hulls of kernels from your teeth for hours.

Arreglados are toasted rolls served with small pieces of meat on top. *Ceviche* is marinated raw fish. Both are among the many delicacies served in Costa Rica. *Gallos* are tortillas rolled into a cone and stuffed with a cheese or meat filling. Like many snacks in Costa Rica, gallos are "environmentally friendly" because you simply eat the wrapping (the tortilla) with the food!

A tempting variety of tropical fruit grows in Costa Rica. You should try as many kinds as possible during your stay in the country. The *chirimoya*, a green fruit native to Ecuador and Peru, tastes like a mixture of pears and mangoes. *Platanos* are cooking bananas found everywhere in Costa Rica.

The fruit banana, raised for export, is not very popular in the country. The lowland *piña* (pineapple) is often enjoyed as a dessert or as juice. Connoisseurs drink pineapple juice mixed with coconut cream and rum as *piña coladas* – served, if at all possible, by the pool or seaside under a shady palm-thatched roof.

Vitamin-rich *guayabas* (guavas), *granadillos* (passion fruit) and *carambolas* (five-pointed star fruit), are served as refreshing desserts or nibbled between meals. *Mamones* (rambutan) resemble lychees in taste but have long stiff bristles on the outside, and the *pejibaye* is a red fruit from a variety of palm tree.

Street vendors sell coconuts as well as strange and exotic fruit drinks. Some of these are quite adventurous looking, as, for example, the juice of the fruit of the cashew nut, which is called the *marañon* in Costa Rica.

METRIC CONVERSION

Metric Unit	US Equivalent
Meter (m)	39.37 in.
Kilometer (km)	0.6241 mi.
Square Meter (sq m)	10.76 sq. ft.
Hectare (ha)	2.471 acres
Square Kilometer (sq km)	0.386 sq. mi.
Kilogram (kg)	2.2 lbs.
Liter (l)	1.05 qt.

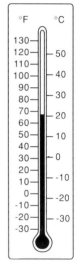

TRAVEL PREPARATIONS

Entry Formalities

To enter Costa Rica visitors need a passport that is valid for at least six months. No visa is required for stays of up to 90 days.

All non-Costa Rican travelers must fill out a *Tarjeta de Ingreso* (tourist card) which they receive on the plane or at the point of entry. Personal data include: reason for trip, length of stay, and address of hotel where you will be staying. The length of your stay in Costa Rica may be extended for an additional 90 days. To aviod the extension procedure, you can spend at least 72 hours in Panama or Nicaragua. Visitors who intend to remain more than 180 days require a visa that can be obtained at diplomatic representatives of Costa Rica (see Embassies).

Upon entry visitors (especially backpackers) are frequently asked to show return tickets or proof of financial means for the length of their stay in the country.

Clothing

Loose light cotton or linen clothing, which lets air circulate, is ideal. Long trousers and long-sleeved shirts offer protection from the sun. Shorts are "out." For cool evenings and mornings in the highlands it is good to have a sweater and/or a light jacket. A windproof and waterproof jacket fills this need and can be used for hiking in the rain forest, climbing mountains and on the Caribbean coast.

Good shoes are essential for hiking. Rubber boots are recommended for the rain forest and protection from snakes and small animals. A sun hat that can be easily stored should always be readily available in hand luggage.

Climate and Travel Seasons

Rainy and dry seasons make up the year. The best times to travel are the months from January to March when it is driest. Even during these months sudden tropical showers may occur along the Caribbean coast, near Golfito on the Pacific Coast, and in the northern lowlands.

From May through November rain is probable everywhere, especially in September and October. School holidays in Costa Rica are from December to February and travelers should reserve hotels well in advance during this period.

Currency and Exchanging Money

The Costa Rican currency is called the *colón*. It is written using the symbol *C/*. Coins come in denominations of 1, 2, 5, 10 and 20 colones, bank notes in 50, 100, 200, 500, 1,000 and 5,000 colones. 100 *centimos* make up one colón. These small coins are now seldom seen but are still in circulation as 25 or 50 centimo coins.

It is best to exchange currency upon arrival in the country, and is best to travel with U.S. traveler's checks or cash. The U.S. dollar is the best known foreign currency and is easily convertible. The rate of exchange is US $1 = 272 colones (January 1999). The black market for changing money is officially forbidden but exists, especially in San José. For longer excursions inland you should have plenty of colones. Changing money at provincial banks can be time consuming.

Banks are open weekdays from 9 a.m. to 3 p.m. The exchange office in San José usually stays open longer. Larger hotels, restaurants and travel agents accept credit cards, but often attempt to add seven percent in order to pass their fee onto the customer. *Warning*: When paying, never let your credit card out of your sight! It could result in unpleasant surprises on your bill upon your return home.

Customs

The *Declaración de Aduana* (customs declaration) asks for information about items such as cameras. Each traveler may bring 500 cigarettes or 500 grams of tobacco and three liters of wine or liquor into the country. Officially, only six rolls of film are allowed, but this rule is seldom enforced.

TRAVELING TO COSTA RICA

Flight connectons in San José (Juan Santamaría Airport, tel. 441-0744) with American Airlines, Avianca, Aviateca, British Airways, Condor, Continental Airlines, Iberia, LACSA, Martinair, United Airlines and VARIG. Transportation to/from San José: Red *Tuasa* buses, "Ruta 200 B," take about 30 minutes and cost approximately US $.50; taxis take about 20 minutes and cost US $13.

Cruise ships make it possible to reach Costa Rica by sea. Most ships dock at

Moín near Puerto Limón on the Caribbean coast or at **Puerto Caldera**, south of Puntarenas.

It is possible to reach Costa Rica **overland** from Nicaragua or Panama. From Nicaragua, Peñas Blancas, on the Panamerican Highway, is the main border crossing. It is open only from 8 a.m. to noon and from 1 to 5 p.m. There are no overnight accommodations at the border. From Panama you can cross the border at Paso Canoas, on the Panamericana, or Sixaola and Guabito on the Caribbean coast. The overland route is time consuming and not without its problems.

TRAVELING WITHIN COSTA RICA

By Air: Two Costa Rican airlines, Travelair and SANSA (*Servicio Aereos Nacionales SA*) fly scheduled flights from San José to the following destinations: Quepos, Tambor, Sámara, Nosara, Tamarindo, Liberia, Barra del Colorado, Tortuguero, Ciudad Neily, Golfito, Puerto Jiménez and Palmar Sur.

The planes – some of which are rather small – take off from Juan Santamaría (SANSA) or Aeropuerto Tobias Bolaños (five kilometers outside San José; Travelair) and often allow only 12 kilograms of luggage per passenger. Flights are heavily booked throughout the year, and it is advisable to reserve as early as possible. Reservations can be made at travel agencies and airports.

By Bus: The bus network covers most of Costa Rica. Buses leave constantly from the San José station and travel in all directions. The further you go from densely populated areas, the more seldom the bus connections. Bus travel is inexpensive.

By Car: Half of all foreign visitors rent a car. The choice of car rental agencies in San José and other tourist centers is enormous. There are also considerable price differences between small local and large international rental agencies. In comparing prices be sure to check that tax and insurance are included in the rental price, and ask how high the personal liability is. To rent a car you must be at least 21 years of age, have a valid driving license, passport and credit card. Some companies require a cash deposit. It is advisable to note all damage on the car in the presence of a rental agency representative before leaving the premises.

Anyone who wants to leave the paved roads and travel over the exciting short-cuts and dirt roads should rent a four-wheel-drive vehicle. Many of the roads outside the capital are not suited for normal passenger cars. If there is more than one driver, their names should be in the rental contract to avoid problems in the event of a police check or accident.

Be careful of fake police officers! At police control stops check the metal name tag of the uniformed police officer, and never pay cash fines directly, even when the purported police officer threatens to increase the fine or refuses to allow the car to proceed.

By Train: The 1991 earthquake seriously damaged many of the railway tracks. The famous Atlantic Railroad from San José to Puerto Limón has been closed down. Following the cancellation of the planned sale of the railroad to a Canadian company in 1995 for US $85 million, railway traffic throughout the country has been halted.

By Ship: In addition to ferry crossings, it is possible to book passage on small cruise ships to Pacific island bird sanctuaries. A boat trip on the *canales* to the Tortuguero and Barra del Colorado national parks is both a good transportation alternative and an unforgettable experience. It is also possible to take a luxury yacht to the Isla del Coco to go on a "treasure hunt."

Organized Tours: In addition to travel agents abroad, local agents in San José offer package tours through Costa Rica.

These usually include English-speaking native guides.

PRACTICAL TIPS FROM A TO Z

Accommodation

Most hotels are privately run – not owned by hotel chains. Hotel owners are often in direct contact with their guests, can give them inside tips and can be helpful in solving problems. The private nature of the accommodations gives travel through Costa Rica a very personal note. Only a few hotels can be classified in the internationally-accepted *LUXURY* category (price in excess of US $100 per night). These are only in San José. Many hotels in national parks and their surroundings offer activities such as horseback riding, golf, swimming, fishing, diving, hiking and white-water rafting. Often, such activities or excursions are included in the price along with meals at so-called "sport hotels." Sport hotels belong to the category *MODERATE* (US $25-75 per night).

The *BUDGET* category (US $10-25) includes *cabinas*, apartment hotels (with their own kitchen), bed & breakfasts, small family inns, youth hostels or hotels specializing in backpackers. A tax of 16.4 percent is often added to the posted price of the room.

Alcohol

Alcohol and drinking are not a problem in Costa Rica. Drinking alcoholic beverages in public places is allowed. Drivers are checked for blood alcohol content. The local *cerveza* (beer), rum and Costa Rican coffee liqueur are worth trying.

Camping

Camping is not as widely developed in Costa Rica as it is in Europe or the U.S. Furnishings at the few campgrounds – e.g., near the ranger stations of national parks, at lakes or in front of hotels – are often very modest. High temperatures, swarms of mosquitoes, and cloudbursts can quickly dampen camping enthusiasm. Camping in unauthorized places is not tolerated by farmers, park rangers or police. Besides, it can be unsafe.

Drugs

In the past few years Costa Rica has increasingly become a marketplace for drugs on their way from South to North America. The government is fighting rigorously against this problem. Drug sales and drug consumption are strictly forbidden and severely punished in Costa Rica. International drug dealers can be sentenced to up to 20 years in prison. Consumption of marijuana, cocaine and heroin can mean years in jail.

You should not believe that smoking hashish is legal on the streets of Puerto Limón, Moín and Cahuita simply because Rastas and other local residents do so openly. Even rolling your own cigarettes from tobacco can put you under suspicion.

Electricity

Electrical power in Costa Rica is 110 volts and 60 hertz. Only flat bi-polar plugs, such as those used in the U.S., fit into the wall sockets. If using adaptable 220-volt appliances, switch them to 110 volts. Travelers from the U.K. and other European countries need plug adapters.

Festivals and Holidays

January: Residents of Santa Cruz, Guanacaste celebrate their annual folk festival with bull fighting and popular festivities. The *Copa del Café* tennis tournament is also held during this time.
January 1: New Year's Day
February: *Fiesta de los Diablitos* in Boruca; agricultural fair with bull fights and music in San Isidro de El General.
March: Pilgrimage to Ujarrás; pilgrimage with ox carts (*Día del Boyero*) on the second Sunday of the month in Escazú;

marathon in San José (*Carrera de la Paz*); National Orchid Show in San José.
March 19: *Día de San José* (St. Joseph's Day), patron saint of the capital.
Holy Week (*Semana Santa*) and **Easter**: Celebrated with processions and events starting on Maundy Thursday. Easter Monday and Pentecost Monday are normal work days.
April 11: *Día de Juan Santamaría*; with commemorations and celebrations of Costa Rica's national hero and the battle of Santa Rosa.
May 1: Labor Day
May 17: *Carrera de San Juan* (marathon near Cartago).
June 29: *Día de San Pedro y San Pablo*; church festival in honor of Sts. Peter and Paul.
July 16: In Puntarenas, the feast of *Santa María*, the patron saint of the sea, is celebrated with a procession, decorated fishing boats and a carnival.
July 25: Anniversary of the annexation of Guanacaste, a rural festival.
August: Afro-Costa Rican culture week with concerts, lectures and shows.
August 2: *Virgin de los Angeles*; church holiday in honor of the "Holy Virgin of the Angels," the patron of the country.
August 31: Feast of *San Ramón* in San Ramón; international music festival in San José.
September 15: Independence Day, celebrated with parades and other festivities.
October: The lively *Carnival* of Puerto Limón begins, and the *Fiesta del Maíz* in Upala both begin on the 12th.
October 12: *Día de las Culturas* (Day of the Cultures); Commemoration of Columbus' discovery of the Americas.
November: Coffee-picking contest in the highlands, and international surfing tournament.
November 2: Cemeteries throughout the country are visited.
December 8: *Fiesta de los Negritos* in Boruca with a traditional dance. On the same day: *Día de la Pólvera*, celebrated

with fireworks throughout the country. *Inmaculate Concepcíon de la Virgin María*; Feast of the Immaculate Conception. Catholic Church holiday celebrated throughout the country.

December 12: Procession similar to *Día de la Yeguita*, (festival of the "Small Mare") in Nicoya with Indian customs and folklore.

December 24 - 25: Christmas.

Guides

Local guides offer their services in many national parks, nature preserves and towns. Often they are biologists, ecologists, travel guides and entertainers – all in one. Many speak several foreign languages in addition to Spanish. Good *Guías*, or local guides, can do more than point out animals and plants and identify them. They can delight tourists with their knowledge of many fascinating details. By negotiating the time, route and price of your tour you can test the guide's knowledge of English.

Health and Vaccinations

Health care in Costa Rica is good by Latin American standards. It is better in the big cities than in the country. But even small villages have well-stocked pharmacies where various medicaments for the usual travel maladies, such as diarrhea, insect bites and sunburn, can be found. You should always use insect repellent. It is a good idea to take salt tablets to guard against excessive mineral loss through perspiration.

Vaccinations are not mandatory for travel to Costa Rica. Along the Caribbean coast there have been individual cases of malaria. Check with a doctor specializing in tropical medicine or a tropical medical institute before taking prophylactic malaria medication. Signing up for travel health insurance makes good sense.

Diarrhea can be prevented by taking a few precautions: Do not eat salads, ice cream, unwashed or unpeeled fruit (also because of pesticides) and avoid unclean water (e.g., tap water).

Hospitals

Clinics and hospitals are listed in the *Guidepost* sections of individual chapters. They are furnished with modern technical equipment. Hundreds of Americans come each year from the U.S. for treatment in Costa Rica because medical costs are cheaper than in the U.S. Treatment must be paid for in cash upon leaving the hospital. Foreign medical health insurance is not recognized. It is advisable to have foreign health insurance that reimburses travelers for foreign treatment upon presentation of a receipt.

Opening Hours

Most shops are open Monday through Friday from 8 a.m. to 6 p.m. Many are also open Saturdays from 8 a.m. to 6 p.m. Public offices close at 3:30 or 4:30 p.m., and take time for a siesta between 11:30 a.m. and 1:30 p.m. Banks are generally only open Monday through Friday from 9 a.m. to 3 p.m.

Photography

Photographers should bring with them: film, spare batteries, flash attachments, tripods and special lens, filters (UV and polarization filter). These items are very expensive or rarely found in Costa Rica. Film is often improperly stored or sold after its expiration date. In addition to plenty of 100-ASA film, photographers should pack a few rolls of 400 ASA film for the shady rain forest.

If you buy film in Costa Rica watch for the expiration date. Protect it from excessive heat and sunlight, especially when changing film. On boats and excursions into the humid jungle, protect film and photo equipment from dampness.

Photos are best taken early in the morning and late in the afternoon, when the light is not as strong and animals in the national parks are most active.

A flash is useful in the dense rain forest and for portraits of people with dark skin on the Atlantic coast. In any case, you should always ask permission before clicking the shutter by saying: "*¿Con permiso?*" or "*¿Puedo tomar una foto?*"

If you need to buy photo equipment the best two places are: Kim Color (Paseo Colón, Calle 38) and IFSA Industrias Fotograficas (Calle 2, Avenida 5) in San José.

Post and Telephones

The *correos* (post offices) are clearly marked everywhere with white signs bearing blue-red writing. Costa Rica has very beautiful special edition postage stamps. A letter or post card to the U.S. or to Europe requires 10-14 days.

Letters to be picked up should be sent to the General Post Office in San José with "*Correo Restante*" clearly written on the envelope and the last name of the recipient underlined. The person to whom it is sent needs a passport to pick up the forwarded mail.

Some post offices have telephones where it is possible to make calls within Costa Rica. Otherwise, the *Instituto Costarricense de Electricidad y Telecomunicaciónes* (ICE) is responsible. Telephone numbers in Costa Rica contain seven digits. There are no area codes. A minimum of three minutes is charged for overseas calls, regardless of the time actually used. The country code for Costa Rica is + 506.

Press

In San José and other large cities, newspaper boys sell papers on the streets, or newspapers are available in book stores. The principle papers are: *La Nacional*, *La República* (which contains entertainment information) and *Diario*. The *Tico Times,* which comes out on Fridays, is the only English-language newspaper in Costa Rica and is especially popular for its extensive calender of events. International newspapers are available in

some bookstores (e.g., Librería Lehmann in San José).

Restaurants / Menus

Most restaurants are open from noon to midnight, often with a break between 3 p.m. and 6 p.m. Many restaurants close Sundays or Mondays. When paying by credit card you should not let the card out of your sight. Criminals frequently make copies of credit cards.

aguacate	avocado
ají	chili pepper
ajo	garlic
albóndigas	meat dumpling
alcachofas	artichokes
arreglado	meat paté
arroz	rice
atún	tuna fish
camarones	shrimp
carne	meat
cebolla	onion
cerdo	pork
chivo	kid
chuleta	cutlet
coco/pipa	coconut
coliflor	cauliflower
cordero	lamb
elote	corn-on-the-cob
empanada	meat-filled pastry
ensalada de fruta	fruit salad
espárragos	asparagus
flan	caramel-topped custard
frijoles	beans
gallo pinto	fried rice with beans
helado	ice cream
higado	liver
hongos	mushrooms
huevos fritos	fried eggs
huevos revueltos	scrambled eggs
jamón	ham
leche	milk
lenguado	sole
lomo/lomito	steak/filet
mantequilla	butter
naranja	orange
natilla	cream
ostras	oysters

palmitos	hearts of palm
pan	bread
pan integral	whole wheat bread
papas fritas	french fries
pato	duck
pavo	turkey
plátanos	cooking bananas
piña	pinapple
pollo	chicken
pulpo	octopus
queso	cheese
queso frito	breaded cheese
res	beef
salchicha asada	grilled sausage
salsa	sauce
sandía	watermelon
sopa	soup
tortilla	corn pancake
trucha	trout
verduras	vegetables

Security

Costa Rica is not regarded as a dangerous land for travelers within Central America, and there are at present no travel warnings from foreign governments. The kidnapping of two female European tourists in 1996 created international headlines but ended without bloodshed.

Certain areas of San José (e.g., Coca Cola, where hold-ups, especially at night, are frequent) are dangerous. Pickpockets seek their victims among foreigners. It pays to be careful, especially in major cities, in the tourist centers, and in larger towns along the Caribbean coast.

In San José the areas to be especially careful in are in and around the Coca Cola bus terminal, in the streets north of the *Parque Central* and in the red-light district. Thieves in these areas take advantage of the noise, crowds and distractions to steal wallets, cameras and purses. It is a good precaution to make copies of travel documents and credit cards and leave these, along with numbers of traveler's checks, in your hotel or in another safe place.

Shopping

Shopping at the stands around the Plaza de la Cultura and the Mercado Central in San José is especially fun. In many other towns and villages, open-air and weekly markets tempt tourists as well as locals.

Souvenirs are sold in many San José shops and in Sarchí, northwest of Alajuela, where many shops specialize in handicrafts.

Newspapers, magazines, books (especially about local flora and fauna) and maps are available at Librería Lehmann or Librería Universal in San José.

Taxis

Taxis in Costa Rica are not expensive. An average trip within San José cost less than US $3. Taxis are regulated by the government and taxi drivers are required by law to use their meters (*maria*) for trips under 12 kilometers.

Drivers often do not do this, explaining that their *maria* is out of order in the hope of getting a better price for the trip. After 10 p.m. there is a 20 percent night surcharge. San José has more taxis than any other city in Costa Rica. The bright red taxis are easiest to find at the Parque Central on Avenida 2. Taxis that wait in front of major hotels are usually more expensive. A trip from the airport to San José costs around US $13 and takes about 20 minutes even in heavy traffic.

Ticoisms

Ticos love the diminutive form in language. Unlike their Latin American neighbors they do not build the diminutive using the suffix *ito* or *itto*. Instead, they add *tico* to many words. In this way from the word gato (tomcat) they make a *gatico* or a *gatitico* (a little tom kitten).

Terms of endearment such as *Negrito* (Little Blacky), *Gordito* (Little Fatty) and *mi Amor* (my love) are frequently used when the person addressed is neither black, fat, a dear friend nor a lover.

Here is a list of some frequent ticoisms (expressions unique to Costa Rica):

¡Adiós!	hello
bomba	gas station
buena nota	great!
¿Hay campo? . .	Is this (seat) still free?
cien metros	one city block
una cuadra	one city block
¿Como andas? .	How are you? (polite)
maje	young buddy
pura vida . .	super! great! ("pure life!")
¡Que Dios te pague!	May God reward you! (polite thanks)
¡Que horror!	How awful! (expression of sympathy)
salado	pity, tough luck!
¡Upe!	Anybody home?
vos	informal form of "you"

Time Difference

Costa Rica is six hours behind Greenwich Mean Time.

Due to its proximity to the Equator the times of the sunrise (6 a.m.) and sunset (6 p.m.) vary little.

Tipping

Hotels and restaurants generally add 10 percent (the amount required by law) to their bills for tips (*propina*). When that is the case no further tip is necessary, but waiters are happy if the amount is rounded off. Prices listed on menus do not include 10 percent tip or 13 percent tax. These are added to the bill.

When the price of a taxi ride has been negotiated, no tip need be added. But when the meter is used, the driver expects a tip of approximately 10 percent.

Women Traveling Alone

Women are generally respected in Costa Rican society. Many *machos*, however, seem to regard women traveling without a male escort as an invitation to a sexual encounter.

Obscene comments, knowing glances, suggestive motions and wolf whistles are common experiences for women traveling alone. Ticas ignore such remarks, but sometimes a verbal exchange becomes inevitable. Decent clothing and complying with the customs of the country are advised.

EMBASSIES

Embassies in San José

U.S.: Pavas, tel. 220-3939. **Canada:** Officentro Ejecutivo La Sabana Detras de La Contraloria, Sabana Sur, tel. 296-4149, fax. 296-4270. **U.K.**: Apartado 815, Deificio Centro Colon (11th Floor), tel. 258-2025, fax. 233-9938. **Ecuador**: Avenida 2, Calles 19/21, tel. 223-6281. **El Salvador**: Calle 5, Avenida Central, tel. 224-9034. **Guatemala**: Avenida 1, Calles 24/28, tel. 231-6654. **Honduras**: Calle 1, Avenida 52, tel. 234-9502. **Columbia**: Calle 29, Avenida 1, tel. 221-0725. **Mexico**: Avenida 7, Calles 13/15, tel. 222-5528. **Nicaragua**: Avenida Central, Calles 25/27, tel. 233-3479. **Panama**: San Pedro, 6 Blocks south from Higueron, tel. 225-3401. **Peru**: Los Yoses, 2 Blocks west of Auto Mercado, tel. 225-9145. **Venezuela**: Los Yoses, tel. 225-8810.

Costa Rican Embassies Abroad

Canada: 135 York St., suite 208, Ottawa, Ontario KIN5TA, tel. (613) 562-2855, fax. (613) 562 2582. **U.K.**: Flat 1, 14 Lancaster Gate, London, W23LH, tel. (171) 706-8844, fax. (171) 706-8655. **U.S.**: 2112 S-Street NW, Washington, D.C. 20008, tel. (202) 234-2945 or 234-8653, fax. (202) 265-4790 or 234-29466.

TOURIST INFORMATION

San José: The **Instituto Costaricense de Turismo** (ICT) in San José, Plaza de la Cultura, is the best informed office (Calle 5, Avenida Central 2, tel. 222-1090) for up-to-date information about the condition of roads and hiking trails in national parks, bus connections, private inns, *cabinas* and hotels. The office can also provide guides for national parks and nature or game reserves.

Abroad: The Costa Rican tourist industry has founded FUTUROPA, the Foundation for the Advancement of Costa Rican Tourism in Europe. The office is in Germany and also functions in the name of the International Costa Rican Tourism (ICT) office. It is the official center for information in Europe. **Costa Rican Tourist Bureau**, Regentenstr. 17, 51063 Köln, Germany, tel. (+49-221) 310-1841, fax. (+ 49-221) 310-1843.

VOCABULARY

Monday	*lunes*
Tuesday	*martes*
Wednesday	*miércoles*
Thursday	*jueves*
Friday	*viernes*
Saturday	*sábado*
Sunday	*domingo*
today / tomorrow	*hoy / mañana*
yesterday	*ayer*
morning	*por la mañana*
at noon	*al mediodía*
afternoons	*por la tarde*
evenings	*por la noche*
0	*cero*
1	*uno, una*
2	*dos*
3	*tres*
4	*cuatro*
5	*cinco*
6	*seis*
7	*siete*
8	*ocho*
9	*nueve*
10	*diez*
11	*once*
12	*doce*
13	*trece*
14	*catorce*
15	*quinze*
16	*dieciséis*
17	*diecisiete*
18	*dieciochcho*
19	*diecinueve*
20	*veinte*
21	*veintiuno*
22	*veintidós*
30	*treinta*
40	*cuarenta*
50	*cincuenta*
60	*sesenta*
70	*setenta*
80	*ochenta*
90	*noventa*
100	*cien*
200	*doscientos*
500	*quinientos*
1000	*mil*
single room	*habitación sencilla*
double room	*habitación doble*
– with bath	*– con baño*
– shared bath	*– baño compartido / baño común*
toilet	*baño, sanitario*
men	*hombres / señores / caballeros*
women	*mujeres / señoras*
the bill	*la cuenta*
where is...?	*¿Dónde hay...?*
closed	*cerrado*
open	*abierto*
Is this the way to...?	*¿Por aquí se va a?*
straight ahead	*derecho*
right	*a la derecha*
left	*a la izquierda*
street	*carretera*
highway	*autopista*
bus	*camión, autobus*
ticket	*boleto, ticket*
How long does it take?	*¿Cuánto durará...?*
Where does (it) go ...?	*¿Adonde va...?*
Where does (it) come from ...?	*¿De donde viene...?*
good morning	*¡Buenos días!*
good day, good afternoon (from noon to 6 p.m.)	*¡Buenas tardes!*
good evening, good night	*¡Buenas noches!*
yes	*sí*
no	*no*

goodbye . . . . . . *hasta luego, adiós*
excuse me . . . . *perdón*
permit me . . . . *con permiso*
please . . . . *por favor*
thank you
(very much) . . . . . *(muchas) gracias*
you're welcome . . . . *de nada*
I need . . . . *necesito*
is there / there is . . . . *hay*
How much
does ... cost.? . . . . . . *¿Cuánto vale?*
I don't understand . . . *yo no entiendo*
At what time ...? . . . . . *¿A qué hora?*
What time is it? . . . . . *¿Que hora es?*
bottle . . . . *botella*
beer . . . . *cerveza*
wine . . . . *vino*
post office . . . . *correos*
letter . . . . *carta*
post card . . . . *carta postal*
postage stamp . . . . *estampilla*
airmail . . . . *correo aereo*
exchange office . . . . *casa de cambio*
money . . . . *dinero*
coins . . . . *monedas*
bank . . . . *banco*
signature . . . . *firma*
doctor . . . . *médico*
help . . . . *ayuda*
hospital . . . . *hospital*
police . . . . *policía*
sick . . . . *enfermo*
friend . . . . *amigo / a*
husband / wife . . . . *esposo / a*
gas station . . . . *bomba*
gasoline . . . . *gasolina*
airport . . . . *aeropuerto*

AUTHOR

Dr. Klaus Boll studied empirical cultural science, ethnology and ancient history at Tübingen University in Germany. He has worked as a journalist and has lived abroad, primarily in Latin America. He now works as a seminar trainer in international development, and also sometimes acts as a guide for educational trips to Costa Rica.

PHOTOGRAPHERS

Agence Nature (Silvestris) 179
Aitken, Kelvin (Silvestris) 121, 161
Archiv für Kunst und Geschichte,
Berlin 18, 19, 20
Attika Reisen 188
Bauer, Rudolf (Silvestris) 157, 224
Beck, Josef 98
Beck, Josef (Silvestris) 222/223
Boll, Dr. Klaus 234/235
Cierpiol, Bernd cover, 23, 45, 58, 138, 139, 173, 190/191
Eisenschink, Gerhard 8/9, 10/11, 14, 15, 22, 31, 32, 35, 36/37, 38/39, 44, 59, 68/69, 80, 97, 99, 101, 104/105, 110, 111, 112, 114, 116, 117, 118, 119, 124/125, 134, 135, 136, 140, 142, 143, 150/151, 152, 156, 166/167, 177, 178, 181, 183, 184, 185, 195, 194, 196, 197, 201, 204, 206/207, 211, 212, 215, 226, 230, 238
Fogden, Dr. M. (Silvestris) 93
Fründt, Hans-Jürgen 83
Hansen, J. P. (JPH-Naturfilm) 137, 214
Helms, Bernd 21, 51, 94, 174
Heinrich, Rolf 48, 53, 187
Institut für Auslandsbeziehungen,
Stuttgart 225
Jakobi, Karl Heinz (Silvestris) 146
Kalden, Gerhard (Silvestris) 61, 73, 175
Kirst, Detlev 12, 16, 25, 26, 27, 30, 34, 47, 50, 52, 55, 56, 57, 60, 64, 75, 76, 77, 78, 91, 92, 96, 108, 115, 130, 131, 133, 144, 145, 147, 160, 163, 168, 218, 227, 231, 232, 233
Legler, Peter (Silvestris) 180
NHPA (Silvestris) 220/221, 229
Poblete, José F. 65, 192
Rosendahl, Dr. W. 88, 159, 176, 237
Roth, Bernd D. (Mainbild) 100, 132
Sohns, J. u. C. (Silvestris) 113, 208
Stankiewicz, Thomas 29, 40, 46, 54, 49, 70, 72, 203, 236
Sunset (Silvestris) 106, 228
Wendler, Martin (Silvestris) 24, 62, 81, 82, 86/87, 120, 126, 164, 216, 239
Wothe, Konrad (Silvestris) 84, 95.